The statements made by the individuals interviewed in this book reflect their individual viewpoints and should not be construed as the views of the publisher. The material contained in this book is presented only for informational purposes. The publisher and the authors do not condone or advocate in any way the use of prohibited substances or illegal activity of any kind.

Cover and end paper images, title design style, and "Pot Culture Picks" design style copyright © Bambu Sales

Editor: Susan Homer
Photo Editor: Meg Handler
Designer: Neil Egan
Spot Illustrations: Steve Marcus
Production Manager: MacAdam Smith and Jacquie Poirier
Cataloging-in-Publication data has been applied for and is available from the Library of Congress.
ISBN 978-0-8109-9440-9
Text copyright © 2007 Shirley Halperin and Steve Bloom
www.potculturebook.com

Printed and bound in China
10 9 8 7 6

Abrams Image books are available at special discounts when purchased in quantity for premiums and promotions as well as fundraising or educational use. Special editions can also be created to specification. For details, contact specialmarkets@hnabooks.com or the address below.

HNA
harry n. abrams, inc.
a subsidiary of La Martinière Groupe
115 West 18th Street
New York, NY 10011
www.hnabooks.com

Pot Culture

The A–Z Guide to Stoner Language & Life

Shirley Halperin & Steve Bloom
Foreword by Tommy Chong

ABRAMS IMAGE, NEW YORK

Contents

Pot Culture Picks: Your Guide to the Best in Stoner Movies, TV, Music, Travel & More 145

Stony Recipes 209

Weed Sites on the Web 215
Index 216
Photography Credits 222
Quotation Sources 223
Acknowledgments 224

Foreword (or Forward)

BY TOMMY CHONG

Hey man, the dude and dudette requested I lay down a taste for their take on the way homies rap and get down in the "hood." In other words, they asked me to mention a few unknown facts about the way language has been affected by pot or at least that's what I am going to do. To begin with, let us realize pot, cannabis, marijuana, hemp has been with us longer than we have been with it. God mentions it in the Bible when He says, "I will raise up for them a plant of renown." And Saint John the Divine describes a tree whose leaves "were for the healing of the nations."

So pot was here when man first began to communicate with the spoken word. One could imagine our early ancestors warming themselves beside a fire of hemp cuttings, laughing all red-eyed at some stupid caveman acting out a funny hunting sequence while munching on a dinosaur bone. And probably the first word uttered could well have been 'ere as he passed the bone to the guy next to him.

In our modern day society, however, I would venture to say that jails, prisons, and places of incarceration have contributed more to the "hip" language style than we care to admit. Prisoners have always had their own secret language in order to hide their activities from the authorities. Look how the baggy clothes favored by rappers and young black teenagers came directly from the city jails in this country—caused by uncaring prison trustees giving new prisoners oversize clothes, and boots, and no belts to make their stay in prison more uncomfortable. This clothing insult turned into a badge of honor by the homies on the outside, emulating the homies on the inside. The language took on the same slant. The term *man* for instance as in "hey man," a phrase used a few million times by me and my old partner Cheech, was a reaction in the forties and the fifties by the black jazz musicians to the derogatory term *boy*, which was used by white racists when they addressed black men.

I imagine many phrases used by jazz players derived from prison because so many jazz players were incarcerated for various drug-related offenses including the smoking of "reefer," "mary jane," "tea," etc. The writers of this book, Shirley Halperin and Steve Bloom, will take you through this very hip journey, and when you come out the other end, you will be able to understand the language and culture "mo better" so if you ever find yourself "in the slammer" for any reason you will be able to "get down wid the brothers (or sisters)" and maybe save your ass in more ways than one.

One word of advice though before you hurt yourself. Be very careful where you use this vocabulary. Try one phrase at a time and only among friends. People in this culture tend to be very territorial when it comes to their "language" and since we are dealing with an outlaw culture, violence factors into the equation as in, "Say what? I'll pop a cap in your ass" or "you talking that fake shit." And as I learned in jail, don't make eye contact with someone unless you know them, and remember that everyone is a potential snitch, including you. Oh yeah! If you are going to jail, wear extra underwear when you self-surrender because sometimes it takes days before you get a change of clothes.

I really feel that Shirley and Steve have hit upon a good thing with *Pot Culture* because by the time the book hits the shelves the language will have changed and a new edition will be needed. In the meantime, though, enjoy the read, and if you finish this book and feel like reading another book, check out *The I Chong*. It is available and I really need the money for my "support a dumb ass lawyer" charity that I have been running for the past few years ...

Ya all stay cool now ... 'ear?

Welcome to Pot Culture

Something we've learned, after years of working in magazines and traveling all over the world, is that stoners are naturally drawn to other stoners. And when they find themselves in an unfamiliar environment, they seek each other out. Those with experience learn a fail-safe mating dance, where common reference points and a unique language decide who does—or doesn't—partake. It's sociology in action, and after seeing it time and time again, it became the inspiration for this book.

When we started writing *Pot Culture*, we had a lot of preconceived notions of what the book would end up being. We didn't want it to read like a deep discourse on botany or politics, but rather, a more light-hearted approach to the culture surrounding pot as a pastime. First and foremost, we thought of a compendium that would itemize and define the various tools and terms that any self-respecting stoner should know—like how to differentiate between a pipe, a poker, and a pope, or how to transform an apple into a pipe. Then, we thought of a manual that would show not only how to roll a joint, but what to roll it with, where to smoke it, what to listen to while you're puffing, how to make the most out of the roach, and so on. And lastly, we thought of a manifesto that would list, explain, and illustrate the basic tenets of a stoner's life—basically everything you've ever wanted to know about pot but were too stoned to ask. As these elements started coming together, we turned our attention to popular culture—to movies, music, and television, three media that have a long history of stoner-friendly entertainment, mostly good, but some really bad. As our brains spat out ideas, we kept a singular mission in mind: It's about the person as much as it's about the plant.

There are plenty of bud books out there for enthusiasts to drool over and lots of cultivation manuals for exceptionally motivated risk takers. This book is neither. *Pot Culture* is about the people who make up this counterculture, which, according to government figures, numbers twenty-five million general users and five million daily users in the U.S. alone. Though stoners are a diverse demographic that transcends typical race, gender, socioeconomic, and age barriers, its population shares common artistic interests, mannerisms, and a unique and ever-expanding language. If you like to pack a bowl and sit back and watch *Fast Times at Ridgemont High* for the umpteenth time—whether you live in Billings, Montana, New York City, or anywhere in between—you are not alone. And big movie studios have openly picked up on this fact: Just look at the number of pot-heavy films that have come out in the past ten years (*Half Baked, Harold & Kumar Go to White Castle, How High, Road Trip, Tenacious D in The Pick of Destiny,* and *Knocked Up*). In music, references to "reefer" date back to the 1920s, and with the popularity of rap, new slang—like "chronic" and "blaze"—has entered the mainstream lexicon like never before. Television has been a bit sneakier. *That '70s Show* had its main characters sit in a circle with smoke wafting above their heads on every episode for eight seasons, but never showed a single puff. Pretty much the only place on the small screen where you could get away with showing a joint, bong, or bag was on animated shows like *The Simpsons*.

That was, until *Weeds* came along. The Showtime series

about a suburban mom—turned—pot dealer hit home for people like us—along with millions of in-the-closet stoners—for its unbiased look at how pot permeates all segments of society. This phenomenon was another motivator for our book, perhaps because it seemed to signal the end of the "Just Say No" era. Nancy Reagan's decade-long sound bite was largely the reason stoners evolved from the normal, good-loving youth of the 1970s to criminals in the 1980s and beyond. And for what? A drug war that has cost U.S. taxpayers billions of dollars, proved futile, and filled our prisons with nonviolent offenders? That blocks access to medicine that can ease the pain of cancer and AIDS patients? That persecutes well-adjusted, employed, and responsible Americans like you?

Let's face it: The U.S. government's marijuana laws, rooted in the 1937 Marihuana Tax Act, which in effect prohibited use of the plant, are archaic and tragically out of touch. Despite the fact that there's plenty of evidence suggesting that it's nonaddictive, nontoxic, and medically beneficial, marijuana continues to be listed as a Schedule I drug in the Controlled Substances Act, alongside heroin—which is indisputably addictive. In most states, if you get caught with a dime bag, you could be looking at jail time. If you smoke regularly, you've ostensibly removed yourself from the employment pool of dozens of corporations that test for drugs. On the flip side, there's alcohol—a legal, addictive substance that is responsible for nearly 100,000 deaths every year, not to mention the violence and driving-related fatalities that all too often accompany its use. In contrast, even daily use of marijuana, studies have suggested, is not harmful to long-term health. We may have gotten used to this hypocrisy, but that doesn't make it right. We could go on forever debating irrational laws and debunking marijuana myths, but that is only part of what this book is about. Our main goal has been to make *Pot Culture* fun to read. Sure, you'll find choice nug-

gets where we rail against pot propaganda, but for the most part what follows is our stab at defining the stoner lifestyle as it stands today, as it has been influenced by the past, and as it continues to transform.

From A to Z, we've compiled nearly five hundred definitions of marijuana-related terms—stoner slang, names of people and places, titles of songs and movies—as well as sifted through decades of stoner entertainment, rating bands, albums, songs, movies, and TV shows. We've enlisted some of our favorite celebrities to offer advice and reveal their innermost stoner secrets. (Who better to explain how to roll a blunt than Redman?) We've included bongs, papers, grinders, munchies, vaporizers, etiquette, drug-test tips, grow basics, top strains, books, colleges, drug lyrics, and so much more. Curated by two lifelong professional stoners, this trippy treasure trove we lovingly call *Pot Culture* hopefully will sit on your coffee table or be carried in your knapsack for years to come.

Shirley Halperin & Steve Bloom
May 2007

Stoner Etiquette 101

THIRTEEN RULES FOR BEING A POLITE AND PROPER POTHEAD

1 Always share. Even if you have only a small amount of weed. It's the stoner way.

2 Be prepared. Take a couple of minutes to break up your buds by hand or in a grinder before you pack them or roll them up.

3 Pass to the left. It's the Indian way, dude. Ho!

4 Offer to a friend first. You don't have to do this every time, but it's a nice gesture and will always make that person feel special.

5 Know the pot's potency. When smoking out a group, be aware of the strength of what you're offering and forewarn anyone who's not a regular toker. You can even suggest the number of hits he or she could safely handle.

6 Puff, puff, pass is OK. Puff, puff, puff, pass? Not cool. Don't Bogart that joint, my friend. Keep it moving.

7 If you don't have weed of your own, ask politely. You're tapped out and find yourself with tokers who don't know you're dry. Ask if you can have a hit and wait patiently until it comes around to you. Don't jump into the stoner circle uninvited.

8 Don't scorch the bowl. When smoking out of a pipe or bong, make sure to light a corner of the bowl and to leave a little green stuff for the next stoner.

9 Flush the toilet. Passing a bong with leftover or backwash smoke is not cool. Empty the chamber by either finishing your hit or removing the stem and blowing through the opening to clear it.

10 Give the tobacco warning. If you prefer to mix tobacco with your weed (as many Europeans do), alert your smoking partners first. Just because someone smokes pot doesn't necessarily mean he or she is down with cigarettes.

11 Watch the spit. Let's all keep our saliva to ourselves. No need to swap spit if you're not dating the guy or girl you're smoking with, right? A common (and much appreciated) technique: Use your fingers (or a fist, chillum-style) as a barrier between your lips and the bowl or joint.

12 Keep it clean. Clean out your paraphernalia often. Replace the bong water after several uses, give your glass a good pipe cleaning occasionally and, if you prefer joints or blunts, wash your hands.

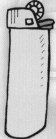

13 Don't pocket someone else's lighter. Stoners love to (inadvertently) steal other people's lighters. No matter how high you are, try to keep track of whose lighter is whose.

Classic Strains

Acapulco Gold (Mexico)

Colombian Gold

Durban Poison (South Africa)

Lamb's Bread (Jamaica)

Matanuska Thunderfuck (Alaska)

Maui Wowie (Hawaii)

Panama Red (Panama)

Thai Stick (Thailand)

Durban Poison

A

ACAPULCO GOLD / *ah-cuh-pull-co-gold* / *n.* 1. Vintage sativa strain from Acapulco (a Mexican resort city on the Pacific Coast) that dates back to the 1960s when marijuana smuggling from Mexico to the U.S. became popular. 2. Name of a documentary film directed by Burt Brinckerhoff and released in 1978 about various methods of growing and smuggling marijuana. 3. Title of a song, "That Acapulco Gold," and album by obscure California psychedelic rock band the Rainy Daze (1967). The song was cowritten by John Carter and Tim Gilbert. 4. Title of a song, "Acapulco Goldie," written by Shel Silverstein and recorded by Dr. Hook & the Medicine Show (1973): "You run away with me, Acapulco Gold." ALSO SEE: CLASSIC STRAINS (P. 11).

ACID / *ass-id* / *n.* SEE ALBERT HOFMANN; LSD; TRIP.

AFGHANI / *aff-gan-y* / *n.* An original indica strain grown in Afghanistan's mountainous regions, this sturdy yielder is available from Dutch seed companies such as Afghani Seeds. It flowers in fifty to sixty days and has 15 to 20 percent THC content.

AFROMAN (B. 1974) California-born rapper (né Joseph Foreman) whose big hit "Because I Got High" (2001) instantly downgraded the intelligence of the entire stoner populace thanks to lyrics like "I messed up my entire life, because I got high." Afroman has released several more albums including *4 RO:20* and *Drunk 'n' High*.

AK-47 / *a-kay-for-tee-sev-en* / *n.* Created by the Dutch company Serious Seeds, AK-47 is an easy-to-grow, mostly sativa strain with Thai, Mexican, Afghani, and Colombian genetics. Both heavy and cerebral, the strain grows to a medium height with thick clusters of buds that have a fruity aroma and a sandalwood taste. It flowers in sixty-five to seventy-five days and has 21 percent THC content. ALSO SEE: ALL-TIME GREATEST STRAINS (P. 124).

ALEDA / *ah-lead-a* / *n.* Brazilian company founded in 2005 that manufactures transparent rolling papers used for

Afroman (left) and *Clerks'* star Jason Mewes (right) in 2001

Green vinyl single of Afroman's "Because I Got High"

How to Make an Apple Pipe

🍁 BY JONAH HILL

He's played pivotal pothead roles in many a stoner comedy (The 40-Year-Old Virgin, Accepted, Grandma's Boy, and Knocked Up). Here the hilarious Jonah Hill (by his own admission a joint man, but not much of a roller), shares how to make the same apple pipe used in The 40-Year-Old Virgin.

Step 1: "The best apple to use is a big, juicy one."

Step 2: "Twist off the stem."

Step 3: "Using a pen, pencil or, if you're in dire straits, a knife, make your first hole through the top—or the head—of the apple. Burrow through to the core—about halfway down. This will become your bowl."

Step 4: "The second hole you make should be halfway down from the top of the apple, in the back. You want to puncture and dig until the two tunnels meet or you 'break on through to the other side,' as Jim Morrison would say."

Step 5: "The third hole should be a quarter of the way to the left or right of the second hole—choose whichever side feels most comfortable. This is the carb. Again, you want to burrow to the core like you did on the other side. You can feel yourself 'break on through' when it happens."

Step 6: "Wipe the apple dry, put the pot in the bowl, and light it up. It's a delicious hit that tastes like apple-flavored smoke, and it's all natural. This is Mother Nature's finest way to smoke marijuana."

smoking. Made from refined eucalyptus wood-pulp cellulose, Aleda transparent paper contains glycerin, which accounts for its shiny and soft appearance. Other companies such as Smokeclear, Paper Trip, and 1Back also manufacture transparent sheets. ALSO SEE: CLEAR; GREAT STONER INNOVATIONS (P. 137); GUIDE TO ROLLING PAPERS (P. 116); NUDIES; SWAYZE.

ALLMAN BROTHERS BAND Generally credited with creating the Southern rock sound (along with Lynyrd Skynyrd), the Allman Brothers—Duane (guitar) and Greg (vocals/keyboards)—were founded in 1969 in Jacksonville, Florida. Signed by Capricorn Records, the band—which also consisted of Dickey Betts (guitar), Berry Oakley (bass), and two drummers, Butch Trucks and Jaimo Johanson—relocated to Macon, Georgia, home base for the label and ground zero for the burgeoning Southern rock explosion. After just three albums, including the highly regarded *At Fillmore East* (1971) live double-LP set, tragedy struck the group when Duane Allman died in a motorcycle accident on October 29, 1971. A little more than a year later, Oakley suffered a similarly fatal bike crash. After several band breakups and reunions, they returned in 1989 with new members Warren Haynes (guitar) and Allen Woody (bass), who died of heart failure in 2000, and have been touring ever since. In 2000 Trucks's nephew Derek replaced Betts on guitar. ALSO SEE: MORE JAM BANDS (P. 107).

AMERICANS FOR SAFE ACCESS (ASA) Oakland, California–based offshoot of CAN, ASA was founded by Steph Sherer in 2002 and focuses entirely on issues relating to medical marijuana. It claims 30,000 members and chapters and affiliates in more than forty states. ALSO SEE: CANNABIS ACTION NETWORK; MEDICAL MARIJUANA.

AMSTERDAM Leading tourist destination for stoners, thanks to relaxed drug laws in the Netherlands, which allow the sale and consumption of small quantities of marijuana. The 700-plus-year-old city, with its serene canals and slanted houses, boasts more than four hundred coffeeshops (smoking bars) each with its own theme and unique vibe. But be forewarned: Europeans like to mix their weed with tobacco, which explains how they can afford to roll those

massive cone joints. Nickname: Amsterjam. ALSO SEE: AMSTERDAM COFFEESHOPS (P. 41); THE SEVEN STONER WONDERS OF THE WORLD (P. 76).

APPLE PIPE / *ap-ul-pipe* / *n.* Also called an apple bong, it is made by burrowing into an apple and creating two separate pathways that connect inside. The top of the apple is scooped out to resemble the depth of a bowl, and the pot is placed within this bowl and lit. Pipes can also be made with other fruits and vegetables such as pears and carrots. ALSO SEE: HOW TO MAKE A CARROT PIPE (P. 79); HOW TO MAKE AN APPLE PIPE (P. 12).

AQUALUNG / *ahk-wa-lung* / *n.* Slang for a gravity bong. ALSO SEE: BUCKET BONG; GRAVITY BONG.

AQUA PIPE / *ahk-wuh-pipe* / *n.* Transportable, carb-less, plastic, mini-bong, which is approximately five inches tall. It retails for $15 to $20. Water is added to the chamber, and the

Above: Coffeeshop T-Boat in Amsterdam's Waterlooplein district dates back to the 1960s
Below: Amsterdam is a biker's paradise

Aquapipe

Jazz pioneer Louis Armstrong, circa 1948

"We always looked at pot as a sort of medicine, a cheap drunk and with much better thoughts than one that's full of liquor."
—**Louis Armstrong,** musician

lid, which contains a bowl for the pot, is screwed onto the top. Once the stem, from which you puff, is raised to a ninety-degree angle, your water-filtered hit is ready to go.

ARMSTRONG, LOUIS (1901–1971) One of the founders of jazz, the New Orleans trumpeter seldom went a day without smoking pot—or "gage" and "muggles" as he liked to call it. The first popular musician to get busted for marijuana, he was arrested for smoking and for possession outside a Los Angeles nightclub in 1931 and spent nine days in jail. In 1954 he wrote President Dwight Eisenhower and asked him to legalize marijuana. ALSO SEE: FAMOUS POT BUSTS (P. 192); REEFER JAZZ CLASSICS (P. 190).

ASH / *ash* / *n.* The remnants of incinerated buds and paper. Devoid of THC content and color, ash should not be smoked again but rather disposed of neatly. ALSO SEE: CASHED.

B

BAG / *bag* / *n.* 1. The most common mode of transport for small quantities of marijuana (less than one ounce) and popularized with the advent of the plastic ziplock seal, which was first test-marketed in 1968. Cheaper nonzip sandwich bags are another option, but your buds may lose freshness as air seeps in, plus your dealer will have to lick the bag shut. 2. A generic term for any quantity of weed that one has on his or her person, as in, "You sure that's an eighth? That bag looks a little light, dude."

BAGGIES / *bag-eez* / *pl. n.* Plastic bags that can be used specifically to carry pot. Baggies range in size and can be as small as one-by-one inch (to accommodate a nickel bag's worth) or as big as the largest freezer-bag size.

BAKED / *bayk'd* / *adj.* The state of being fully high, as in, "Stick a fork in me. I'm so baked, dude." ALSO SEE: BLASTED; BLAZED; BURNT; BUZZED; CRISPY; FRIED; HIGH; LIT; LOADED; RIPPED; STONED; TOASTED; WASTED; ZONKED; ZOOTED.

BAMBU / *bam-boo* / *n.* One of the oldest brands of rolling paper, Bambu's naturally gummed papers originated in Spain in 1764 and are among the most popular in the U.S. and abroad. The brand is known for its Big Bambu line, Double Wide size, Pure Hemp, and flavored papers. The cover of the package, which features a dapper man smoking, known only as Mr. Bambu, was immortalized by Cheech & Chong, first on the cover of their comedy album, *Big Bambu* (1972), and later on the poster advertising their classic film, *Up in Smoke* (1978). Both images are graphic plays on the design of the Bambu pack. ALSO SEE: THE GREATEST POT-

Derry, proprietor of Barney's Coffeshop in Amsterdam

THEMED ALBUM COVERS (P. 182); GUIDE TO ROLLING PAPERS (P. 116).

BARNEY'S Originally known as Barney's Breakfast Bar for its all-day English-breakfast-style menu, the coffeeshop has changed names and expanded to include Barney's Lounge, Barney's Brasserie, and Barney's Farm (for seeds). Just mere blocks from Amsterdam's Centraal Station, this stoner institution is owned by a transplanted Irishman known simply as Derry who stocks award-winning strains, such as Sweet Tooth, Laughing Buddha, Morning Glory, and White Widow. ALSO SEE: AMSTERDAM COFFEESHOPS (P. 41).

BAT / *batt* / *n.* Synonym for a one-hitter or single-use smoking device, this term (a.k.a. batter) is most often associated with the wooden dugout, into which it's inserted, allowing the user to scoop up enough weed from the bottom for at least one hit, and maybe even two. ALSO SEE: DUGOUT; ONE-HITTER; ONE-HITTER GUIDE (P. 102); ONEIE.

B.C. Short for British Columbia, Canada's left-leaning province on the Pacific coast boasts stoner capital Vancouver and more than 20,000 illegal grow-ops. The B.C. cannabis industry is valued at seven billion dollars per year. The name "B.C. Bud" generally refers to strains grown in the province, and not to one particular strain. Outside Vancouver, the prime growing regions are the Kootenay Rockies and the Gulf Islands. ALSO SEE: VANCOUVER.

BEASTERS / *beest-urz* / *n.* American term for generic Canadian cannabis, usually midrange in quality.

BEATLES, THE SEE PAGES 16–17.

BEER BONG / *beer-bahng* / *n.* A plastic funnel connected to a tube, popular at parties (particularly fraternity parties). Beer is poured into the funnel, while the tube is plugged with a thumb and raised straight up. When the thumb is removed, gravity releases the beer from the funnel, down the tube, and into a waiting esophagus. A beer bong is similar to a keg stand.

BHANG / *bong* / *n.* 1. Term for marijuana in India. Cannabis flowers and leaves are either turned into hash paste for eating (in the form of bhang candies and drinks) or powder for smoking. Also known as ganga and siddhi. 2. Thai word from which *bong* is derived, it describes a cylindrical container made out of bamboo.

BHANG LASSI / *bong-la-see* / *n.* Popular Indian drink made of bhang, yoghurt, and ice water. Another common bhang drink is made with thandai (almond, spice, milk, and sugar). Such drinks are sold in government-authorized bhang shops in the northern Indian cities of Varanasi, Puri, Jaisalmer, and Pushkar.

BINGER / *bing-err* / *n.* Shorthand and slang for a bong hit, sometimes implying a small or solo hit, as in, "Load me up a binger, dude."

A beer bong in action

"I enjoy it [pot] once in a while. There's nothing wrong with that. Everything in moderation."
—Jennifer Aniston,
actress

The Beatles

Perhaps the greatest rock band of all time, the Beatles shook, rattled, and rolled the 1960s generation, leaving their indelible mark during a frenetic nine-year stretch that began in 1962 when drummer Ringo Starr joined songwriters John Lennon (rhythm guitar), Paul McCartney (bass), and George Harrison (lead guitar). After the early years of Beatlemania, when the group had a phenomenal run of Top 10 hits starting with "I Want to Hold Your Hand" (1963), they began experimenting with drugs (Bob Dylan turned them on to pot in 1964) and musical styles, leading them to create the psychedelic masterpieces *Sgt. Pepper's Lonely Hearts Club Band* (1967), *Magical Mystery Tour* (1967), and *The White Album* (1968). Lennon and McCartney drifted apart when Lennon divorced his first wife, Cynthia, and became inseparable from his second wife, Yoko Ono. The Beatles recorded their last album, *Abbey Road* (1969), separately, with Lennon providing the first side and McCartney the second. Meanwhile, Harrison discovered LSD and journeyed to India, where he adopted a Hindu philosophy, which led to a solo career that included *The Concert for Bangladesh* superstar benefit concert and triple-album set in 1972. Starr went solo as well, scoring hit singles with "You're Sixteen" (1974) and "No Song" (1975), which featured the lyric, "No no no, I don't smoke it no more." McCartney transitioned with his own band, Wings, throughout the 1970s. Lennon recorded a series of solo albums before dropping out of sight in 1975 for the next five years. During this time, he fought the U.S. campaign to deport him over his 1968 pot bust in England—and won.

Lennon's early 1970s radical years saw him perform a benefit for pot activist John Sinclair in 1971 and produce David Peel's album *The Pope Smokes Dope* in 1973. But McCartney was the real pothead of the group, as he proved by getting arrested at the Tokyo airport in 1980 with nearly half a pound of marijuana and spending a week in jail. He and his wife Linda Eastman both enjoyed their weed until she died of cancer in 1998. McCartney has claimed the Beatles' song "Got to Get You Into My Life" was his ode to marijuana. He also composed "Let Me Roll It" for Wings in 1973. He's been arrested three other times for marijuana possession and has called for decriminalization on many occasions. Eastman was arrested twice. After Eastman's death, McCartney married Heather Mills, who encouraged him to stop smoking pot. They've since had a high-profile divorce. Lennon reemerged in 1980 with the album *Double Fantasy*, featuring Ono. Sadly, shortly after the album's release, he was murdered by Mark David Chapman. Harrison died of lung cancer in 2001. The two surviving Beatles, McCartney and Starr, continue to tour separately with their respective bands.

☘ Drug References in ☘ Beatles Songs

1. "Lucy in the Sky with Diamonds": This *Sgt. Pepper's Lonely Hearts Club Band* (1967) epic is widely believed to be a clever play on the abbreviation LSD. Lennon repeatedly denied it was intentional but rather spoke matter-of-factly about it being inspired by a drawing his first son Julian had handed him. ("Here's Lucy, here's the sky, and this is a diamond," Julian supposedly said at the time.)

2. "With A Little Help from My Friends": This song precedes "Lucy in the Sky with Diamonds" on *Sgt. Pepper's*, making it the Beatles' most powerful one-two drug-song punch. "I get by with a little help from my friends," Starr sings. "I get high with a little help from my friends / Gonna try with a little help from my friends."

3. "I Am the Walrus": The infamous ending of this psychedelic masterpiece from *Magical Mystery Tour* (1967) repeats the line, "Smoke pot, smoke pot, everybody smoke pot." Also, the song contains the "I

"I buried Paul" lyric. However, you have to play it backward on vinyl to hear it.

4. "A Day In the Life": Another track from *Sgt. Pepper's*, this song contains the lyric, "I'd love to turn you on." Once again interpreted by certain segments of the media as Lennon and the Beatles promoting the use of LSD, it was swiftly banned by the BBC.

5. "Got to Get You Into My Life": In Barry Miles's biography of Paul McCartney, *Many Years from Now* (1997), McCartney explains that this song on *Revolver* (1966) was his ode to marijuana: "I was alone, I took a ride / I didn't know what I would find there / Another road where maybe I could see some other kind of mind there / Ooh, then I suddenly see you / Ooh, did I tell you I need you / Every single day of my life."

6. "Tomorrow Never Knows": "Turn off your mind, relax and float downstream" is the first line of this song penned primarily by Lennon and placed last on *Revolver*. The use of backward guitar and trippy loops perfectly complement the song's spiritual premise, which is also believed to reference an LSD trip. It's been said that Lennon told producer George Martin he wanted to sound like the Dalai Lama screaming from a mountaintop.

7. "Doctor Robert": This song is said to reference a certain Dr. Robert, a member of the 1960s London jet set and a dentist with whom Lennon, Harrison, and their wives allegedly had dinner one night. As the story goes, their coffee was spiked with LSD and the mysterious Dr. Robert came to life in the form of a song, which was subsequently included on *Revolver* (1966).

8. "She Said, She Said": Inspired by an acid trip taken by Lennon in Los Angeles while the Beatles were on tour, as legend has it, Peter Fonda (relatively

The Fab Four—(clockwise from top left) George Harrison, Ringo Star, John Lennon, and Paul McCartney —during the "Our World" broadcast at EMI Studios in 1967, where they sang "All You Need Is Love" for an international television audience of 400 million

unknown at the time, certainly to Lennon) was at this particular party and kept whispering into Lennon's ear, "I know what it's like to be dead," over and over again. The line apparently referred to one of Fonda's own trips and was later immortalized on *Revolver*.

9. "I Want To Hold Your Hand": Perhaps the first-ever Beatles' drug reference, at least according to Bob Dylan. As the story goes, this song on *Meet the Beatles* (1964) was a favorite of Dylan's, and at his first meeting with the Fab Four, he told them how much he liked it, especially the suggestive line, "I get high, I get high, I get high!" Of course, the actual line was "I

can't hide," and, in fact, the Beatles had never tried marijuana up until that point. Dylan took it upon himself to introduce them to pot at the Delmonico Hotel in 1964.

10. "Girl": This song appeared on *Rubber Soul* (1965), the first album the Beatles recorded after they started smoking pot. It contains the peculiar sound of what may or may not be a breathy, deep hit from a joint before each chorus. It is also debated whether or not Lennon is mumbling in the background, "Smoke it or sniff it, don't shoot up," and whether the word "tit" is disguised in the background vocals.

Chris Robinson, lead singer and cofounder of the Black Crowes, performs at the HORDE Tour in 1995

BLACK CROWES, THE Atlanta hippie rockers who took the marijuana world by storm in 1992 when they headlined the Atlanta Pot Festival. Lead singer Chris Robinson attended the MTV Video Awards wearing pot-leaf-adorned pants, and Black Crowes–brand rolling papers were sold at concerts. The band had major hits with "Hard to Handle" and "Jealous Again" in 1990, and *The Southern Harmony and Musical Companion* (1992) is generally considered the best of their six studio albums. In 1995 they recorded a version of Bob Dylan's "Rainy Day Women #12 & 35" ("Everybody must get stoned") on *Hempilation: Freedom Is NORML*. Robinson, who founded the band with his older brother Rich, married actress Kate Hudson (daughter of Goldie Hawn) in 2000. They have one child and divorced in 2006. The Black Crowes, after breaking up in 2002, reunited in 2005. ALSO SEE: GREATEST SMOKING SONGS (P. 125); STONER BANDS (P. 177).

BLACK, JACK (B. 1969) This modern-day Jeff Spicoli born in Redondo Beach, California, can make you laugh just by raising an eyebrow. His first major movie role was as the record-store clerk in *High Fidelity* (2000). He earned his cannabis "cred" with *Bongwater* (1997), but it was *Orange County* (2002)—his Lance character mixes up his pharmaceuticals, misplaces his clean drug-test pee, and burns down a college building while on Ecstasy—that established him as a fully formed stoner. His career as a lead actor was launched with *School of Rock* (2003) followed by a starring role in *King Kong* (2005) and another lead turn in *Nacho Libre* (2006). When Black's not acting in movies, he's rocking out with Kyle Gass in their band, Tenacious D. The duo first appeared in their own HBO series in 1999, and in 2006 they costarred in the thoroughly stony *Tenacious D in the Pick of Destiny*. Tenacious D performed at a NORML benefit concert in Los Angeles in 2003. Black also portrayed Russell Putnam, "*High Times* investigative reporter," in a *Saturday Night Live* skit in 2003. ALSO SEE: COMEDIES TO WATCH WHILE YOU'RE STONED (P. 156).

BLAST, BLASTED / *blahstt, blahstt-ed* / *n., adj.* 1. Having a "blast" is to have a good time. 2. Being extremely high, as in, "Dude, I'm blasted," derived from the term "blast

Jack Black wears the Wake & Bake Pizzeria T-shirt seen in *Tenacious D in The Pick of Destiny*

grower DJ Short, it flowers in fifty-five to sixty days and has 18 to 20 percent THC content. ALSO SEE: ALL-TIME GREATEST STRAINS (P. 124); CANNABIS CUP STRAINS (P. 31).

BLUNT / *bluhnt* / *n.* 1. Marijuana rolled in the tobacco leaf from a cigar. Blunts were first created in Jamaica and became popular with African Americans and the hip-hop community in the late 1980s. Cheap cigars such as Phillies, El Producto, and White Owl are commonly used. In Jamaica a fresh tobacco leaf used for a blunt is called a *fronta*. Individual cigar sheets known as "blunt wraps" became popular in the late 1990s. While blunts smoke clean and slow, and can be passed around many times, nontobacco smokers shy away from them because of their dizzying effect. Rappers have popularized them in song, with hits like Redman's "How to Roll a Blunt," Cypress Hill's "Spark Another Owl," and Missy Elliot's "Pass the Blunt." As an adjective, to be blunted is to be high on a blunt. 2. A skateboarding and surfing magazine based in South Africa. ALSO SEE: BLUNTED HIP-HOP CLASSICS (P. 184); FRONTA LEAF; HOW TO ROLL A BLUNT (P. 20).

BOGART / *bo-gart* / *v.* To hold on to a joint for too long. This hippie term is derived from Hollywood star Humphrey Bogart, who was known to talk with a cigarette in his hand or his mouth, and popularized in the stoner classic *Easy Rider* (1969) with the song, "Don't Bogart Me," by Fraternity of Man: "You've been hanging on to it / And I sure would like a hit / Don't bogart that joint, my friend / Pass it over to me." ALSO SEE: A BRIEF HISTORY OF THE GREATEST MARIJUANA SONGS (P. 178); GREATEST SMOKING SONGS (P. 125).

BOMB, THE / *bom-the* / *n.* The best marijuana available, as in, "This is the bomb, dude." Or even more colloquially, "This iz da bomb."

BONE / *bohn* / *n. or v.* 1. Slang for a joint, due to its thin shape and white color, as in, "Let's smoke a bone." 2. Slang for having sexual intercourse.

BONG / *bhang* / *n.* A bong is a water pipe used for inhaling marijuana and other smokeable substances by filtering heat and smoke through liquid. When used, the smoke

Humphrey bogarts that cigarette

Bong

off." ALSO SEE: BAKED; BLAZED; BURNT; BUZZED; CRISPY; FRIED; HIGH; LIT; LOADED; RIPPED; STONED; TOASTED; WASTED; ZONKED; ZOOTED.

BLAZE, BLAZED / *blayz, blayzd* / *v., n., or adj.* 1. To smoke pot. 2. A large fire. 3. Hip-hop terminology for being high, as in, "Yo, son, I'm blazed." 4. To forge ahead, as in, "He blazed a trail for others to follow." 5. Character Johnny Blaze from video game *Def Jam Vendetta* played by Method Man. ALSO SEE: BAKED; BLASTED; BURNT; BUZZED; CRISPY; FRIED; HIGH; LIT; LOADED; RIPPED; STONED; TOASTED; WASTED; ZONKED; ZOOTED.

BLUEBERRY / *bloo-berry* / *n.* A sweet-smelling, mostly indica strain composed of Purple Thai in combination with Afghani. Dense and stout, it cures to a lavender-blue shade and gives a pleasantly euphoric high. Created by Canadian

How to Roll a Blunt

🍁 BY REDMAN

Back in 1993 rapper Redman was one of the first to hype blunts—marijuana rolled in cigar paper—when he wrote the song, "How to Roll a Blunt." When it comes to his favorite smoking method, Redman prefers Backwoods, which come in a pouch, and Vanilla Dutch Masters. He smokes an average of eighteen blunts per day. Using a Dutch Masters cigar, here Redman explains how he likes to roll a blunt.

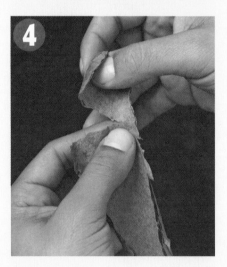

Step 1: "This should take about four minutes. I use both cigar papers, because without that second layer of paper your blunt burns like a paper bag."

Step 2: "Split the Dutch with your fingers, carefully opening it up lengthwise with your thumbs. I don't use scissors or a knife."

Step 3: "Remove the ground tobacco."

Step 4: "I tear the ass off. That's the rounded part at the end. A lot of people roll it with this part on. In the hood we call it the cancer. Make sure you take this off or your blunt will taste like shit. It's too much extra paper."

Step 5: "Don't lick the whole paper. Just lick the edges, because some of the edges are rough. I call this 'edgin' it. You gotta edge it. I like to be neat about my shit, but no blunt is gonna be perfect."

Step 6: "Break up the weed with your hands or a grinder. I prefer Sour Diesel, Haze, and Strawberry Cough. Make sure there are no stems to poke holes in the blunt."

Step 7: "Roll it up just like it's paper."

Step 8: "Trim the edge here and there just to touch it up."

Step 9: "Roll it nice and tight. Lick the top layer and let it dry on its own. No need to dry it with a lighter. Some people like their blunts round. With a blunt you have a lot of air in it. That's why I like to flatten my blunts."

Step 10: "Fire it up!"

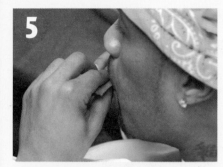

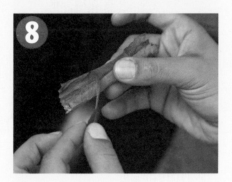

The mushroom fountain at the Bonnaroo Music & Arts Festival in Tennessee

collects in a chamber, where a combination of pressure and air, released through a carb, allows it to be inhaled fully in a single breath (called a hit or pull). A report issued by the Multidisciplinary Association for Psychedelic Studies (MAPS) claims that water pipes actually filter out more THC than potentially harmful tars, which requires that one smoke more in order to reach his or her desired high. But it's also been proven that filtering smoke, whether tobacco or cannabis, does reduce the amount of toxic carcinogens one would ingest into the lungs through unfiltered vehicles (such as a cigarette or joint), making it the healthier way to smoke. Bongs come in a variety of shapes, sizes, and materials, from the acrylic mainstay Graffix to the more expensive and elaborate glass models pioneered by craftsmen like Bob Snodgrass and Jerome Baker. When ice is inserted—creating an ice bong—the hit is cooled for an extra-tingly sensation. Bongs can be made at home out of wood, bamboo, clay, a plastic soda bottle, an aluminum can (can bong), or in a pail or tub (gravity bong). Extolled by Cypress Hill on: "Hits from the Bong" (1992). ALSO SEE: ANATOMY OF A BONG (P.23); BUBBLER; GLASS VS. PLASTIC (P. 59); GRAFFIX; GRAVITY BONG; HOOKAH; ICE BONG; ROOR; WATER PIPE.

BONG HIT / bhang-hitt / n. The act of clearing a bong chamber of smoke by inhaling. ALSO SEE: BINGER; HIT; PULL; RIP.

BONGHITTERS / bhang-hih-turz / pl. n. High Times' softball team, founded in 1991, by John Holmstrom. From 1991 to 2007, the team won 75 percent of its games versus such opponents as Rolling Stone, The Wall Street Journal, and The Onion.

BONG WATER / bhang-wah-ter / n. Brown water left after a bong hit. The more pulls, the nastier—and smellier—it gets until the stench reaches full-on rank. 2. New York–based underground rock group, Bongwater, from 1985–1992, consisting of actress Ann Magnuson and Shimmy Disc label founder Mark Kramer. Their four albums include the popular Double Bummer. 3. Novel (1995) by Michael Hornburg about stoners from Portland, Oregon, who move to New York. 4. Movie adaptation (1997) of the novel, starring Luke Wilson (who deals pot), Jack Black (who grows pot), Alicia Witt, Brittany Murphy, Amy Locaine, Andy Dick, Jamie Kennedy, Scott Caan, and Patricia Wettig.

BONNAROO / *Bon-eh-roo* / *n.* Music and arts festival that's become the prime destination for 80,000 jam-band fans every June since 2002. It's no wonder—in Cajun *bonnaroo* means "a really good time." Founded by the New Orleans–based promotion company Superfly Presents, the four-day festival is held on a farm in Manchester, Tennessee (which is sixty-five miles south of Nashville), features multiple stages with events going sixteen hours a day, and a camping area that extends for miles. Among the top performers to have played this festival are Bob Dylan, Radiohead, Tom Petty, Neil Young, and Dave Matthews Band. ALSO SEE: STONER FESTIVALS (P. 196).

BOO / *bu* / *n.* 1. Slang for marijuana, as in, "Let's smoke some boo." 2. Derisive chant. 3. Song by Usher and Alicia Keys, "My Boo" (2004).

BORDER STASH / *bored-dur-stash* / *n.* When crossing a border by car, the act of hiding your stash in a spot at a nearby town or exit so that it can be picked up on the way back.

BOSTON FREEDOM RALLY One of the longest-running protest rallies in America lights up the Boston Common every third Saturday of September with speeches, music, and marijuana. Since its inception in 1992, crowds of up to 50,000 have gathered to see bands like Letters to Cleo, the 360's, and David Peel, and to express their support for marijuana-law reform. ALSO SEE: HASH BASH; RALLY; SEATTLE HEMPFEST; SMOKE-IN; U.S. POT RALLIES (P. 200).

BOWL / *bole* / *n.* 1. Another name for a pipe, as in, "Smoke a bowl?" 2. The concave carrier (usually metal or glass) in a bong or bubbler into which pot is placed to be smoked. ALSO SEE: ANATOMY OF A BONG (P. 23); PIPE OPTIONS (P. 110).

BREEDING / *bree-dinjh* / *v.* Creating a distinct marijuana strain by crossing two or more varieties, as in, "Strawberry Fields × Haze = Strawberry Cough."

BRICK / *brihck* / *n.* Large quantity of low-grade marijuana (usually a kilo) that has been compressed for easier transport, a.k.a. brick weed. The brick form is most often

Anatomy of a Bong

Mouthpiece: The opening at the top of the chamber over which you place your mouth in order to inhale.

Ice Pincher: A ridge inside the upper part of the chamber that holds ice used to cool the hit just before it reaches the user's mouth.

Carb: A small hole on the back or side of the chamber, positioned where a hand would rest comfortably. When the carb is closed (sealed with a finger), the smoke from the burning bowl is collected and held within the chamber. When it is opened (by removing the finger), the smoke is released, and as the bong hitter inhales, drawn up through the mouthpiece into the mouth.

Chamber: The container in which the water is stored and the smoke is collected, also sometimes called the tube. Some bongs have multiple chambers for extra impact.

Base: The bottom of the bong, sometimes part of the chamber and sometimes a separate piece. The base, typically the heaviest part of the apparatus, anchors the bong and keeps it from tipping over.

Bowl: The cradle that sits on top of the stem and holds the buds that are about to be smoked. Depending on the design of the bong, some bowls are fused onto the stem while others screw into it. When the bowl can be separated from the stem, a rubber washer is positioned between the two to prevent air leakage.

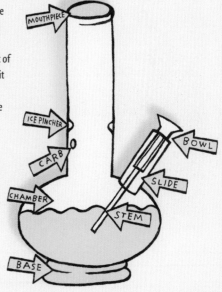

Slide: Often a feature of glass bongs, a slide (male) is a small thin tube that fits inside the stem (female) and is connected to the bowl. Pulling the slide out of the stem replicates the effect of a carb by releasing pressure and air.

Stem: A narrow tube, usually made of glass or metal that passes through a hole in the wall of the chamber and connects the bowl to the base. The slide (male) fits into the stem (female). The suction created when inhaling filters the burn, eliminating toxins but also slightly weakening the THC's impact.

Brownies

used to smuggle schwag out of Mexico, Colombia, and other Latin American countries. 2. Atlanta-based funk band Brick had a hit with "Dazz" on *Good High* (1976). The album cover features pot leaves on a kilo of weed. ALSO SEE: DITCH WEED; THE GREATEST POT-THEMED ALBUM COVERS (P. 182); KILO; SCHWAG.

BROWNIE / *brown-nee* / *n.* A baked good based on any variation of the traditional recipe, but with the addition of pot, hash, or cannabutter. A pot-brownie high is often described as more intense than your average smoking high, and is generally thought to be more of a body high than a head high. That's likely because the THC is absorbed through the stomach before reaching the brain. Casual stoners often eat pot brownies recreationally, but these treats have a medicinal purpose as well. Those afflicted with a disease such as AIDS or who are undergoing chemotherapy can use them as a way to induce hunger or ease nausea. ALSO SEE: CANNABUTTER; MEDICAL EDIBLES (P. 57); SPACE CAKE.

BUBBLE GUM / *buhb-ul-gumm* / *n.* A mostly indica strain, a.k.a. Bubblelicious, first developed by U.S. growers in Indiana, then in New England, before Dutch seed companies such as Serious began adding it to their catalogues. A short plant with large leaves and dense buds, it has a sweet smell and taste, hence its name. It flowers in fifty-six to sixty-three days and has 21 percent THC content.

BUBBLE HASH / *buhb-ul-hash* / *n.* A hash so pure it bubbles when heated, it is made using an ice-water extraction technique developed by Amsterdam native Milla Jansen. Milla's "Ice-O-Lator" literally isolates trichomes, or resin glands, from freshly trimmed marijuana leaves and shakes them. Her "Ice-O-Lator Hash Bags" (updated by Fresh Headies in Canada, and renamed "Bubble Bags") require cold water, ice, and cannabis. After being sieved through several different size bags, the prized green residue is ready to smoke. The same process can be done in an oscillating-type machine, such as Milla's Bubbleator, without using bags. ALSO SEE: CHARAS; HASH; HASH OIL; ISOLATOR HASH; KIF; NEDERHASH; TRICHOMES.

BUBBLER / *buhb-ler* / *n.* A mini-bong or glass water pipe with no removable parts, often called a hammer or a sidecar, depending on its shape. Fill the chamber with a small amount of water and smoke using the carburetor.

Glass bubbler

BUBBLE ROLL / *buhb-ul-role* / *n.* A joint made of the best possible marijuana rolled in a flattened, thin sheet of homemade bubble hash. This extravagant delicacy requires seven to ten grams of hash (at $50 per gram) and seven to fourteen grams of bud. It's also known as a Mendocino cigar.

BUCKET BONG / *buk-ett-bhang* / *n.* Gravity bong where the smoking cylinder is plunged into a bucket of water as opposed to a bathtub.

BUD / *buhd* / *n.* 1. The flower of the marijuana plant. When mature and fully dried, it's smoked for maximum enjoyment. 2. Slang for a friend, as in "Hey bud, let's party." ALSO SEE: KEEPING YOUR BUDS FRESH (P. 25).

Sour Diesel bud

BUDDHA / boo-dah / n. 1. Hip-hop term for marijuana, as in, "Don't miss out on what you're passing / You're missing the hootah / Of the funky Buddha" (Cypress Hill, "How I Could Just Kill a Man," 1991). 2. Name given to Siddhartha Gautama (c. 563–c. 483 BC), prince of the Shakya nation in Nepal, when he achieved enlightenment. He is also known as Shakyamuni Buddha and "The Awakened One of the Shakya Clan." 3. One who practices Buddhism and achieves enlightenment.

BULLDOG, THE / buhl-dawg-the / n. One of Amsterdam's original coffeeshops—where marijuana and hash are legally sold—and also one of Amsterdam's biggest tourist traps. Though many shops have long surpassed it in quality, its primo Leidseplein location keeps it in the thick of things. Two additional Amsterdam shops and a hotel add up to a major marijuana success story. ALSO SEE: AMSTERDAM COFFEESHOPS (P. 41).

The Bulldog coffeeshop in Amsterdam's Leidseplein district

Keeping Your Buds Fresh

1 Ditch the plastic baggie: It will only dry out your buds faster, wasting valuable THC.

2 Use an airtight jar: You can buy one specially designed for weed or use a screw-top mason jar, which comes in various sizes and sells for $2 and up. Recycled tomato sauce jars work just as well. Weed-specific glass jars can cost anywhere from $10 to $80, depending on their size. Another option is a small Tupperware-like container, which sells for less than $5, or the specially designed vacuum-sealable Tightvac.

3 Store in a cool spot away from direct sunlight: Some like to keep their jars in the fridge or freezer. While this is not necessary to ensure freshness, it certainly won't hurt your buds.

4 If you want to keep the buds extramoist: Don't use orange peels (they may mold your stash). Instead, add a small humidifier disk to the container. Disks can be bought at most head shops for around $3.

5 Don't constantly open and close your pot containers: Air will ultimately dry out your stash and downgrade the overall quality.

BULLET / *bul-lit* / *n.* A compact metal pipe shaped sort of like a bullet, it has a screw-off top that contains a bowl, and a small hole for discreet lighting and the minimization of

Burning Man statue

smoke. Considered a one-hitter because of its size (it will fit snugly into the palm of your hand), be forewarned: It packs quite a wallop. ALSO SEE: ONE-HITTER GUIDE (P. 102).

BUMMER / *bum-her* / *n.* Hippie term for a downer or bad thing that has happened, as in, "Bummer, dude." ALSO SEE: DRAG.

BURN, BURNED, BURNT / *burrn* / *n., adj., or v.* 1. Term for the smokeability of a joint, as in "This is a good burn." A poorly rolled joint or still-drying marijuana can result in a "bad burn." 2. In the case of a pot deal, to sell inferior marijuana or to short the buyer by providing "less weight" than stated, commonly referred to as "getting burned." 3. To smoke a joint, as in, "Let's burn one." 4. Ben Harper song, "Burn One Down" (1995): "Let us burn one / From end to end / And pass it over / To me my friend / Burn it long, well burn it slow / To light me up before I go." 5. To be overly high, as in, "I'm burnt, dude." ALSO SEE: BAKED; BLAZED; BUZZED; CRISPY; FRIED; HIGH; LIT; LOADED; RIPPED; STONED; TOASTED; WASTED; ZONKED; ZOOTED.

BURNER / *burr-ner* / *n.* A 1970s term for a pothead or a stoner, as in, "He's OK, dude. He's a burner."

BURNING MAN / *burr-ningh-mon* / *n.* Founded in San Francisco by Larry Harvey and Jerry James in 1986, this festival originally took place at San Francisco's Baker Beach on the summer solstice, culminating in the ritualistic burning of a wooden "man," an iconic structure that has grown from eight to forty feet high over the years. Since 1990 Burning Man's following of alternative-culture freaks now converges at Black Rock City, Nevada, for eight days in September. More than 35,000 people attend this annual art-driven campout in the desert ninety miles northeast of Reno. ALSO SEE: STONER FESTIVALS (P. 196).

BURNOUT / *burrn-out* / *n.* High school catchall term for an individual who abuses drugs, alcohol, and/or cigarettes. Often associated with excessive marijuana use, as in, "He's a burnout."

BURROUGHS, WILLIAM S. (1914–1997) A founding member of the Beat Generation (along with Jack Kerouac and Allen Ginsberg), he was born in St. Louis, is revered by rock and rollers like Kurt Cobain, and wrote the psychedelic

Beat legend William S. Burroughs

classic, *Naked Lunch* (1959). Famous for his cut-up writing style, where pages are randomly mixed, he also wrote *The Soft Machine* (1961) and *Nova Express* (1964). He fled to Mexico in 1947 after authorities raided his marijuana farm in Texas. Arrested there in 1951, he was charged with the shooting death of his common-law wife, Joan Vollmer. He appeared in the films *Chappaqua* (1966) and *Drugstore Cowboy* (1989). His novel *Naked Lunch* (1959) was adapted into a movie by David Cronenberg in 1991. His spoken-word recordings include *Dead City Radio* (1990), *The Priest They Called Him* (1992) with Cobain, and *Spare Ass Annie and Other Tales* (1993) with Disposable Heroes of Hiphoprisy. A longtime heroin user who wrote *Junkie* (1953), he died of a heart attack at the age of eighty-three. ALSO SEE: EASY RIDERS, RAGING BEATS (P. 54).

BUST / *buhsst* / *n.* 1. Arrest for marijuana or other drugs. Common phrase: "This is a bust!" 2. Sculpture of a person's head and shoulders. 3. A woman's breasts. 4. An alternative women's magazine launched in 1993. ALSO SEE: DEALING WITH A DRUG TEST (P. 49); ROAD RULES.

Road Rules

(OR, HOW NOT TO GET BUSTED ON THE HIGHWAY)

A car is the most likely place to get busted. Once you're pulled over by the police, you have virtually no rights. Here's how to travel smart on the highway.

1 **Don't drive under the influence:** Smoke up *before* you enter the vehicle. Preferably, way before.

2 **If you insist on toking in the car:** Have a designated driver. Joints (they look like cigarettes) rather than pipes are preferable for passengers. Do not roll in the car.

3 **If you must carry:** It's generally recommended to have less than an eighth of an ounce.

4 **Be a smart stoner:** Make sure your car is in good shape (no headlight malfunctions) and that your license and registration are up-to-date. Avoid bumper stickers that might tip off the police.

5 **Keep your cool:** If you do get pulled over, stay calm and collected. If the police ask you to get out of the car, do not refuse. If they ask to search the car, you really don't have much of a choice, so be polite and hope for the best.

The Byrds—(left to right) Skip Battin, Roger McGuinn, Gene Parsons, and Clarence White—circa 1971

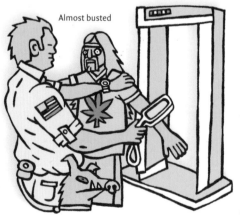

Almost busted

BUSTED / *buss-tid* / *adj.*   1. Having been arrested for marijuana or other drugs.   2. Having been caught in the act of doing something wrong by a parent or other authority figure, as in, "You're so busted!"   ALSO SEE: DEALING WITH A DRUG TEST (P. 49); ROAD RULES (P. 27).

BUTLER / *butt-ler* / *v. or n.* The act of breaking up buds by hand into a finer, easy-to-roll form. Used as a noun, the term refers to the individual who takes on the responsibility of removing unwanted stems and breaking up hard nugs with precision, and then either rolling the marijuana into joints or gladly serving it up in bong hits.

BUZZ, BUZZED / *buhz, buhzd* / *n. or adj.* 1. To be slightly intoxicated, as in, "Thanks, dude. I've got a good buzz going." Used as an adjective, "buzzed" describes feeling good, but not necessarily wasted or loaded.   2. Hype surrounding the newfound popularity of something that's up and coming, such as a particular band and their music or a scene from a movie. ALSO SEE: BAKED; BLASTED; BLAZED; BURNT; CRISPY; FRIED; HIGH; LIT; LOADED; RIPPED; STONED; TOASTED; WASTED; ZONKED; ZOOTED.

BYRDS, THE A groundbreaking band formed in 1964, whose original lineup included David Crosby, Chris Hillman, and Roger McGuinn. The Byrds defined the psychedelic folk-pop sound of the 1960s with stony hits like "Eight Miles High." But it was when Gram Parsons joined the lineup in 1968 that they veered in another direction and country rock—later popularized by Crosby, Stills & Nash, the Grateful Dead, Poco, and the Eagles—was born. The Byrds were the first longhairs to ever play the Grand Ole Opry, and Nashville was never the same.

How to Make a Can Pipe

🍁 BY **STEVE-O**

The costar of Jackass and Wildboyz, and a full-time prankster, Steve-O explains how to construct his preferred smoking device, the can pipe, in a matter of seconds.

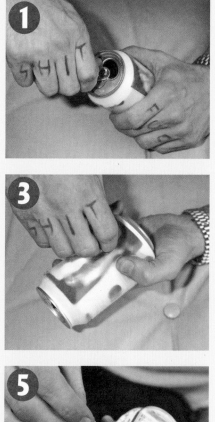

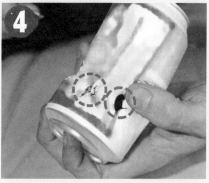

Step 1: "Get a standard aluminum can. The only kinds that are no good are the really heavy ones that are hard to poke a hole through, like a pineapple juice can. I prefer a Budweiser can."

Step 2: "The next thing you're looking for is a puncturing device. You can use a girl's earring, keys, or a knife. If you try it with a pen, the pen can go all the way through, making the hole too big. I prefer to snap the tab off the can, then break the tab in half so it's pointy and use it to poke the perfect size hole."

Step 3: "Indent the can at one end and poke a hole into it for the bowl."

Step 4: "Poke a carb in the side of the can."

Step 5: "Pack the bowl."

Step 6: "Light, and ignite. Inhale through the opening at the top. It's not really a harsher hit. When people try my can pipes, they're always like, 'No way, dude—that actually works good.' I get really good reviews. The other great thing about the can pipe is, if you're caught, you can always step on the can and really crush it down. All of a sudden, there's nothing to get caught with."

C

Cañamo

CALYX / *cal-licks* / *n.* Botanical term for a flower, fruit or, in the case of marijuana, the bud.

CAÑAMO / *con-ya- moe* / *n.* Spanish marijuana magazine published in Barcelona since 1997. *Cañamo* is the Spanish term for hemp.

CAN PIPE / *kan-pipe* / *n.* A homemade smoking device constructed from an aluminum can (beer or soda). The side of the can is bent slightly, then small holes are punctured into it to allow smoke to collect inside. The addition of a carb, or another hole punctured into the opposite side, provides added pressure, which helps push the hit through the metal, slightly lessening its harshness. ALSO SEE: HOW TO MAKE A CAN PIPE (P. 29).

CANNABINOIDS / *kan-a-bi-noydz* / *pl. n.* The chemical compounds in cannabis that interact with cell membranes known as cannabinoid receptors to produce the high and other effects of marijuana. Cannabinoid receptors are located primarily in the brain and the immune system, and were first discovered in 1988. Before then, the effects of marijuana on cell membranes were considered nonspecific. Tetrahydocannabinol (THC), the psychoactive cannabinoid in marijuana, provides the cerebral high as well as pain relief. Nonpsychoactive cannabidiol (CBD) relieves nausea and convulsions. Moderately psychoactive cannabinol (CBN) acts as a sedative. Pharmaceutical manufacturers have begun to separate out the numerous cannabinoids to create specific cannabis-based medications, such as Sativex.

CANNABIS / *kan-a-bis* / *n.* Plant species originally cultivated in China, it was classified in 1753 by Carolus Linnaeus as *Cannabis sativa*. This classification was amended in 1785 by Jean-Baptiste Lamarck to include *Cannabis indica* and again in 1924 by Janischevsky to include *Cannabis ruderalis*. In the 1970s botanist Richard Schultes concluded that these were three unique species rather than a genus: *Cannabis sativa*—the tallest of the three, with thin leaves and wide spaces between branches—is traditionally grown in subtropical countries such as Jamaica, Colombia, Mexico, and Thailand. It provides a cerebral, uplifting high. Favorite sativas include Haze and Maui Wowie. *Cannabis indica*—short and bushy, with wide leaves—is traditionally grown in mountainous countries like Pakistan, India, and Afghanistan. It provides a heavy, sleep-inducing high. Favorite indicas include Kush and Northern Lights. The THC content of indicas generally exceeds that of sativas. *Cannabis ruderalis*—a dwarf-size species—is traditionally cultivated in the harsh climates of Russia, Latvia, and Lithuania. Seldom grown for smoking purposes due to its low THC content and yield, ruderalis is occasionally crossed with its sister species.

CANNABIS ACTION NETWORK (CAN) A youthful offshoot of NORML is devoted to grassroots organizing. Founded in 1989 by Debby Goldsberry, the organization soon moved from Lexington, Kentucky, to Berkeley, California, where members helped pass local bills supporting medical marijuana and deprioritization, as well as Proposition 215 in 1996. It opened one of Berkeley's first medical marijuana dispensaries in 1998, the Berkeley Patients Group, and in 2005 and 2006 respectively started the Los Angeles Patients and Caregivers Group and the California Patients Group, which was raided by the DEA in 2007.

CANNABIS CULTURE Canada's first marijuana magazine, it was founded by Marc Emery in 1994 in Vancouver and originally titled *Cannabis Canada*. Emery funded the magazine with his seed company, Emery Seeds Direct, until he and two associates were arrested in 2005 by U.S. and Canadian authorities for selling seeds south of the border. Efforts to extradite the trio, known as "The BC3," are ongoing. Despite loss of revenues, the magazine continues to be published on a bi-monthly basis.

Cannabis Culture

Cannabis Cup Strains

Pot Culture PICKS

🌿 **Super Silver Haze:** Winner of two consecutive Cannabis Cups (1998, 1999), this mostly sativa Haze hybrid is derived from Skunk, Northern Lights, and Haze genetics. The strain helped put the Green House coffeeshop and seed company on the Amsterdam map.

🌿 **Skunk #1:** This first-ever winner of the Cannabis Cup (1988) is one of the great strains, but crossbreeding over the years has made it less available and somewhat hard to find.

🌿 **Blueberry:** Fruity-flavored mostly indica winner of the Cannabis Cup (2000)—a rare win for the Noon, one of Amsterdam's smaller coffeeshops—this strain is available from numerous seed companies.

🌿 **Sweet Tooth:** This powerful, mostly indica winner of the Cannabis Cup (2001) was the first indicator that Barney's would give the Green House some real competition. Sweet Tooth was created by BC grower Breeder Steve.

🌿 **Jack Herer:** This mostly sativa Haze hybrid named after hemp activist Jack Herer won the Cannabis Cup (1994) the year it was introduced by Sensi Seeds, one of Amsterdam's original and most venerable seed companies.

Skunk #1

The Art of Scoring

BY MATCHBOX TWENTY'S ROB THOMAS

With more than a decade's worth of bong-hitting tours behind him, Matchbox Twenty's frontman gives *Pot Culture* his highly experienced assessment of the art of how to suss out a stoner and score when you're dry.

Rob Thomas, with bud, in 2005

"The thing about pot is, no matter where you are in the world, you'll find that the people smoking it are generally kind, friendly, peace-loving folks. But this isn't to say that stoners are all hippies like the ones portrayed in the media. If that were the case, it would be easy to find weed anywhere. Just walk up to the first head you see, make the universal 'two fingers to the lips' sign, and you'll be hooked up. But the truth is that all kinds of people are stoners: lawyers,

"That group of gigglers huddled around the trunk of a Volvo? Stoners!"

Fortune 500 businessmen, housewives, the fifty-something dude who lives next door and wears lemon sweaters and white shoes. But because of the stigma surrounding our favorite ritual, people have to keep it to themselves. This means that if you want to search out the other heads in your surroundings, you have to become a pot-smoking Crime Dog McGruff. Now, it's easier to hook up at parties and weddings than offices and funerals, but these rules really can apply anywhere. So before you say, 'I can't do it' or 'It's too complicated,' or 'Hey, aren't you the guy from the Goo Goo Dolls?' I urge you to try them out."

What to Do If You're at a Social Event

Find some overzealous partygoers and point out that they must be on pot: "Most of the time, a fellow stoner will respond that he wishes that he could be high as well, and the connection is made."

Use alcohol to bridge the conversation: "Make a comment about how strong the drinks are and how yours reminds you of a time when you smoked pot. Say it around a suspected head and wait for results."

If you smoke tobacco: "While you're hanging outside with the other smokers, make a comment about how you don't really usually smoke anymore. Cigarettes, that is."

Take a stroll: "Go for a quick walk around the parking lot. That group of gigglers huddled around the trunk of a Volvo? Stoners!"

If you smell the sweet cheeba: "All you need to do is find the source and 99 percent of the time, they will just pass it to you if you take your place in the circle."

Examine the look: "Judging someone by his or her clothing isn't always the wrong way to go, but it has to be age appropriate. The fifty-year-old guy with the ponytail and the diamond stud in his 'I'm-not-gay' ear is probably a safe bet."

Last Resorts

The "pot friend": "There's nothing better than someone who is a genuine friend *and* a hookup, but sometimes your hookup is a 'pot friend.' He's a good guy, but you probably wouldn't be sitting in his living room listening to his band's demo tapes if you weren't in need. Fifteen minutes is about all you need to catch up with said pot friend. He's doing fine. He has a gig at the Junkyard on Thursday. You'll try to make it if you can. You're pretty busy. The place looks nice. Well, gotta go!"

The sketchy part of town: "The absolute last thing you should do is walk down to the corner of Stab Me Avenue and Beat Me Street and start asking shady people if they know where you can find some really good stuff, man. I can't say I haven't been there. You just don't want to be."

Home Delivery

"If scoring is a persistent issue for you, maybe consider moving to a major city where delivery services take almost all of the worry away. The weed is a bit more expensive, but it's well worth the extra cash to have the goods delivered right to your door. Let the guy on the bike worry about it."

Cannabis cups with strains in competition

Cannabutter

CANNABIS CUP *High Times'* marijuana-judging contest in Amsterdam. This annual event was first held in 1988 to determine the best Dutch cannabis seed strains. Founded by longtime *High Times* editor in chief Steven Hager, it was opened to the public in 1994, and has since grown to accommodate 3,000 "judges" every November during Thanksgiving week. Judges visit participating coffeeshops (as many as twenty-five) and sample the nominated strains for four days before voting. Repeat winners include the Green House, Barney's, Sensi Seeds, and Soma Seeds. The Cup also features live music, cultivation seminars, a hemp expo, and nightly parties. ALSO SEE: AMSTERDAM COFFEESHOPS (P. 41); CANNABIS CUP STRAINS (P. 31).

CANNABUTTER / *ka-na-butt-urr* / *n.* A marijuana-infused food made by various methods, all of which involve cooking ground pot in melted butter or oil and allowing it to decarboxylate. Once fully absorbed, it is cooled and ready for use in any kind of recipe. ALSO SEE: MEDICAL EDIBLES (P. 57); RECIPES (P.209).

CANOE / *ken-new* / *n.* A badly burning joint, it is caused by excess air pockets or seeds, either of which force the joint to run or rupture prematurely. It usually starts with a bad roll, resulting in a misshapen joint that lets in too much air and triggers an uneven burn. The same effect can occur as a result of rolling without first removing the seeds. A rupture starts as a small hole and quickly expands, enveloping a good part of the joint. The best way to deal with a canoe is to burn it off. ALSO SEE: DE-SEED.

CARB / *kahrb* / *n.* Believed to have gotten its name from *carburetor*, the car engine technology that fuses air with fuel, this small circular opening found on most bongs and glass pipes is your own manually operated internal combustion system. It acts as the trigger by which smoke is blasted into your system. ALSO SEE: ANATOMY OF A BONG (P. 23).

Canoe

Timothy Leary (left) and Neal Cassady (right) on the Further bus during its stop at Leary's house in Millbrook, New York, in 1964

Dave Chappelle in 1998

CASHED / *kash'd* / *adj.* When a bowl is depleted of smoke-able marijuana and all that's left is ash, as in, "Load up another, dude, this bowl is cashed." The term is also used to describe a lighter that is out of fluid.

CASSADY, NEAL (1926–1968) Before the crazy gonzo antics of Hunter S. Thompson, there was Neal Cassady, who though not a writer himself, was presented by Jack Kerouac as the speed-talking, whirling dervish of the Beat Generation. Born in Salt Lake City and raised in Denver, he hustled for a living and stole cars. After meeting Kerouac in 1946, the two embarked on cross-country adventures that Kerouac later chronicled in *On the Road* (1957) and *Visions of Cody* (1973). Cassady married Carolyn Robinson in 1948. He was arrested in San Francisco for selling marijuana to a narc in 1958 and spent nearly two years in California's San Quentin prison. In 1968 he bridged the gap between the Beats and the hippies when he joined Ken Kesey's Merry Pranksters in the early 1960s, and was featured in Tom Wolfe's *Electric Kool-Aid Acid Test* (1968). He was found comatose next to railroad tracks in Mexico and died shortly thereafter. His autobiography *The First Third* came out posthumously in 1971.

"Marijuana should definitely be legal. Booze is a hundred times worse."
—**Rodney Dangerfield,** comedian

In 1972 Grateful Dead lyricist John Perry Barlow offered his tribute to the Beat legend in the song "Cassidy": "Blow the horn, tap the tambourine / Close the gap on the dark years in between / You and me, Cassidy." A biopic starring Tate Donovan is scheduled to be released in 2008. ALSO SEE: EASY RIDERS, RAGING BEATS (P. 54).

CERVANTES, JORGE (B. 1954) *High Times'* cultivation columnist born in Washington State has long resided in Barcelona. He is the author of numerous grow books, including *Indoor Marijuana Horticulture* (1983), which has evolved over the years into multiple revised editions and been retitled *Marijuana Horticulture: The Indoor/Outdoor Medical Grower's Bible* (2006). His "Jorge's Rx" question-and-answer *High Times* column replaced Ed Rosenthal's "Ask Ed" in 1999. *High Times* has produced and released *Jorge Cervantes' Ultimate Grow* DVDs (2006 and 2007).

CHALICE / *chall-is* / *n.* 1. A water pipe generally made out of a coconut shell and popular among Rastafarians in Jamaica. A plastic tube and bowl are attached to the shell. Marijuana and tobacco are chopped finely and placed in the bowl to smoke. Among Rastas, ganja is considered a sacrament. 2. A drinking cup or goblet used for wine consumption in Christian religious ceremonies to signify the sacrament of Holy Communion. ALSO SEE: GANJA REGGAE CLASSICS (P. 186).

CHAMBER / *chaim-burr* / *n.* The long, tubelike part of the bong that connects the stem to the mouthpiece. Once smoke from a lit bowl is collected and the chamber is full, the smoke—a.k.a. the hit—can be inhaled in one shot. ALSO SEE: ANATOMY OF A BONG (P. 23).

CHAPPELLE, DAVE (B. 1973) Star and cowriter of *Half Baked* (1998), one of the most popular stoner movies of all time. Born in Washington, D.C., he began his career as a stand-up comedian. After *Half Baked* he appeared in several other movies, including *Undercover Brother* (2002), before his hugely popular *Chappelle's Show* on Comedy Central took off in 2003. Breaking every racial taboo and making sure to include plenty of drug humor (like the faux ad for a nontoxic chronic called O 'Dweeds), *Chappelle's Show* became an immediate cult classic. After two seasons, however, the star suddenly quit the show and returned to stand-up. In 2006 he starred in the music documentary *Dave Chappelle's Block Party.* ALSO SEE: HALF BAKED; MUSIC MOVIES (P. 168); MUST-SEE STONER TV SHOWS (P. 170); STONY COMEDIANS.

CHARAS / *charr-us* / *n.* This holiest of handmade hash

Stony Comedians

In addition to Dave Chappelle, here are a few more pot jokesters.

Doug Benson: One of the three stony minds responsible for the off-Broadway hit, *The Marijuana-Logues.* An acerbic commentator on VH1's *Best Week Ever,* as a stand-up comedian most of his jokes are pot-oriented.

George Carlin: Lenny Bruce and Carlin were the first comics to talk about pot. In "Grass Swept the Neighborhood" (1973), Carlin reminisced about when marijuana started to replace alcohol as people's drug of choice. On the cover of *Toledo Window Box* (1974), Carlin wore a T-shirt with a window box filled with pot plants.

Tommy Chong: He literally defined pot humor first as a stand-up comedian (with partner Cheech Marin) and later in films like *Up in Smoke* and on TV's *That '70s Show.*

Sacha Baron Cohen: As Ali G on *Da Ali G Show* and in *Ali G Indahouse,* he represents

George Carlin, circa 1971

marijuana smokers, rolling a spliff in one hand and dealing with police harassment. But as Borat, he doesn't smoke.

Bill Maher: The most politically active comic today, he regularly articulates the thoughts of millions of stoners with one prevailing message: Legalize it!

Amy Poehler: The *Saturday Night Live* standout almost always delivers the pot joke on "Weekend Update." She got her start with the sketch comedy group, the Upright Citizens Brigade.

Joe Rogan: The host of TV's *Fear Factor* (2001–2006), he has made a name for himself on the stand-up comedy circuit espousing marijuana and other psychedelics, and occasionally mixing it up with rivals like Carlos Mencia.

Sarah Silverman: She showed a fondness for bong hits in her stand-up film *Jesus is Magic,* while on her Comedy Central show, *The Sarah Silverman Program,* she's all about cookies and cough syrup.

Jon Stewart: Sly pot references on *The Daily Show with Jon Stewart* keep the stoner nation tuned in daily, and his cameo in *Half Baked,* as he regularly reminds viewers, is legendary.

STONER COMIC LEGENDS (R. I. P.): Lenny Bruce, Rodney Dangerfield, Bill Hicks, Sam Kinison, and Richard Pryor

Cheech & Chong

The Abbott and Costello of pot, Richard "Cheech" Marin and Tommy Chong joined forces in Vancouver in 1969 when Chong, a native Canadian of Asian descent, recruited Marin, a Mexican-American, to be his comedy partner. They made five comedy albums (including 1972's *Big Bambu* with a gigantic rolling paper inside) and six movies, starting with *Up in Smoke* (1978), the granddaddy of all stoner movies. Once the duo stopped making movies together in 1985, Marin shed the stoner reputation with roles in mainstream movies (*Tin Cup* and *Cars*) and on TV series (*Nash Bridges* and *Judging Amy*). Chong practically played himself on *That '70s Show* as the head-shop owner Leo. In 2003 Chong's bong company, Chong Glass, was raided. Arrested for selling paraphernalia across state lines, he served a nine-month sentence. Chong periodically performs at comedy clubs with his wife, Shelby. ALSO SEE: A BRIEF HISTORY OF STONER MOVIES (P. 146); CLASSIC STONER DIALOGUES (P. 154); TOMMY CHONG; OPERATION PIPE DREAMS; STONER CHARACTER ACTORS (P. 152); UP IN SMOKE.

🌿 Stoned & Stoneder: 🌿 Rating Cheech & Chong Movies

Up in Smoke (1978): Without a doubt Richard "Cheech" Marin and Tommy Chong's best movie was the result of years of stand-up performances and many comedy albums. Directed by Lou Adler, the film begins with Cheech (Pedro) picking up hitchhiker Chong (Anthony Stoner, or just simply "Man"). Chong pulls out a ridiculously large doobie and lights it up, prompting Cheech to ask, "Is that a joint? That looks like a quarter pounder." Much of the movie is spent lampooning the police (Stacy Keach plays Sgt. Stednanko). Another memorable scene features a van that is made out of weed and somehow manages to cross the border from Mexico into the U.S. 🌿🌿🌿🌿

Cheech & Chong's Next Movie (1980): The misadventures of Cheech & Chong continue in this follow-up to *Up in Smoke*. Cheech doubles as his hayseed cousin Red, who carries a duffel bag of weed everywhere he goes. Paul Reubens ("Pee Wee Herman") is memorable as the exasperated hotel clerk; Chong's wife, Shelby, and Rita Wilson also make appearances. 🌿🌿🌿

Cheech & Chong's Nice Dreams (1981): Directed by Chong, the dopey duo rips off a pot grower and then, masquerading as ice-cream vendors, sells the stuff out of an ice-cream truck. The cast includes Reubens, Sandra Bernhard, Keach, Shelby Chong, and Timothy Leary in a cameo. 🌿🌿🌿

Still Smokin' (1983): Cheech & Chong go to Amsterdam for a film festival that doesn't happen. 🌿🌿

Cheech & Chong's The Corsican Brothers (1984): This non-pot-related movie set in prerevolutionary France and directed by Chong marked the beginning of the end for the world's greatest stoner duo. A family affair for Chong, he cast his wife, Shelby, and daughters, Rae Dawn and Robbi. After the mockumentary *Get Out of My Room* (1985), directed by Marin, Cheech & Chong would never again appear together on the silver screen. 🌿

Cheech & Chong in *Nice Dreams*

ONLY
THE
BEST

est Qua
ICE REAMS

.50
.50
PAK .75
NDWICH .75
AKE·SHAKE .75

🍁 How to Use a Chillum 🍁

Smoking a chillum (a pipe long used in Hindu ceremonies), whether made of clay, glass, or wood, is a natural act for the seasoned stoner but can be challenging to the novice. If you are able to master a chillum, you will get one of the strongest hits you've ever experienced. Here's how to do it.

1 Make sure you have a small stone, or, if need be, a screen, to keep your pot or hash mix from falling through the bowl.

2 Pack the chillum with ground buds, not too tightly, but not too loosely either.

3 Place the chillum between your index and middle fingers on your left hand (reverse this if you are left-handed), as close to your knuckles as possible. Hold it there snugly, lean your head back, and face straight up. Make a fist with your left hand, and with your open right hand, clasp your left hand, creating a ball so that no air can escape when you inhale. Place your mouth at the hole created by your curled left hand, and have a friend light the bowl. Take a deep drag. If you're doing everything right, no air will escape, and you'll get a powerful hit.

Note: If you are smoking solo, light the bowl, then create the ball with both hands as described above and inhale. Say a simple prayer to Shiva as you blast off.

An Indian sadhu smokes a chillum

by Tone Loc with "Cheeba Cheeba" (1988). 2. Cheba Hut: chain of sub shops that sells "toasted" sandwiches.

CHEECH & CHONG SEE PAGE 36.

CHEF RA (1950–2006) Born James Wilson Jr. in Charleston, West Virginia, and christened Chef RA when he began writing a ganja food column called "Psychedelic Kitchen" for *High Times* in 1988, the Urbana, Illinois–based marijuana activist taught several generations of stoners how to cook with pot. He appeared in two *High Times'* video and DVD productions: *Chef RA Escapes Babylon* (1992) and *Chef RA: Ganja Gourmet* (2004). He died of a heart attack on December 26, 2006.

CHERRY / *chair-ee* / *n.* The burning ember at the end of a joint or bowl. It is called a cherry because the round coal burns hot and red.

CHILD'S GARDEN OF GRASS, A Comedic marijuana handbook written by Jack S. Margolis and Richard Clorfene in 1969 and adapted into a comedy album by Margolis, Jere Alan Brian, and Ron Jacobs in 1971. ALSO SEE: POT BOOKS THROUGH THE AGES (P. 206).

is cultivated in the Himalayan regions of India, Jammu and Kashmir, and Pakistan and smoked by India's religious sadhus, who pray to the Hindu god Lord Shiva. Made by touching ripe cannabis plants with your hands, the gooey residue, known as cream, is then scraped off, mixed with tobacco, and smoked in chillum pipes. Manali in the Indian state of Himachel Pradesh bordering Nepal and Peshewer in northeast Pakistan produce this highest of delicacies.

CHEEBA / *chee-bah* / *n.* 1. Slang for marijuana, as in, "Let's smoke some cheeba." Popularized in song by Harlem Underground with "Smokin' Cheeba Cheeba" (1976) and

CHILLUM / *chil-em* / *n.* Pipe made from ceramic, glass, or cow's horn and used by Hindu sadhus during ritualistic smoking of charas in India. Sometimes mixed with tobacco, the charas is smoked through cupped hands so that the pipe doesn't touch the lips. Spiritual stoners have adopted this technique, which includes saying praises to Shiva, such as "Boom Shiva." ALSO SEE: HOW TO USE A CHILLUM (P. 38).

CHONG, TOMMY (B. 1938) Born Thomas Chong B. Kin in Edmonton, Alberta, Canada, to a Chinese-Canadian father and a Scottish-Canadian mother. Together with Richard "Cheech" Marin, he formed Cheech & Chong, the greatest pot-comedy duo of all time. He has six children (including actress Rae Dawn) and has been married to his wife, Shelby, with whom he has performed, since 1975. In 2006 he was the subject of Josh Gilbert's documentary *a/k/a Tommy Chong* and authored *The I Chong: Meditations from the Joint*. He also wrote the foreword to this book. ALSO SEE: A BRIEF HISTORY OF STONER MOVIES (P. 146); CHEECH & CHONG (P. 36); DOCUMENTARIES (P. 166); OPERATION PIPE DREAMS; STONER LEGENDS (P. 194); STONY COMEDIANS (P. 35); UP IN SMOKE.

CHRISTIANIA Self-governed neighborhood in the Christianshavn area of Copenhagen, once known as "The Amsterdam of Scandinavia," it is famous for its lax possession and distribution laws. After serving as a military site in the 1940s and 1950s, it became a hippie haven in the 1960s and later formed its own collective based on the progressive idea of a free society. In 1971 its residents won an independence of sorts, and were allowed to determine their own governing laws based on consensus. At the heart of this new Christiania, also known as Freetown Christiania, is the notorious "Pusher Street," which used to be lined with stalls openly selling hash. In 2004 the stalls were all but shut down in a police crackdown and, ever since, opposition to the drug trade has effectively kept them from returning. Still, high-end hash remains a staple of the area, which is inhabited by approximately 850 residents. Hard drugs, guns, violence, and cars are not allowed, which gives the eighty-five-acre area a quaint, village-type feel.

CHRONIC / *kraw-nik* / *n.* 1. Hip-hop term for ultrapotent marijuana, first noted in 1992 with the title of Dr. Dre's album *The Chronic*. Other musical references include Snoop Dogg's "Chronic Break" and Kottonmouth Kings' "We Got the Chronic." 2. High-end quality kind bud, as in, "Dawg, this is the chronic!" 3. Generic, mostly indica, strain available from Serious Seeds in Holland. Flowers in fifty-six to sixty-three days and has 8 to 15 percent THC content. ALSO SEE: THE GREATEST POT-THEMED ALBUM COVERS (P. 182); KIND.

CHRONIC CANDY / *kraw-nik-kan-dee* / *n.* Florida manufacturer of hemp-based lollipops. They offer three flavors: O.G. Chronic (green), Train Wreck (blue), and Kush (purple). They also sell Chronic Ice Herbal Iced Tea and bath-and-body products. The New York City Council condemned sale of the candies in 2004, calling them "sickening" and accusing the company of "targeting to children." Owner Tony "Montana" Van Pelt replied, "Hemp candy has been around since 1920."

CHUFF / *chuff* / *v.* To expel air suddenly in a fashion halfway between a cough and a huff. It's what happens when you hold your hit a little too long and cough without opening your mouth.

CLEAR / *kleer* / *v.* 1. To flush a hit all the way through your bong, pipe, or one-hitter, so that leftover smoke is inhaled from the chamber and any stale smoke is removed. 2. To get rid of an obstruction that is clogging a bowl. 3. Another name for cellulose-based rolling sheets or papers. ALSO SEE: ALEDA; BONG HIT; NUDIE; SWAYZE.

CLONE / *clohne* / *n.* Cutting from a plant, which when placed in a rooting medium such as rockwool, perlite, sand, vermiculite, dirt, or simply water, produces an identical version of that plant. All marijuana clones are taken from female plants.

CLUB / *cluhb* / *n.* Brand of rolling papers manufactured by S. D. Modiano, an Italian company founded in 1870. Originally produced without gum and known for its extremely thin sheets, these papers have long been the favorite of connoisseurs. The package features a red-bearded man reading a newspaper while smoking a cigarette or joint.

"America's view on weed is ridiculous. I mean— are you kidding me? If everyone smoked weed, the world would be a better place."
— **Kirsten Dunst,** actress

"Marijuana should be legalized. It's ridiculous that it isn't."

—**Robert Altman,**
director

COACHELLA / *ko-a-chel-la* / *n*. Shorthand for the Coachella Valley Music and Arts Festival, an annual spring weekend gathering, in the desert town of Indio, California, (outside Palm Springs) since 1999, which draws more than 60,000 fans and features the best in alternative music both past and present. Considered closest in vibe to European festivals like Roskilde and Glastonbury, the organizers' one rule is that they don't book "aggressive" bands. Tool, the Red Hot Chili Peppers, or the Pixies are about as heavy as it gets. ALSO SEE: STONER FESTIVALS (P. 196).

COFFEESHOP / *kaw-fee-shop* / *n*. In all countries other than the Netherlands, it's where you get your daily dose of caffeine. But in Amsterdam and throughout Holland, it's your one-stop shop for quality marijuana sold in small

Paradise Coffeeshop
in Amsterdam

quantities or as pre-rolled spliffs. Hash, space cakes, and cookies are also available for purchase as are other food and drinks. Just walking down the street in Amsterdam you can smell one of these retail outlets a block away. Nonsmoking laws appear to threaten them, but most likely they'll survive the European Union's disdain for liberal Dutch pot policies. ALSO SEE: AMSTERDAM COFFEESHOPS (P. 41); BARNEY'S COFFEESHOP; THE BULLDOG; CANNABIS CUP; THE GRASSHOPPER; THE GREEN HOUSE.

COLA / *ko-la* / *n*. 1. The long flower or bud at the top of a marijuana plant. 2. Spanish slang *colitas* means little buds or little tails, derived from the opening line of a song by the Eagles, "Hotel California" (1976): "On a dark desert highway, cool wind in my hair / Warm smell of colitas, rising up through the air." 3. Carbonated beverage, such as Coca-Cola, Pepsi-Cola, or R.C. Cola.

COLOMBIAN GOLD / *ko-lum-bee-an-goald* / *n*. A classic, pure sativa strain from the original South American pot capital, it takes six months to grow outdoors and produces huge colas. It has a minty, hashlike flavor and was bred with Acapulco Gold and Afghani to create Skunk #1. Now available only as a hybrid, it is crossed with indicas like White Widow. ALSO SEE: CLASSIC STRAINS (P. 11).

COMPASSION CLUB / *come-pash-in-club* / *n*. 1. Dispensary, clinic, or community center where medical marijuana is provided to patients. More common in Canada, as in the B.C. Compassion Club Society, a cannabis dispensary may operate within a club. 2. Organization that assists those in need. ALSO SEE: DISPENSARY; MEDICAL EDIBLES (P. 57); MEDICAL MARIJUANA.

CONE / *cohn* / *n*. Joint rolled in a conical shape, usually with a filter. Cone joints are common in Europe and Jamaica. ALSO SEE: SPLIFF.

CONTACT HIGH / *kon-takt-hi* / *n*. Term used to describe the reaction to breathing in a nearby person's marijuana smoke. To achieve this kind of high, you are not directly taking part in the toking.

COP / *kahp* / *n. or v*. 1. Slang for a police officer. The term's original meaning, dating back to the early 1700s, was to seize or capture. In the mid-1800s, the word "copper"

Reggae artist Rocker T smokes a huge cone joint

was first used in England and the U.S. to describe some-one who catches criminals. This term was later shortened to cop. 2. To obtain, steal, or take, as in, "Dude, I'm running low. Can I cop a joint off you?" 3. To admit, as in, "I did smoke the last of your weed, dude. I'll cop to that."

COTTONMOUTH / kot-ten-mouth / n. 1. The sensation of unquenchable thirst after serious toking, where your tongue feels as dry as sandpaper. The best bet for relief: water (as opposed to a sugary soda). Beer's not bad either. 2. Word used in the names of two bands: Cottonmouth, Texas, and Kottonmouth Kings. ALSO SEE: KOTTONMOUTH KINGS.

COUCH-LOCK / kouch-lawk / n. A colloquial stonerism to describe the state of feeling so high you can't get off the couch.

CREEPER / kree-purr / n. Common term used in and around Florida to describe the kind of high that comes on slowly (it creeps up on you). The buds themselves are often referred to as crippy weed. ALSO SEE: KRYPTO.

CRISPY / kris-pee / adj. 1. A sensation akin to feel-ing "toasty" or "toasted," it's the point at which you are comfortably high and may not necessarily need to smoke any more. 2. In terms of food, it's a word used to de-scribe a hard or brittle texture that causes whatever you are eating to crunch in your mouth. ALSO SEE: BAKED; BLASTED; BLAZED; BURNT; BUZZED; FRIED; HIGH; LIT;

Amsterdam Coffeeshops

Pot Culture PICKS

C

Barney's: Winner of many Cannabis Cups, stop here for English-style breakfasts (that means eggs and potatoes) any time of the day as well as for vaporizer hits dispensed at the bar.
BEST STRAINS: Sweet Tooth, Morning Glory, Laughing Buddah
LOCATION: Haarlemmerstraat 102

Bluebird: Known as the best hash shop in Amsterdam, you can take a tour of all the hash-producing countries—from Nepal to Morocco—in a couple of visits. Or one *really* long one.
BEST HASHES: Mazar-i-Sharif, Nepali Cream, Malana Cream
LOCATION: St. Antoniesbreestraat 41

De Dampkring: The shop was featured in *Ocean's 12* and named a strain after the movie. It's best known for delicious strains and big crowds.
BEST STRAINS: NYC Diesel, Mako Haze, Amethyst

LOCATION: Handboogstraat 29

The Green House: The three Green Houses in Amsterdam are favorites of anyone who's attended the Cannabis Cup, which has awarded the shop and its seed company more than thirty trophies over the years.
BEST STRAINS: Super Silver Haze, White Rhino, Hawaiian Snow
LOCATIONS: Tolstraat 91, O.Z. Voorburgwal 191, Waterlooplein 345

Rokerij: Their first and main shop is located in the Leidseplein section near the museums, Vondel Park, and the Melkweg Paradiso rock club. Always crowded, its Middle Eastern decor will make you want to curl up with a hookah in the corner. In the past few years, Rokerij has expanded to three additional shops.
BEST STRAINS: Rokerij Haze, Stardust, White Widow
LOCATIONS: Leidsestraat 41, Singel 8, Amstel 8, Elandsgracht 53

Coffeeshop menu

41

Pot-Parazzi

CELEBRITY STONERS CAUGHT IN THE ACT

Charlize Theron: The Oscar-winning actress demonstrates proper use of the apple pipe at a backyard birthday party in Santa Monica in 2001. What, nobody had papers?

Charlize Theron

Ryan Phillippe: The *Flags of Our Fathers* star reverses the usual smoke-and-munchies pattern. After chowing down at a seafood restaurant in Pacific Palisades, California, the hunky actor ducks into his car to take a hit off a metal pipe.

Ryan Phillippe

Mischa Barton: The *OC* actress partakes, in a car no less. Clearly, a bad demonstration of keeping it "on the d.l.," especially with the pot-parazzi following you.

Mischa Barton

Paris Hilton: The hotel heiress who spent nearly a month in jail in 2007 for DUI and driving with a suspended license has been photographed numerous times smoking and carrying weed.

Paris Hilton
(below and right)

Cameron Diaz and **Drew Barrymore:** While vacationing together in Hawaii, A-list actresses and longtime friends Cameron Diaz and Drew Barrymore share a time-out and a toke on Kauai's Anini Beach.

Drew Barrymore (left) and
Cameron Diaz (right)

LOADED; RIPPED; STONED; TOASTY; WASTED; ZONKED; ZOOTED.

CRUNCHY / *krun-chee* / *adj.* 1. A somewhat derogatory modifier for a person who is also known as a hippie or Deadhead, or, some would add, an environmentalist or overall liberal. 2. In terms of food, a word used to describe something that, when chewed, produces an audible sound.

CRUTCH / *kruhch* / *n.* 1. British term for the filter tip used at the end of a spliff when "skinning up." ALSO SEE: FILTER; FILTER TIP; SKIN.

CRYSTALS / *cris-tylz* / *pl. n.* 1. Resin glands or trichomes that accumulate on the outer layer of cannabis flowers or buds and look like snow or powder—the more crystals, the stronger the marijuana. 2. Clear igneous rocks sought by hippies and New Agers. 3. In the singular form, the term can refer to crystal methamphetamine (crystal meth, for short). ALSO SEE: TRICHOMES.

Crystals

CULTIVATION / *kull-ti-vay-shun* / *n.* The act of growing fruit or flowers, indoors or outdoors, organically or hydroponically. ALSO SEE: GET GROWING (P. 64).

CURING / *keyor-ing* / *pres. part. of cure* The last stage in the marijuana drying process when buds are placed in glass jars (preferably mason jars) or wooden boxes for two to four

Cypress Hill—B-Real (front right), Sen Dog (front left), and DJ Muggs (back seat)—in 1991

weeks. This process improves the taste, smell, and smokeability. ALSO SEE: MASON JAR.

CUTTING SEE CLONE.

CYPRESS HILL The most popular pro-marijuana hip-hop group of all time. They hail from Los Angeles and include rappers B-Real (Louis Freese) and Sen Dog (Senen Reyes), both of Hispanic heritage, and DJ Muggs (Lawrence Muggerud), a transplanted Italian-American from New York. In 1992 NORML designated Cypress Hill its spokesgroup. The band's eponymously titled debut album (1991) includes such marijuana anthems as "Stoned is the Way of the Walk," "Light Another," and "Something for the Blunted." In 1993 the group had their biggest hit with "Insane in the Brain" from *Black Sunday*, which also features "I Wanna Get High" and "Hits from the Bong." In 1994 they added percussionist Eric Bobo, the son of salsa legend Willie Bobo, to the group. From 1995 to 2004 they released five more studio albums. ALSO SEE: BLUNTED HIP-HOP CLASSICS (P. 184); THE GREATEST POT-THEMED ALBUM COVERS (P. 182); STONER BANDS (P. 177).

"The ultimate twenty-year plan is to be living in the Caribbean, writing, living off the land, eating from the ocean, and probably smoking herb."
—Ryan Phillippe,
actor

Rules of Dealer Etiquette

1 Keep it on the q.t.: If you must discuss specifics via phone, e-mail, or text prior to a purchase, use code words previously agreed upon by you and your dealer.

2 Know what you want: Whether it's going to be delivered or picked up, know what grade you plan on buying and how much of it you want.

3 Smelling is OK, sampling is not: Though there are dealers who allow buyers to try the goods before committing, to ask to sample a particular strain can put the dealer in an awkward spot since it may cut into his or her profit margin.

4 Steer clear of the IOU: Try to take only what you can afford. Though many dealers will extend an unofficial line of credit, running a bill can be bad news, especially if your dealer is also a friend.

5 Have your cash ready: There is nothing more annoying to a dealer than a mid-transaction ATM run.

6 Do it on the d.l.: If you must complete a transaction in a public place, like the street or a park (*not* recommended), try to find a more low-key spot around the corner or in the car, somewhere out of the sight line of random passersby.

7 Offer to smoke out your hookup: If the transaction goes down in a private space where you can freely smoke, offer the dealer a puff out of your recently bought bag. It's common stoner courtesy.

8 Sharing your dealer: When a stoner friend contacts you inquiring about your dealer's number, ask the dealer first if he or she is looking for new customers. Only when you get the go-ahead should you offer the dealer's number.

9 Don't bring friends with you: Dealers are notoriously and understandably paranoid. They don't appreciate new faces showing up and checking out their business. Ask first if it's OK to let a friend tag along. If the dealer says no, that means no.

10 No pinching allowed: If you are the dealer, don't pinch. It's just not cool, dude.

D

DAHAB / *dah-hob* / *n.* Bedouin seaside village on the southern tip of Egypt's Sinai Peninsula. *Dahab* means "gold" in Arabic. Over the past twenty years it has become the Middle East's bohemian destination, thanks to its two-mile strip of hippie-friendly beach camps (sleep and eat tent-style) and hookah bars (they call water pipes "shish"). A newspaper roll of Bedouin buds—a half-ounce of stemmy, dry, and leafy shake (they are grown in the most arid of climates, after all)—can be scored by literally asking anyone, except for the one "town" cop, and costs about $20. The laid-back desert high is well worth the trip. ALSO SEE: STONER BEACHES (P. 202).

DANK / *danck* / *n. or adj.* 1. Slang for high-quality marijuana, as in, "That weed is dank" or "Who's got the diggity dank?" Also slang for anything perceived to be good, as in, "That concert was dank, dude." 2. Damp and humid. 3. Thank you in Dutch.

DAZED AND CONFUSED 1. Title of the 1993 indie film directed by Richard Linklater about a group of high school stoners in Austin, Texas, circa 1976, starring Ben Affleck and Matthew McConaughey in early roles. The film also features Rory Cochrane as the ultimate stoner, Slater, who waxes eloquent about George and Martha Washington's pot-smoking habits. 2. Title of a song written and originally performed by American singer-songwriter Jake Holmes who, in 1967, opened for the Yardbirds (featuring Jimmy Page) on a U.S. tour. Impressed by the song, Page reworked it and performed it in the Yardbirds' live shows. He eventually rerecorded it with his next band, Led Zeppelin, in 1968, and the song appeared on the band's debut album, *Led Zeppelin* (1969). Though hailed as a drug anthem for its opening line, "Been dazed and confused for so long," it is, according to Holmes, actually a love story about a girl who can't decide whether to stay with him or not. 3. Name of a monthly British style magazine founded in 1991 and devoted to covering of-the-moment fashion, music, and art scenes, as well as social and political issues. ALSO SEE: A BRIEF HISTORY OF STONER MOVIES (P. 146); DAZED AND CONFUSED: TEN YEARS AFTER (P. 46); LED ZEPPELIN; TALKING DAZED WITH MATTHEW MCCONAUGHEY (P. 47).

DEADHEADS / *ded-hedz* / *pl. n.* Followers of the legendary Grateful Dead. The term refers to casual fans and those who actually traveled from show to show, on tour, fully embracing the nomadic, self-sustaining lifestyle until the band stopped performing after the death of Jerry Garcia in 1995. ALSO SEE: THE GRATEFUL DEAD; HEAD(S).

DEALER / *deel-urr* / *n.* 1. In stoner culture, the person supplying the pot, be he or she a professional or just a pal. 2. A person, company, or retail establishment in the business of selling a product. 3. In gambling, the person who deals the cards during a table game, a.k.a. croupier. ALSO SEE: RULES OF DEALER ETIQUETTE (P. 44).

DECRIMINALIZATION / *dee-krim-in-uh-li-zay-shun* / *n.* When laws governing marijuana are changed to reduce the penalties for possession of small quantities (usually below one ounce) to noncriminal status. The first state to decriminalize was Oregon in 1973, followed by California, New York, Ohio, Nebraska, Minnesota, Colorado, Mississippi, Alaska, Maine, North Carolina, and Nevada.

DEPRIORITIZATION / *dee-prye-or-ih-tih-zay-shun* / *n.* Easing marijuana regulation to the point where it's considered the lowest priority of law enforcement. It is usually

Deadheads dance at Berkeley's Greek Theater

passed on the local level, such as in Ann Arbor, Michigan, where possession is subject to a $25 fine.

DE-SEED / *de-seed* / *v.* To rid your schwag of seeds. This sometimes tedious process is necessary because, when burned, seeds not only smell and taste bad, but cause joints to canoe or rupture. ALSO SEE: CANOE; SCHWAG; SIFT; VINTAGE VINYL: ALBUMS FOR ROLLING & LISTENING (P. 48).

DIME BAG / *dyme-bhag* / *n.* 1. The term for a $10 amount of marijuana, it is the cousin of the nickel bag, the term for a $5 amount. 2. Part of the nickname (Dimebag Darrell) for Pantera guitarist Darrell Abbott, who was killed by a deranged fan in 2004. ALSO SEE: NICKEL BAG.

DISPENSARY / *dis-pen-sir-ee* / *n.* A retail outlet for medical

De-seeding

Dazed and Confused

TEN YEARS AFTER

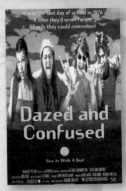

At this classic stoner movie's tenth-year reunion party in Austin, Texas (at the Moontower, dude!), in 2003, *Pot Culture* asked the stars of *Dazed and Confused* some burning questions.

Pot Culture: What were you really smoking in the movie?

Joey Lauren Adams (Simone): It was a kind of oregano that tasted really bad. But during the last scene in the movie when we're driving to get Aerosmith tickets, we were so stoned. Fortunately, no one had any lines!

PC: Who was the inspiration for your character Wooderson, the lovable 1970s greaser dude?

Matthew McConaughey (Wooderson): It was [based on] who I thought my older brother, Pat, was. When I was ten, he was seventeen, and when I saw him leaning against a brick wall in school one afternoon, smoking a cigarette with his leg up, he looked about seven feet tall. He was the coolest, man.

PC: Were you as mean as your character Darla when you were in school?

Parker Posey (Darla): When I was in high school, I looked up to the bad girls. They were always cool and doing reckless things. I was drawn to their troubled-ness, but I would never do what they did. I repressed it and got to play a part where I could express that side.

PC: What was up with Mitch touching the bridge of his nose all the time?

Wiley Wiggins (Mitch): For ten years, people have been asking me that. Don't people do nervous, twitchy things in real life? Nobody asked me to do it, but when they edited the film, they kept it in.

Best Buds: (left to right) Rory Cochrane (Slater), Jason London (Randall), and Sasha Jensen (Don)

Wiley Wiggins (Mitch) and Christin Hinojosa (Sabrina)

Talking Dazed

WITH MATTHEW McCONAUGHEY

As *Dazed and Confused*'s girl-chasing, hot-rodding stoner-greaser Wooderson, Matthew McConaughey, in his first major film role, stole virtually every scene he was in. Now one of Hollywood's most in-demand actors, thanks to box office successes like *We Are Marshall* and *The Wedding Planner*, McConaughey reflects on the movie that made him a star.

Pot Culture: Do people come up to you and quote lines from *Dazed and Confused*?

Matthew McConaughey: All the time. They'll say, "Hey, man, got a joint?" Or, "Wanna play some foosball?" Or they'll just walk by and go, "That's why I love those high school girls, man..." and they'll wait for me to finish [the line]. They'll keep walking and just raise their arm like, I don't want nothing, just a little exchange. *Dazed* fans are the coolest.

PC: Does everyone just presume that you're a stoner?

MM: I don't know. Ever since I was born, my whole family's always thought I was the hippie of the clan. For me, whether I'm smoking or not, I always feel nice and stony.

PC: Where do you think your character Wooderson would be now?

MM: He's DJing at his local community radio station where he's got his own gig and doin' all right. And I think he's married and he's got two girls. Wooderson's got a lot of things figured out in a really good way. I like that guy.

PC: Back when you made the movie in 1993, did you think it would end up being a cult classic?

MM: No, I didn't think about it. It was my first film and I didn't know what the hell I was doing, anyway. But I remember sitting there, watching what was going on and thinking, "This feels right."

"For me, whether I'm smoking or not, I always feel nice and stony."

Matthew McConaughey as Wooderson

Vintage Vinyl

FOR ROLLING AND LISTENING

Back when vinyl LPs were the only music-listening option, many album covers also served as surfaces on which to de-seed or prepare pot. Even better were double albums and gatefolds with trippy artwork. The following classic albums are stoner staples worth listening to and rolling on (if you can find them):

The Beatles: *Sgt. Pepper's Lonely Hearts Club Band; Magical Mystery Tour;* and *The White Album*

Black Sabbath: *Paranoid*

Bob Marley: *Burnin'*

Earth, Wind & Fire: *Gratitude*

Funkadelic: *One Nation Under a Groove*

Grateful Dead: *Live Dead; Europe '72*

Hüsker Dü: *Zen Arcade*

Jimi Hendrix: *Electric Ladyland*

Led Zeppelin: *Houses of the Holy*

MC5: *High Time*

Miles Davis: *Bitches Brew*

The Stooges: *Fun House*

The Who: *Quadrophenia; Tommy*

Above: *Houses of the Holy* by Led Zeppelin (1973)
Below: Vintage color vinyl

marijuana. They are primarily located in California, where patients with legal medical cards can obtain marijuana and other cannabis products such as edibles and clones at reasonable prices. Some double as community centers, with activities for patients. ALSO SEE: COMPASSION CLUB; MEDICAL EDIBLES (P. 57); MEDICAL MARIJUANA.

DITCH WEED / *dich-weed* / *n.* 1. Feral hemp still found in parts of the American Midwest. Plants are usually tall and contain very low levels of THC. They are sometimes harvested by overzealous potheads and sold as schwag. Smoking it will most likely cause a headache. 2. Another name for schwag or brick weed, the term signifies leafy, dry pot with an abundance of stems and seeds, and a low potency. ALSO SEE: BRICK WEED; HEMP; SCHWAG.

D.L. / *dee-ell* / *n.* Abbreviation for "down low," which, in stoner culture, can describe the strategic passing of a joint, discreet sneaking of a toke, or careful completion of a cash transaction, as in, "Keep it on the d.l., dude." The term derives from urban vernacular for something done covertly or under the radar. The abbreviation originated in hip-hop culture and gained popularity when R. Kelly released the song "Down Low (Nobody Has to Know)" (1996).

DMT The abbreviation for dimethyltriptamine, a powerful hallucinogen that can be smoked, injected, snorted, or eaten. Smoking is the most common method and results in a brief trip lasting ten to thirty minutes. Visuals occur internally with eyes closed. Some people, such as author Terence McKenna, report out-of-body experiences and contact with aliens. It is a main ingredient in the Amazon hallucinogen ayahuasca, but is prohibited in the U.S. where it is classified as a Schedule I drug.

DOOB / *dube* / *n.* Short for doobie (see next page), as in, "Dude, you got a doob on you?"

DOOBAGE / *dube-edge* / *n.* Slang for any quantity of pot. The term is used famously in *The Breakfast Club* (1985), when burnout Bender (played by Judd Nelson) asks for his stash back after hiding it in the pants of geek Brian Johnson (Anthony Michael Hall). "So Ahab, kybo mein doobage," Bender says before smoking out the rest of the detention crew in the school library.

DOOBIE / *doo-bee* / *n*. 1. Hippie term for a joint, as in, "Spark up that doobie, dude." Some believe the term derived from the children's TV show *Romper Room* (aired 1953 to 1994), which featured the jive-talking bumblebee character, Mr. Do-Be ("Do be good boys and girls to your parents…"). 2. Part of the name of a popular 1970s rock group, the Doobie Brothers. 3. *High Times* music awards show, The Doobies, first held in 2000.

DOORS, THE SEE P. 50.

DOPE / *doap* / *n. or adj*. 1. General term for drugs, as in, "Who's got the dope?" First applied to marijuana, as in, "You wanna smoke some dope?" Gradually evolved to mean heroin, as in, "Let's shoot some dope." 2. African-American slang for good, as in, "That's dope." 3. Slang for information, as in, Cecil Adams's syndicated column "The Straight Dope," published since 1973. 4. New York–based metal band formed in 1999 by Edsel Dope. 5. *Doop*: the Dutch word for sauce or gravy. 6. Early American usage: syrup topping for ice cream; syrup base for cola-flavored soft drink; syrup base for the original Coca-Cola recipe (which includes a small amount of cocaine). 7. Someone who is not very smart. 8. Dopey: one of the Seven Dwarfs. 9. Doper: negative term for a drug user.

DOSE / *dohse* / *n*. 1. An amount of a drug as recommended by a physician, a prescription, or over-the-counter medicines, such as Aspirin. 2. One hit of LSD. 3. As a verb, the act of giving LSD to another person. It can also mean to surreptitiously give LSD to another person.

DOWNER / *dao–nur* / *n*. A person or event that causes dissatisfaction or unhappiness, as in, "You're a downer, dude." ALSO SEE: BUMMER; DRAG.

DRAG / *draagg* / *n. or v*. 1. A hit off a tobacco cigarette (as opposed to a marijuana joint). 2. A downer or bummer, as in, "What a drag, dude." 3. A term originating in the theater to describe when a male dresses like a female. 4. To pull something across a groundlike surface. 5. To force a movement, as in, "Dude, I had to be dragged out of bed after last night." ALSO SEE: BUMMER; DOWNER.

DRAW / *draugh* / *v. or n*. To inhale marijuana or tobacco smoke into the lungs. Referenced in the song "One Draw" (1981) performed by Rita Marley and written by Bob Marley. 2. A hit of marijuana. 3. To make a piece of art by using your hand and a pen, pencil, marker, or crayons. ALSO SEE: BRITISH POT SLANG (P .130); GANJA REGGAE CLASSICS (P. 186); HIT; INHALE; PUFF; PULL; RIP; SMOKE; TOKE.

DRUG ENFORCEMENT ADMINISTRATION (DEA) The nemesis of drug users everywhere, this federal agency was founded as part the Controlled Substances Act of 1970,

☘ Dealing with a Drug Test ☘

After cops and nosy neighbors, drug tests are anathema to pot smokers. Since marijuana can stay in body tissues for thirty days after use, here is the dope on drug tests.

1 Stop smoking: If you know a test is coming, that's the best strategy. If you're a daily smoker, clean out for at least a month prior to the test. If you're a weekend toker, clean out for one-to-two weeks prior.

2 Drink lots of water: The key is to dilute the urine sample. Drink a gallon of water the night before and again the morning of the test.

3 Household products don't work: Myths abound that Mountain Dew, vinegar, niacin, and goldenseal can thwart a drug test. They can't.

4 Shop for a drug-test solution: Companies like Clear Choice promise to help you beat a drug test with their products. Users report that these potions work. Some companies also offer home-testing kits.

5 If you're really desperate: Some stoners have been known to strap on the Whizzanator, a fake phallus that pees synthetic urine. Unfortunately, this device is only an option for dudes.

The Doors

Los Angeles band—formed in 1965 by UCLA film students, singer-poet Jim Morrison and keyboardist Ray Manzarek (later joined by guitarist Robbie Krieger and drummer John Densmore)—whose name references a verse in William Blake's poem, "The Marriage of Heaven and Hell" ("If the doors of perception were cleansed, everything would appear to man as it is: infinite") and in turn was used by Aldous Huxley for the title of a book on mescaline, *The Doors of Perception* (1954). The band skirted the lines between rock, psychedelia, and performance art with organ-led melodies, epic arrangements, and dramatic delivery. Their first hit, "Light My Fire," went to Number 1 in July 1967, the height of the Summer of Love. Two months later the band that had started out playing gigs on the Sunset Strip was asked to perform on *The Ed Sullivan Show* with the condition they would change one line of "Light My Fire" ("Girl we couldn't get much higher"). Morrison ignored the request, and instead, emphasized the word *higher* during their live performance, infuriating Sullivan, who never invited them back on the show. Their next four albums all came in at the top of the charts with Morrison's now-legendary stage antics pushing their popularity to unprecedented heights. Their career was thwarted, however, by Morrison's alcoholism and hard drug use. In 1971 Morrison died in Paris from a heroin overdose. Oliver Stone's movie *The Doors* (1991), starring Val Kilmer as Morrison, chronicles the band's short career.

My First Time BY RAY MANZAREK

Here, the man responsible for the Doors' endlessly trippy keyboard melodies and solos writes about his maiden voyage with pot, both on his own and with the legendary 1960s rock band.

D

The Doors—(clockwise from left) Robbie Krieger, John Densmore, Ray Manzarek, and Jim Morrison—posing with POT graffiti tag in Los Angeles in 1969

"I was in the U.S. Army, one of several thousand Americans stationed in Southeast Asia before the start of the Vietnam War. It was 1963 and I got sent to Korat, Thailand, to a military base out in the boonies. I don't think anyone knew what was going on there—typical military, spend hundreds of thousands of dollars and nothing was happening—but it was in the high desert, up on a plateau, and the perfect place to try marijuana for the first time.

"I got some ganja from my houseboy—these Thai locals would come do your laundry and clean your barracks for a couple of dollars. I exchanged a carton of American cigarettes that cost me two dollars—he would double his money when he sold them in town—and he brought me Thai Sticks stuffed into a can of Saltine crackers.

"It was a Saturday night and there was nothing to do, so we decided, 'Let's smoke this stuff!' We bought some Cokes and pound cake from a little snack stand, sat down in the shade and proceeded to roll up a couple of joints. I didn't know how to roll—and never learned—so this guy did it instead. As we smoked, he said, 'Hold it in your lungs.' I did and it was nice and smooth, no real coughing or anything. I exhaled and passed the joint. Then I said, 'Roll another, my friend.' The second was a very mellow, nice high. Then after about fifteen minutes, it started to really come on. As I recall, I put my head back and little by little, my tongue would uncurl out of my mouth until it was extended as far as it could possibly go. And I was sitting there in a reclining position, stoned out of my mind, with my tongue all the way out of my mouth, hanging down, and I had to push it back in. This went on for the next four hours. I would say, 'Oh my God, give me another Coke. I'm as dry as I can possibly be, and while you're at it, give me two more pieces of that luscious, divinely delicious, lemony pound cake.' It was the best thing I had eaten in my entire life—and washing it down with Coca-Cola on a Saturday night in the middle of Thailand, I had become a stoner and stayed that way for the next fifteen years.

"The Doors really were a band of potheads."
—Ray Manzarek

"A little while later, in the fall of 1965, Jim [Morrison], John [Densmore], Robbie [Krieger], and I smoked the first time we ever played together as the Doors. We rolled a joint, passed it around, and everybody took a couple of hits. Then, we played 'Moonlight Drive,' the very first song Jim sang to me on Venice Beach. Being stoned and with the four of us playing together, I had transcended. I went to a place I had never been before. Robbie played bottleneck guitar that sounded like a sitar. Morrison just went crazy. At the end of the song, I said, 'Listen guys, I have played music all my life, but this is the first time I have ever understood what it meant to play music.' Whether it was Robbie's bottleneck, the song, or the marijuana, the Doors had finally come together."

51

which categorized all drugs, illegal and legal, in numerous schedules: I, II, III, and so on. Marijuana is considered a Schedule I drug, meaning it has no acceptable use according to the federal government. Petitions to reschedule marijuana—one means of legalizing it—have been repeatedly denied. The organization employs 11,000 people, 5,000 of whom are "special agents," a.k.a. "narcs." ALSO SEE: NARC.

DRUG POLICY ALLIANCE (DPA) Created in 2000 with the merger of the Drug Policy Foundation (formed by Arnold Trebach in 1987) and the Lindesmith Center (formed by Ethan Nadelmann in 1994), it is funded by liberal philanthropist George Soros and supports the legalization of all illicit drugs, with a special emphasis on marijuana. Nadelmann remains the executive director.

DRUG TEST / *drug-test* / *n.* One of the big successes of the Reagan-era war on drugs was when the federal government encouraged private corporations to drug-test their employees. Pot smokers have become the chief target due to the fact that THC may remain in the bloodstream for thirty to forty-five days. The ultimate invasion of privacy, drug testing has evolved from urine samples (the most common form) to hair and saliva samples. ALSO SEE: DEALING WITH A DRUG TEST (P. 49).

DRY / *dreye* / *adj.* 1. What happens to marijuana when air seeps in and sucks the moisture out of the buds and the leaves. 2. The absence of marijuana (or alcohol) or to run out of either, as in, "I'm totally dry, dude—can you hook me up?"

DUDE / *dood* / *n.* One of the most frequently used words in the stoner lexicon, it can refer to a male or female and, depending on the inflection, imply a call to attention ("Dude, check this out"). It is also another way of saying "right on," as in, "You won $2,000 in Blackjack? Dude!" Or it can simply be a general acknowledgment of another person, friend, or recent acquaintance, as in, "Hey, dude, got any weed?" Appearance of the word dates back to 1883 in the U.S., where it was used to describe a sharply dressed man, and to 1887 in Europe, where it simply referred to a man. In the decades to come, the word was adopted by cowboy cul-

Dude

Bob Dylan performing in 1965

ture, though it was often intended as a derogatory term for Easterners venturing out West to engage in the cowboy experience. (A "dude ranch" served as a vacation destination as much as it functioned as a working farm.) Still, many Western movies of the early twentieth century contain characters named or referred to as "dudes." In *Easy Rider* (1969), Peter Fonda's character defines a "dude" as a "nice guy." Sean Penn's Jeff Spicoli character in *Fast Times at Ridgemont High*

(1982) famously sprinkles all conversations with the term as did Keanu Reeves's Ted and Alex Winter's Bill in *Bill & Ted's Excellent Adventure* (1989). In *The Big Lebowski* (1998), the main character played by Jeff Bridges is known as "The Dude." In 2000 *Dude, Where's My Car?* was a major hit. Today, the word remains a constant in hippie culture (though the female form, dudette, never really caught on).

DUGOUT / *dug-out* / *n.* A wooden receptacle with a slide-off top that contains two barreled areas—one that fits a metal bat or one-hitter and the other for ground-up marijuana—carefully designed to hide your pipe and stash, and to generally look innocuous to the average security guard or bag checker. ALSO SEE: BAT; ONE-HITTER; ONE-HITTER GUIDE (P. 102); ONEIE.

Dugout

DURBAN POISON / *derr-bun-poy-zun* / *n.* 1. Classic pure sativa outdoor strain from South Africa's Rift Valley. Lanky with thin leaves and an anise smell, it can be grown indoors successfully from Dutch seeds cultivated in Holland. It flowers in fifty-six to sixty-three days and has 9 percent THC content. 2. British band formed in 2003.

DYLAN, BOB (B. 1941) Born Robert Zimmerman in Duluth, Minnesota, America's greatest living troubadour continues to tour and release quality albums more than four decades after his self-titled debut came out in 1962. He shook up the folk world when he went electric at the Newport Folk Festival in 1965. A year later, he penned the smoker's anthem, "Rainy Day Women #12 & 35," with the chorus, "Everybody must get stoned." Despite being noted for turning the Beatles on to pot in 1964, he's carefully refrained from advocating marijuana use over the years. ALSO SEE: DOCUMENTARIES (P. 166); POT (OR NOT?) SONGS (P. 99).

EASY RIDER Legendary 1969 road movie starring Dennis Hopper as Billy and Peter Fonda as Wyatt, or "Captain America," two bikers who "went looking for America and couldn't find it anywhere," it remains the greatest drug movie of all time and a lasting document of 1960s counterculture. Featuring Jack Nicholson in his breakout role as the drunk lawyer George who frees the duo from jail and joins the ride, the film's classic bonfire scene shows him getting turned on to pot for the first time. Later on, Hopper and Fonda head to New Orleans and drop acid during Mardi Gras. ALSO SEE: A BRIEF HISTORY OF DRUGGY DRAMAS (P. 154); CLASSIC STONER DIALOGUES (P. 152); EASY RIDERS, RAGING BEATS (P. 54); STONER CHARACTER ACTORS (P. 150).

Dennis Hopper (left), Peter Fonda (center), and Jack Nicholson (right) in *Easy Rider*.

ECSTASY / *ex-sta-see* / *n.* The street name for methylenedioxymethamphetamine or MDMA, an entacogen used by psychiatrists as a therapeutic tool before it was made

EASY RIDERS, RAGING BEATS

In our homage to Peter Biskind's terrific book, *Easy Riders, Raging Bulls* (1998), here we present four iconoclastic 1960s-era actors and six writers who spirited the Beat movement.

William S. Burroughs: Author of *Naked Lunch* (1959) and a longtime heroin user, he was an essential member of the Beats fraternity. He died in 1997.

Neal Cassady: Jack Kerouac's muse and road-trip partner, he was fictionalized as Dean Moriarty in *On the Road* (1957) and later joined the Merry Pranksters, driving their Further bus across the country. Arrested for marijuana in 1958, he was jailed until 1960. He died in 1968.

Bruce Dern: Father of Laura, he is not well known for his roles in counterculture classics *The Trip* (1967) and *Psych-Out* (1968) with Jack Nicholson, Peter Fonda, Dennis Hopper, and Susan Strasberg, but he should be.

Lawrence Ferlinghetti: The oldest-living Beat (born in 1919) and a poet in his own right (*Coney Island of the Mind*, 1958), he founded the City Lights bookstore in San Francisco in 1953.

Peter Fonda: Son of Henry and father of Bridget, he costarred in *The Trip* (1967) and *Easy Rider* (1969) and many years later appeared in the biker movie *Wild Hogs* (2007).

Allen Ginsberg: The poet laureate of the Beat Generation startled the world with *Howl* (1956) and *Kaddish* (1961), his open homosexuality, and his embrace of marijuana. He died in 1997.

Dennis Hopper: He directed *Easy Rider* (1969) and *The Last Movie* (1971), and appeared in *The Trip* (1968) and *Easy Rider*, where he forged his reputation as one of Hollywood's raging stoners.

Herbert Huncke: He coined the term "Beat"—for living on the margin. A petty criminal, jailbird, and heroin addict born in 1915, he was to William S. Burroughs what Neal Cassady was to Jack Kerouac. He died in 1996.

Jack Kerouac: The author of *On the Road* (1957), he put the Beat Generation on the map with his improvisational writing style and cool-cat characters. He died in 1969.

Jack Nicholson: Back when he was a B-movie actor, Nicholson wrote *The Trip* (1967) and *Head* (1968) before his breakout role in *Easy Rider* (1969). Since then, he's become simply "Jack," Hollywood's beloved bad boy.

William S. Burroughs (left) and Jack Kerouac (right) in 1953

illegal in 1985. Also known as X or XTC, it is a mood-elevating drug—not a hallucinogen—swallowed in tablet form (a normal dose is 100 to 125 mg) that takes thirty minutes to an hour to kick in. The brain chemical serotonin is released and acts as an antidepressant, spurring feelings of euphoria, warmth, and empathy. The Ecstasy peak wears off in four to six hours. Physiologically, the drug elevates body temperature, which can put users at risk of dehydration or heatstroke, particularly when combined with alcohol. Still, Ecstasy is a popular indulgence at late-night dance parties and raves all over the world.

EIGHTH / *ay-dth* / *n.* A measurement of weight denoting one-eighth of an ounce (3.5 grams) of marijuana, as in, "Can I get an eighth?" The most common size of an individual portion for recreational use, its price can range from $35 to $75 per bag. ALSO SEE: GRAM; O.Z.; Q.P.; QUARTER.

ELASTALUNG / *ee-last-uh-lung* / *n.* Slang for a lung of exceptional capacity. The term originated in central New Jersey circa 1988 and is also used to describe the kind of person who

can absorb the hugest of hits without so much as a chuff.

EMERALD TRIANGLE, THE Nickname for the area in northwestern California containing Humboldt, Mendocino, and Trinity counties. This tricounty area is known for producing some of the best marijuana cultivated in the U.S. ALSO SEE: HUMBOLT COUNTY; MENDOCINO COUNTY; TRINITY COUNTY.

ENTHEOGENS / *nth-e-yogins* / *pl. n.* Alternate term for hallucinogens or psychedelic drugs coined in 1979 by a group of ethnobotanists including R. Gordon Wasson and Richard Schultes, and intended to primarily denote the natural vision-producing substances used in shamanic or religious ceremonies.

E-Z WIDER / *ease-ee-why-der* / *n.* Rolling-paper company founded in 1971 by Robert Stiller. Made from French paper

with natural Arabic gum, these papers are available in multiple sizes and flavors (strawberry and banana), and a variety of ingredients (hemp and wheat straw). Stiller sold the company to Rizla+ for $6.2 million in 1979 and purchased Green Mountain Coffee with the profits. ALSO SEE: GUIDE TO ROLLING PAPERS (P. 116).

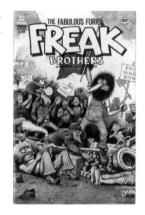

The Fabulous Furry Freak Brothers

FABULOUS FURRY FREAK BROTHERS, THE Hippie comic strip created by Gilbert Shelton in 1968 and by Shelton with Paul Mavrides since 1978. It features three dope-smoking characters: Fat Freddy, Freewheelin' Franklin, and Phineas T. Freakears. Similar in style and spirit to R. Crumb's work, the comics are compiled in numerous books and have appeared in *High Times* and *Playboy*.

FAST TIMES AT RIDGEMONT HIGH Blond-haired, dimwitted Jeff Spicoli (played by Sean Penn) never wears a shirt,

Best Buds: Sean Penn flanked by Eric Stoltz (left) and Anthony Edwards (right) in *Fast Times at Ridgemont High*

hardly ever goes to class, and always uses the word *dude* in Amy Heckerling's 1982 coming-of-age flick about a group of L.A. teens. Spicoli, the dopey surfer who emerges from a smoke-filled van, is one of Hollywood's most lovable and enduring stoners, thanks to Cameron Crowe's book and script. In addition to Penn, the film stars Jennifer Jason Leigh, Phoebe Cates, and Judge Reinhold. ALSO SEE: A BRIEF HISTORY OF STONER MOVIES (P. 146); STONER CHARACTER ACTORS (P. 150).

Dutch-rolled fatty

FATTY / *phat-tee* / *n.* 1. A particularly large joint, usually rolled by growers or those who possess mass quantities of marijuana. Also spelled fattie or phattie and expanded to phattie boom batty. 2. An overweight person. 3. In hip-hop, *phat* means good. ALSO SEE: CONE; JOINT; SPLIFF.

FILTER / *phil-turr* / *n. or v.* 1. A barrier between a smoke-able substance like tobacco or marijuana and the smoker's mouth, it prevents burning of the lips and provides a passageway that slightly lessens the impact of the about-to-be-inhaled smoke. 2. Removing unwanted materials by first passing a substance through a purifying element. ALSO SEE: CRUTCH; FILTER TIP.

FILTER TIP / *phil-turr-tip* / *n.* Small cutout of medium-stock paper or a prefabricated cigarette tip that, when placed at the end of a piece of rolling paper, can be rolled into it. A filter tip creates a more powerful, cleaner hit and also prevents a joint from becoming a roach. It comes in a variety of sizes, materials, and themes and can be used in joints or blunts. Popular manufacturers include Zig-Zag, Rips, and Swan.

Packaged filter tips

FIRE / *fie-er* / *n.* Flame to light a joint or bowl, using a lighter or match, as in, "Who has some fire?"

FLUFF / *fluph* / *n.* 1. Light, airy buds; the opposite of dense nugs. 2. Used in the title of the Phish song "Fluffhead" on the band's debut album, *Junta* (1988), whose lyrics include the lines, "Fluff came to my door asking me for change / His eyes were clear and pure but his mind was so deranged." 3. Short for Marshmallow Fluff, a spreadable form of the confection that, when combined with peanut butter and two slices of bread, becomes a Fluffernutter sandwich, a favorite munchie of the 1970s.

FONDA, PETER SEE A BRIEF HISTORY OF DRUGGY DRAMAS (P. 154); CLASSIC STONER DIALOGUES (P. 152); EASY RIDER; EASY RIDERS, RAGING BEATS (P. 54).

FORÇADE, TOM (1945–1978) Born Gary Goodson in Phoenix, Arizona, he renamed himself Thomas King Forçade and moved to New York where he started the Underground Press Syndicate and the High Times bookstore in 1970 before founding *High Times*. A marijuana smuggler and political activist, he funded the magazine with illegal money and published the first issue in 1974. He committed suicide in 1978. The magazine is still owned by Forçade (pronounced "forsod") family members and associates.

FRESHY / *fresh-ee* / *n.* A newly packed, all-green bowl from which the first hit is taken, as in, "Hold up, dude—I'll pack you a freshy."

FRIED / *fryd* / *adj.* 1. Sensation of feeling overloaded or burnt out from excessive smoking, as in, "Dude, I couldn't possibly take another hit, I'm so fried!" 2. Word used to describe food cooked in hot fat or oil. ALSO SEE: BAKED; BLASTED; BLAZED; BURNT; BUZZED; CRISPY; HIGH; LIT; LOADED; RIPPED; STONED; TOASTED; WASTED; ZONKED; ZOOTED.

FRONTA LEAF / *frahn-tuh leef* / *n.* Jamaican name for a fresh tobacco leaf used to roll marijuana. The original form of blunts, they are also known as fronto leaf.

FUNNY CIGARETTE / *fun-knee-sig-ah-rhett* / *n.* 1. Code words for a marijuana joint, the term was used predominantly in the 1920s and 1930s at the time of Prohibition. Today it's considered a nerdy term used by out-of-the-loop parents. 2. An item referenced in the song "Days Go By" by roots rocker J. J. Cale on his 1996 album, *Guitar Man* ("When you light that funny cigarette, would you pass it back to me?"). 3. Title of a song by Austin, Texas–based retro-jazz ensemble Asylum Street Spankers on *Spanks for the Memories* (1996). ALSO SEE: WACKY TOBACKY.

FUZZ / *fuzz* / *n* 1. Slang for police, this term saw use among America's criminal underground in the 1920s and 1930s and is believed to be a shortening of the word *fuzzy*, which in the early twentieth century meant unmanly, incompetent, or soft. 2. Term caught on in Great Britain when

Medical Edibles

Here's a sampling of the delicious food products found in California cannabis dispensaries.

Lollipops: Gaining popularity for their portability and potency, the superstrong suckers sell for about $3 to $5 each. Much like the crippy effect, the buzz comes on slowly.

Potella: A spiked version of the chocolate spread. Not recommended for breakfast if you have anything to do during the day.

Brownies: The original space cake, a brownie is still the most popular edible and is now available in a variety of forms: with or without nuts, vegan, and even flourless.

Tainted Candy Bars: Ultrapotent variations of chocolate favorites, like peanut butter cups and Snickers bars.

Cookies: Available in many flavors, from chocolate chip to oatmeal raisin to peanut butter.

rockers Supergrass released their 1994 hit single, "Caught by the Fuzz," a song about a mate's arrest for possession at the age of fifteen ("Caught by the fuzz, well I was, still on a buzz").

Jerry Garcia, with joint

G

GAGE / *gayj* / *n.* Slang for marijuana, this term was popular among jazz musicians in the 1930s and 1940s.

GALBRAITH, GATEWOOD (B. 1947) Perennial "pot candidate" who graduated from the University of Kentucky College of Law in 1977, he has run for governor four times, most recently in 2007. In 1991 Willie Nelson endorsed the pro-hemp candidate, stumping and performing a benefit concert. His autobiography, *The Last Free Man Meets the Synthetic Subversion*, was published in 2004.

GANJA / *gone-jah* / *n.* Jamaican term for marijuana that is widely considered to be derived from the Hindi word *ganga*. Indian Hindus migrated to the West Indies in the twentieth century, bringing the herbal substance and the term with them. Jamaicans adopted the word but changed it to ganja. 2. Jamaican Rastafarians consider it a sacrament and smoke to bring themselves closer to God, or Jah. Many Jamaican artists sing about it, such as in Eek-a-Mouse's "Ganja Smuggling." 3. The second-largest city in Azerbaijan. ALSO SEE: GANJA REGGAE CLASSICS (P. 186); GRASS; HERB; HEMP; MARIJUANA; POT; SMOKE; TREES; WEED.

GARCIA, JERRY (1942–1995) SEE THE GRATEFUL DEAD; MORE JAM BANDS (P. 107); STONER LEGENDS (P. 194).

GIGGLES, THE / *gig-ulz* / *n.* An uncontrollable laughing fit spurred by a really good high.

GINSBERG, ALLEN (1926–1997) Beat-generation poet born in New Jersey, who wrote *Howl* and *Kaddish*, among many other works. Ginsberg was a longtime associate of

Poet Allen Ginsberg, among the first to publicly protest in favor of pot, in 1966

Jack Kerouac, William S. Burroughs, and other Beat-era luminaries. In 1966 *Atlantic Monthly* published his pot polemic, "The Great Marijuana Hoax: The First Manifesto to End the Bringdown," and he was famously photographed by Ben Fernandez holding the sign, "Pot Is Fun." ALSO SEE: EASY RIDERS, RAGING BEATS (P. 54).

GLASS / *gl-ass* / *n.* Pipes or bongs made out of glass, as opposed to wood or acrylic, first appeared in parking lots of Grateful Dead shows in the late 1980s. Considered a quantum leap in the history of smoking, these devices offer a cleaner, smoother way to inhale.

Elaborate glass pipe

Glass vs. Plastic

It is a common dilemma: Splurge on the $50-plus glass bong or stick with the more affordable acrylic model? Here is our assessment.

Glass Pros:

Tastier hit: Smoking out of glass just tastes better. This has to do with the fact that glass, which can be cleaned, lessens the amount of resin that builds up in the chamber.

Easier to clean: Pour any combination of Formula 420, rubbing alcohol, salt, and water into your glass bong, leave it for a while, then shake it and scrub. Voilà! Practically any cleaning substance can be used without degrading your bong's surface.

Serve it chilled: OK, so you can make an ice bong with plastic, too, but glass, which serves as a conductor of heat or cold rather than as an insulator, will make your hit cooler by several degrees.

Art you can smoke: Certain hand-blown high-end glass bongs look more like art pieces than functional water pipes. However, once your glass bong is resinated, it may lose some of its luster.

Glass Cons:

It can—and will—break: Ultimately, either you or some stoner friend will knock it over, and chances are, the bowl or stem will break or the chamber will crack. Glass bongs clearly have shorter shelf lives than plastic. Warning: Don't use boiling hot water to clean your bong. It may cause the glass to crack.

Price is a factor: Glass is typically way more expensive than plastic—like four times more expensive (just like what kind bud is to schwag).

Glass is clunky: Whether big or small, glass is a hassle to transport because it can be heavier and is more fragile.

Plastic Pros:

Easy to carry: The plastic (or acrylic) bong is built for endurance and can be easily transported.

It will not shatter: Knock it over, drop it out the window, slam it down on a table, the plastic bong may come apart, but unless you run it over with a car, it won't break.

More affordable: The smallest plastic model, about six inches in length, costs as little as $8, while the largest available for sale can top six feet and cost as much as $75.

Plastic Cons:

The fog factor: Built-up resin will eventually cloud the chamber and repeated scrubbing will degrade it.

Cleaning is a challenge: Boiling water is often the best way to break up collected tar or resin, but with a plastic bong, it may melt the plastic and/or distort the shape.

You're actually smoking through metal: Almost all acrylic bongs contain a metal bowl that inevitably alters the taste, no matter how good your buds are.

Verdict: Glass

Left: glass pipe
Right: plastic pipe

"I did smoke a joint and I did inhale. The bottom line is that's what it was in the '70s, that's what I did."
—**Arnold Schwarzenegger,**
actor, politician

The great innovator is blower Bob Snodgrass, whose intricate, colorful pieces (known as Snoddies) saw widespread use in the 1990s, making his home base of Eugene, Oregon, the glass-pipe capital of America. (It now houses the world-renowned Eugene Glass School.) Other early players in the glass world include Jerome Baker of Jerome Baker Glass and Tommy Chong of Chong Glass, both of whom were busted in the 2003 Justice Department clampdown, Operation Pipe Dreams, which targeted online and interstate sales of paraphernalia, and specifically manufacturers of glass bongs and pipes. ALSO SEE: BONG; GLASS VS PLASTIC (P. 59); GREAT STONER INNOVATIONS (P. 137); ONE-HITTER GUIDE (P. 102); OPERATION PIPE DREAMS; PIPE OPTIONS (P. 110).

GLOW STICK / glo-stik / n. Plastic tube filled with chemical fluid that emits neonlike light but not heat in a process called chemoluminescence. A common sight at concerts and raves, it was also a favorite of dancing (and tripping) Deadheads and Phishheads entranced by visual trails of colorful sticks tossed in the air, a.k.a. a glowstick war.

GOA Situated on the western coastline of India, this Indian city gained notoriety as a stoner hot spot in the 1960s when hippies first discovered its laid-back vibe and sixty miles of golden beaches. Tourism flourished in the 1980s and 1990s as all-night raves attracted trance-music lovers from all over the world during the peak rave season (September to March). Indian hash (charas) smuggled from Manali and Nepal and most often rolled spliff-style with tobacco, is available year-round for about fifty rupees a gram (just over a dollar) as are a variety of psychedelics. Poorquality Indian marijuana is not worth seeking out. While officially illegal in India, you would never know it in Goa where joints are smoked openly in restaurants, bars, on the street, and at the beach. ALSO SEE: THE SEVEN STONER WONDERS OF THE WORLD (P. 76); STONER BEACHES (P. 202).

GRAFFIX / graph-fix / n. Brand of popular acrylic bongs that is no longer being manufactured. Featuring a cartoon jester as its logo, a Graffix bong was a staple in American basements and dorm rooms throughout the 1970s and 1980s—largely due to its affordability (a one-footer cost between $20 and $40) and durability. Available in a variety of sizes (from one foot to six) and colors (the most prevalent being red and blue), it had a metal stem with a rubber stopper and a drilled-out hole that served as a carb. Today, the company still exists but mainly sells "tobacco accessories" like papers, filters, and rolling machines.

GRAM / grahm / n. The smallest weight of marijuana. One ounce equals twenty-eight grams. ALSO SEE: EIGHTH; O.Z.; Q.P.; QUARTER.

GRASS / grass / n. 1. Slang for marijuana, this term dates back to the 1930s, and was popularized by beatniks in the 1950s and hippies in the 1960s. It is not commonly used today. 2. The title of Ron Mann's 1999 documentary, narrated by Woody Harrelson. 3. The title of an illustrated book by Jack Herer and Al Emmanuel, subtitled *The Official Guide for Assessing the Quality of Marijuana on the 1 to 10 Scale* (1973). ALSO SEE: DOCUMENTARIES (P. 166); GANJA; HEMP; HERB; MARIJUANA; POT; SMOKE; TREES; WEED.

GRASSHOPPER, THE Coffeeshop chain in Holland. Considered more commercial and touristy than many of the smaller shops, it has two locations in Amsterdam and one in Eindhoven.

GRATEFUL DEAD, THE Pioneers of the "San Francisco sound," icons of American counterculture, and a touring phenomenon for almost thirty years, the band known simply as the Dead inspired a stoner scene that numbered in the hundreds of thousands and continues to exist today—long after the death of guitarist Jerry Garcia. Formed in 1965 by Garcia (guitar, vocals), Phil Lesh (bass, vocals), Bob Weir (guitar, vocals), Ron "Pigpen" McKernan (keyboards, vocals), and drummers Bill Kreutzmann and Mickey Hart, the Dead mixed elements of rock, country, bluegrass, and folk, and gave them a psychedelic bent. But it was the band's live shows (*Live/Dead, Europe '72*) with their trademark improvisational free-form "jams" that could go on for as long as forty-five minutes that brought out fans (Deadheads) in droves. By the early 1980s, the parking lots at Dead shows became huge communal gatherings, taking tailgating to a whole new

Arjan Roskam, proprietor of the Green House coffeeshop in Amsterdam

tics), outdoors, or in greenhouses. ALSO SEE: GET GROWING (P. 64); INDOORS; OUTDOORS.

GREEN HOUSE, THE Winner of more than thirty Cannabis Cups, this Amsterdam coffeeshop chain founded in 1992 by Arjan Roskam is known for such strains as Super Silver Haze, White Rhino, and Hawaiian Snow. Roskam quickly expanded his business in 1993 to include a second

The Grateful Dead—(left to right) Bob Weir, Mickey Hart, Jerry Garcia, and Phil Lesh—in San Francisco's Haight-Ashbury in 1968

level. Rows of cars turned into makeshift flea markets and "Shakedown Streets" (inspired by the Dead's 1978 album) where Deadheads sold everything from food (kind veggie burritos, gratefully grilled cheese, and PB and Js) to jewelry, smoking accessories, and kind nugs. Garcia, a pothead who also dabbled in psychedelics (primarily LSD) and heroin later in his life, died in a rehab facility on August 9, 1995. Still, the Dead scene lives on in a variety of jam bands, most notably Phish who inherited much of the hippie fan base following Garcia's death, and Dead offshoots like Phil Lesh and Friends and Bob Weir's Ratdog. ALSO SEE: DEADHEADS; FAMOUS POT BUSTS (P. 192); JERRY GARCIA; MORE JAM BANDS (P. 107).

GRAVITY BONG / grav-i-tee-bhang / n. Homemade smoking device constructed from a two-liter soda bottle with its bottom cut off and a bowl punched into its side. To use, submerge the bottle in a pail of water and light the bowl. Once the bottle is filled with smoke, slowly pull it out of the water while inhaling. The force of lifting the bottle out of the water creates a powerful hit. ALSO SEE: HOW TO MAKE A GRAVITY BONG (P. 62).

GREEN / grean / adj. The color of marijuana, money, and envy. Slang for marijuana, as in, "Who's got the green?" 2. R & B singer Al Green known for classics like "Let's Stay Together," is also code for marijuana, used in phone, e-mail, or text conversations with dealers, as in, "Got any Al Green CDs I can borrow?" ALSO SEE: STONER CODE (P. 82).

GREENHOUSE / grean-haus / n. Area enclosed by glass or plastic used to cultivate plants. Marijuana growers either cultivate indoors (in closets, basements, bedrooms, and at-

G

How to Make a Gravity Bong

🍁 BY CISCO ADLER

Whitestarr frontman and son of legendary producer and director Lou Adler (Up in Smoke) is a medical card-carrying member of the Los Angeles pot elite. Here, he reveals his tried-and-true method of making the best gravity bong.

Step 1: "Get a two-liter bottle of soda and pour out all the liquid that's inside. At the same time, pull a stem-bowl combo from your bong. Metal is easiest to fit."

Step 2: "Unscrew the soda-bottle cap and carefully make a hole in the center, one that's big enough to fit your stem and bowl."

Step 3: "Insert the bowl into the hole and use chewing gum to seal it in place."

Step 4: "Slice off the bottom third of the bottle with a knife or scissors."

Step 5: "Plug your sink and fill it up with cold water. You can also use a bucket."

Step 6: "Screw the cap—with the bowl—back onto the bottle. Pack some weed into the bowl."

Step 7: "Submerge the bottle in water, start lighting, and pull it up. The suction draws smoke into the bottle and you can actually see it collect."

Step 8: "Once the smoke is collected, unscrew the cap-bowl, put your mouth to the opening, and push the bottle down so all the smoke goes into your lungs."

shop and the Green House Seed Company, and in 1997 to include a third shop. Roskam has appeared as the self-styled "King of Cannabis" in several DVDs directed by Kenya Winchell. ALSO SEE: AMSTERDAM COFFEESHOPS (P. 41).

GRINDER / *grine-dur* / *n.* A two-part circular device—originally manufactured by the Canadian company Sweetleaf in 2001—in which tiny strategically placed metal teeth mash buds when pressed against a twistable top. Over the years, metal and plastic grinders have steadily outsold the wooden ones, which tend to get sticky with repeated use. Dozens of companies make grinders that are readily available at any head shop. ALSO SEE: GREAT STONER INNOVATIONS (P. 137); GRINDER GUIDE (P. 63); HOW TO PREPARE YOUR POT (P. 72).

GRINSPOON, LESTER (B. 1928) A leading academic and medical advocate for marijuana, he has spent forty years at Harvard Medical School, where he's currently an associate professor emeritus of psychiatry. He is the author and coauthor (with James B. Bakalar) of numerous books, including the groundbreaking *Marihuana Reconsidered* (1971), *Psychedelic Drugs Reconsidered* (1979), and *Marihuana: The Forbidden Medicine* (1993). He was a member of NORML's advisory board from 1976 to 1984 and on the board of directors from 1996 to 2000. The Australian band Grinspoon is named after him.

GROW / *groh* / *n. or v.* 1. As an noun, the term is used to describe a location where marijuana is being cultivated, a.k.a. a grow-op, for grow operation. 2. As a verb, the act of cultivating plants. ALSO SEE: GET GROWING (P. 64).

GROWROOM / *groh-rume* / *n.* Indoor facsimile of outdoor growing conditions set in a closet, bedroom, basement, or attic and equipped with artificial lights, fans, and exhaust pipes as well as other environmental additives (such as CO_2) needed to cultivate quality marijuana. Also known as a grow, a grow-op or, in Canada, a grow show. ALSO SEE: GET GROWING (P. 64); GROW-OP.

G-13 / *gee-ther-teen* / *n.* Some believe this potent Afghani indica strain was bred either in Mississippi or at the University of Washington, but no one knows for sure. The "G" allegedly stands for government, as in the

🍁 Grinder Guide 🍁

Metal: Whether it's the single twist or the double pull-apart model with a resin catcher (from which you can make kif), the metal grinder is the silver standard in prepping your pot because of its durability and ease of use. 🍁🍁🍁🍁

Plastic: The second-best option, the plastic version with thick pegs is surprisingly strong and grinds to perfection. Plus it's lightweight. 🍁🍁🍁

Electric: Like a coffee grinder, but smaller. On most electric models, you can't see the pot as you grind it. 🍁🍁

Wood: The original grinder is the most troublesome. Reactive to heat and cold, wood expands and contracts according to temperature and humidity, making it difficult to twist. Resin can also collect in the grinder, sticking to the sides and eventually clogging it to the point where it cannot be twisted or even pulled apart. 🍁🍁

U.S. government that grows marijuana at the University of Mississippi in Oxford. The "13" allegedly stands for the thirteenth letter of the alphabet: "M." (M is for marijuana.) Then again, maybe not. What we do know is that it's available as a hybrid such as G-13 × Hash Plant (a.k.a. HP-13) from such seed banks as Mr. Nice. An ounce of it was sold for $2,000 to Kevin Spacey's character Lester in *American Beauty*. The strain flowers in eight to nine weeks and has 25 percent THC content. ALSO SEE: ALL-TIME GREATEST STRAINS (P. 124).

Get Growing

Outdoors

1. The easiest way to learn how to grow marijuana is to put a plant or two out on your back porch, in a window box, on a fire escape, or in your backyard. Start with either a seed or a clone. A seed will take a week or so to sprout. Place it in a wet paper towel. When it sprouts, place the seedling in a small pot filled with organic soil or in a rockwool cube. When it has three sets of leaves, transplant it to a larger pot. Be sure to fertilize the soil with small amounts of bat guano.

2. Planting should be done in the spring after all cold spells are past. If you live in a climate that is warm year-round, you can plant anytime. But most of North America follows a spring-to-fall growing season.

3. If you use clones, you won't need to identify the sex of your plants. They're already female, which is what you want. If you start with nonfeminized seeds, male plants need to be removed once they show their sex. (Male plants can be identified by their pollen sacs. Female plants can be identified when hairs start sprouting from the bud sites.) If you fail to pull the males in time, they will pollinate the females, causing seeds to develop, and the overall crop will be diminished. Unless you're growing a seed crop, you don't want seeds.

4. Once you've determined the females and gotten rid of the males, the plants will continue to fill out over the summer months. One way to prevent the plants from growing too tall is to pinch them back when they're young. Pinching the top leaves will force the

plant to split into two main stalks, creating a smaller, bushier plant.

5. Water your plants daily. Make sure they don't dry out or wilt. Add liquid fertilizer (diluted with water) every other day.

6. Fertilize your plants organically using liquid seaweed formulas. During the early stages, plants need plenty of nitrogen (N). You should get to know the term NPK, which stands for nitrogen, phosphorus, and potassium. More phosphorus is needed during the flowering stage. Potassium is needed throughout all

stages of growth. A standard NPK requirement before flowering is 10-2-5.

7. Once flowering has begun, switch the NPK to 2-10-5. Use a specific fertilizer that's intended for flowering, such as Super Bloom, which you can purchase in most garden supply stores. Don't use chemical fertilizers such as Miracle-Gro.

8. Flowering can take up to three months, depending on whether you're growing a mostly sativa or mostly indica strain. The latter will flower earlier, in eight to ten weeks.

Harvested buds in Mendocino County, California

Outdoor plants grow particularly large in California's Emerald Triangle

9. Two weeks before harvesting, stop using fertilizers and flush the plants with plain water.

10. When your beautiful buds are full, sticky, smelly, and moist, they're almost ready to harvest. Never harvest the kind before its time. To make sure it's ready, use a loupe or magnifying glass to look closely at the trichomes (resin glands). If they are clear and have their mushroom-shaped heads intact, the plant needs a bit more time. If they are opaque and milky (not clear), it's time to cut the plants down. If they've turned amber and most of the heads are gone, it may be too late to salvage your plants.

11. Trim off all the large fan leaves with scissors or pruning shears and manicure the buds. The less leaf the better. This process will require a significant amount of time, depending on how many plants you have. If you have more than you can

handle, ask a close friend or two to come over for a trimming party.

12. When completely manicured, hang the buds upside down on hangers in a closet. Shut the door and keep the interior free of humidity. The buds should be fully dried in anywhere from three to seven days.

13. Make sure the buds are no longer moist before placing them in containers. This is crucial. If you enclose still-drying buds in plastic or glass containers, they might mold, ruining all your hard work. Nothing is worse to a grower than the smell of mold.

14. The buds are ready to smoke. However, you should place the bulk of the crop in containers (mason jars or Tupperware) and allow it to cure. This process will improve the taste and put a finishing touch on the overall quality. *Bon appetit!*

Indoors

1. The object when growing marijuana indoors is to replicate outdoor conditions. Start by picking a secluded spot in your house, such as a closet, attic, or basement.

2. Indoor growing isn't cheap. Your main purchases will be a grow light, which should be from 250 to 1,000 watts, and either a High Pressure Sodium (HPS) or Metal Halide bulb housed by a High Intensity Discharge lamp, a reflector, and a ballast. Most people prefer HPS bulbs. These supplies can easily add up to $500.

3. One thousand watt bulbs are not for beginners. Compact fluorescent bulbs (65 watt) *are*, but they produce smaller plants and buds. Do not use household incandescent lightbulbs.

4. Indoor grow-ops tend to have insect problems. Be prepared with Neem and other organic solutions to eradicate all pests, such as spider mites and whiteflies.

5. Fans and ventilation are extremely important. You need to make sure there is good air circulation and contain odors as much as possible. Creating an exhaust vent is a good idea.

6. You can grow indoors any time of year. During the vegetative stage (before flowering), plants require twenty-four hours a day of light. To begin or to force flowering, you need to create darkness. Set the timer to a 12–12 hour light-dark cycle. Make sure no light seeps into the room during the dark periods.

7. Follow the instructions for growing outdoor plants once flowering begins.

Indoor plants ready to be harvested

Soil vs. Hydro

Most people are more familiar with growing plants of any kind in soil rather than in water. Soil tends to be organic, while hydroponics generally require chemical fertilizers, and buds often retain a chemmy flavor and smell as a result.

The advantage of hydroponics is that you don't need to haul soil around and you can set timers for virtually all functions (such as feeding and light cycles). Overall, it's a much cleaner operation. But hydro systems using wicks, resevoirs, ebb and flow,

or aeroponics are even more expensive than soil-based cultivation. They cost from $200 to $500, not including lights.

Because timers are used for virtually every important function, the hydro farmer doesn't need to be on the premises every day, unlike with soil-based gardens that generally need daily watering (wicks can be used with soil as well). This allows the grower to take some time off, even go on a short vacation while the plants evolve from baby clones to full-blown flowering machines.

Seedling

A tray of seedlings

H

HACK / hak / v. or n. 1. To cough violently or uncontrollably after a big hit of marijuana smoke. 2. To use a computer to break into another digital entity. 3. To cut into pieces. 4. As a noun, someone whose abilities are average at best, as in, "That guy's a hack, dude."

HAIGHT-ASHBURY Key intersection in San Francisco, where Haight and Ashbury streets meet in the neighborhood that was ground zero for the pot-fueled Summer of Love. A bohemian subculture began to take root in the Haight's low-rent Victorian houses in the mid-1960s. One group,

the Diggers, formed an anarchist collective there with "free stores" that gave away all their merchandise. Others smoked pot and played Frisbee on "Hippie Hill" in Golden Gate Park. The nation's first head shop, the Psychedelic Shop, opened in early 1966. *Oracle*, an underground newspaper, launched soon after. By January 1967 the Haight's hippies hosted the Human Be-In: a "gathering of the tribes" with speakers, poetry readings, and psychedelic music that attracted 30,000 people (including Timothy Leary and Allen Ginsberg) to Golden Gate Park. The Haight has also been home to many musicians. The Grateful Dead shared quarters at 710 Ashbury, while Janis Joplin and her boyfriend Country Joe McDonald lived near Fell and Oak streets. The Jefferson Airplane resided in a magnificent Greek-columned structure nearby at 2400 Fulton Street. Although its trippy heyday is a thing of the past, the Haight continues to attract countercultural types with its vintage clothing vendors, memorabilia shops, record stores, and marijuana dispensaries. And if you make eye contact with the dude hanging out on the corner, he just might offer to sell you something leafy and green. ALSO SEE: GRATEFUL DEAD; JEFFERSON AIRPLANE; THE SEVEN STONER WONDERS OF THE WORLD (P. 76).

(Left to right) Tom Wolfe, Jerry Garcia, and the Grateful Dead's manager Rock Scully in San Francisco, circa 1968

Hairs

HAIRS / hares / pl. n. The first sign that a female marijuana plant has begun to flower. The hairs turn various colors—white, red, and purple—depending on the strain and climate and do not indicate potency or quality.

HALF BAKED Stoner comedy starring and cowritten by Dave Chappelle about two friends who steal several pounds of medical marijuana to start a delivery service in order to spring their friend from jail. Only Mary Jane, Chappelle's love interest in the film, wants no part of the stoner lifestyle. With cameos by Snoop Dogg, Willie Nelson, Jon Stewart, and Tommy Chong, this 1998 movie still holds up today. ALSO SEE: A BRIEF HISTORY OF STONER MOVIES (P. 146); DAVE CHAPPELLE.

HALLUCINATE / *ha-loo-si-naight* / *v.* To experience altered perceptions, which can manifest in visual patterns and sensory hyperawareness. Most commonly brought on by psychedelics such as LSD, psilocybin (magic mushrooms), DMT, ecstasy, and peyote. As a noun, a hallucination is the physical result of the altered mind state. ALSO SEE: ALBERT HOFMANN; LSD.

HARRELSON, WOODY (B. 1961) Noted hemp activist and star of many movies (including *The People vs. Larry Flynt* and *Natural Born Killers*), Harrelson was born in Midland, Texas, and got his start on TV as the easy-going bartender Woody on *Cheers*. In 1996 he was arrested in Kentucky for planting hemp seeds. He has stated: "I have very serious problems with a government that doesn't want you to smoke something that makes you euphoric." He is the subject of *Go Further* (2003), a documentary by Ron Mann, and the narrator of Mann's pot-doc, *Grass* (1999).

Woody Harrelson in 1997

HARRISON, GEORGE (1943-2001) SEE THE BEATLES (P. 16).

HASH / *haash* / *n.* Short for the Arabic word *hashish*, it is a substance composed of THC-rich resin, or trichomes, from a female plant. When collected and compressed (either by hand or with a hash press), the resin forms into a hardened concentrate with varying degrees of gooeyness. It can be smoked out of a pipe or bong, rolled with marijuana and/or tobacco in a joint, or used in food. Because much of the world's supply comes from Morocco, Lebanon, Afghanistan, Pakistan, India, and Nepal, use is more prominent in European countries than in the U.S. Stronger than marijuana, it produces more of a body high. It comes in a variety of colors (blond, red, brown, and green) and textures (soft, hard, and creamy). It can also be made at home using oscillating machines and bubble bags. ALSO SEE: BUBBLE HASH; CHARAS; HASH OIL; KIF; NEDERHASH.

Mazar-I-Sharif hash, produced in Afghanistan's fourth largest city

HASH BASH / *haash-baash* / *n.* One of the oldest marijuana rally events in the U.S., it dates back to 1971 and takes place annually at the University of Michigan in Ann Arbor on the first Saturday in April. ALSO SEE: U.S. POT RALLIES (P. 200).

HASH OIL / *haash-oy-el* / *n.* Also known as honey oil, this preparation is made from cannabis leaves and shake. A solvent such as butane or isopropyl alcohol is commonly used to separate the resin glands, or trichomes. The remaining plant material is filtered and then evaporates, leaving a thick, oily, and extremely potent product. It's smoked by dripping the product onto heated charcoals or incense cones and inhaling the resulting smoke through a tube or similar hollow device. ALSO SEE: HASH.

HAZE / *heyz* / *n.* 1. One of the original marijuana strains, created in Santa Cruz, California, in the early 1970s by the Haze Brothers. A pure sativa combining tropical strains from Colombia, Mexico, and South India, it was brought to Amsterdam in 1984 by Sacred Seeds' Sam the Skunkman. The Seed Bank's Neville Schoenmakers bred it with Northern Lights #5 to create Neville's Haze. Many hybrids have followed, including Purple Haze, Super Silver Haze, and Arjan's Haze. Not the best yielder, it produces fluffy buds with a mixed sweet-and-sour taste and a clear, energetic high. It flowers in twelve to fourteen weeks and has 15 percent to

"It's about personal freedom. We should have the right in this country to do what we want, if we don't hurt anybody. Seventy-two million people in this country have smoked pot, eighteen to twenty million in the last year. These people should not be treated as criminals."
— Woody Harrelson,
actor

Stoner Slogans

Legalize It

I Smoke Pot and I Like It a Lot

Keep On the Grass

Hemp Hemp Hooray

Thank You for Pot Smoking

Tune In, Turn On, Drop Out

Puff, Puff, Pass

Puff, Puff, Give

Take Two and Pass

Poke Smot

Can't We All Just Get a Bong?

Bong Hits 4 Jesus

You Don't Get Off 'til You Cough

It's Always 4:20 Somewhere

Got Smurb?

18 percent THC content. The original Haze from the Flying Dutchman has never been hybridized. 2. A state of confusion or of being out of it, as in, "He's in a haze." ALSO SEE: ALL-TIME GREATEST STRAINS (P. 124); CANNABIS CUP STRAINS (P. 31).

HEAD / *hedd* / *n.* 1. Generic term for any group of diehards has seen the most use as a shortened version of Deadhead, pothead, or Phishhead, all signifying a person who subscribes to stoner lifestyle and culture. 2. Title of the Monkees' first and only feature film in 1968, a psychedelic—and some would say nonsensical—tale of their world, written by Jack Nicholson.

Heads

HEADS / *hedz* / *pl. n.* 1. Shortened form of the terms Deadheads or potheads that can also be used to describe any kind of socially connected group, such as metalheads or cokeheads. 2. Canadian pot magazine founded in 2000 and based in Montreal, dedicated to cultivation, travel, and culture.

HEAD SHOP / *hedd-shoppe* / *n.* Retail establishment where one can buy various forms of smoking accessories including papers and paraphernalia. Such shops started popping up in the late 1960s in and around U.S. college towns. Believed to be the first, the Psychedelic Shop on Haight Street in San Francisco opened its doors in January 1966 with an inventory of counterculture books, posters, incense, and bead necklaces, in addition to pipes. Sadly, the location is now home to Fat Slice Pizza. For legal reasons, most head shops operate by advertising that their products are for tobacco use only, sidestepping the paraphernalia laws in most states.

HEMP / *hemmp* / *n.* The nonpsychoactive cousin of cannabis, it dates back 10,000 years to China, where it's still grown as an industrial crop. Fibers inside the plant stalks serve a multitude of purposes, including making paper, rope, clothing, food, and fuel. Used for the original draft of the Declaration of Independence and grown by both George Washington and Thomas Jefferson, it was a popular crop in eighteenth- and nineteenth-century America but was banned in 1937 along with marijuana. Today, hemp remains prohibited in the U.S. in all but one state, North Dakota, which passed legislation allowing farmers to grow it in 1999 and began issuing permits in 2007. It's legal in many countries, including Canada, England, Germany, Russia, Romania, Italy, and China. Because hemp contains minute traces of THC, the U.S. and other countries continue to ban it. Feral plants found today in the American Midwest are actually related to the legal crops grown before 1937. Foreign spellings include *hanf* (German), *haenap*, (Dutch) and *hon-nab* (Arabic). ALSO SEE: DITCH WEED; MARIJUANA; POT.

HEMP FOR VICTORY The title of the U.S. government's fourteen-minute black-and-white film made in 1943 to en-courage farmers to grow hemp for the war effort—despite the fact that it had been prohibited six years earlier. This bit of Americana was discovered by activists Jack Herer and Maria Farrow at the Library of Congress in 1989.

HEMPILATION / *hem-pill-ay-shun* / *n.* Series of benefit compilation albums produced by *High Times* and Capricorn Records on behalf of NORML. *Hempilation: Freedom Is NORML* (1995) features the Black Crowes, Cypress Hill, Blues Traveler, Sublime, 311, and Ziggy Marley & the Melody Makers. *Hempilation 2: Free the Weed* (1998) features Willie Nelson, George Clinton, and Spearhead. The two albums have raised $150,000 for NORML.

HENDRIX, JIMI (1942–1970) Legendary guitarist known for his ear-shredding licks, he took the music world by storm in the late 1960s. With albums like *Are You Experienced?* (1967)—which included such classics as "Hey Joe," "Fire," "Purple Haze," and "Foxy Lady"—and its follow-ups, *Axis: Bold as Love* (1967) and *Electric Ladyland* (1968), his blend

Hemp products

Los Angeles head shop Dementia

Jimi Hendrix jams with his band, The Experience, at San Francisco's Winterland in 1968

☘ How to Prepare Your Pot ☘

Breaking up marijuana is the first step to smoking. Doing this properly will make rolling a joint or blunt easier and provide you with better bowl hits. Here's how to do it right.

Option 1: Get a grinder (metal preferred). Place buds in the smaller half, close it up with the other half, and give it a twist. Shake out the freshly ground weed on a clean surface and smell. Sweet!

Option 2: If for some reason you don't have a grinder handy (you're traveling, for instance, and don't want to carry paraphernalia), use scissors. The main goal is to touch the buds as little as possible, so trichomes (resin glands) don't stick to your fingers and get wasted. Place the buds in a shot glass, dip the scissors into the glass, and snip away neatly. If a shot glass isn't available, then hold the bud in your hand and carefully scissor it.

Option 3: No grinder or scissors? It's time to go old-school and break up the buds with your hands. That's why they call it a green thumb.

pot to LSD. He was arrested in May of 1969 at the Toronto airport when hash and heroin were found in his luggage (he was acquitted). He died in London on September 18, 1970, by asphyxiating on his own vomit. The autopsy revealed he had drunk several glasses of wine and ingested nine Vesperax sleeping pills.

HERB / *urb* / *n.* 1. Any plant whose leaves or seeds are used for flavoring or medicine. 2. Slang for marijuana, commonly used among Jamaican Rastas, as in, "Who's got the herb?" ALSO SEE: GANJA REGGAE CLASSICS (P. 186); GRASS; POT; WEED.

HERER, JACK (B. 1939) 1. Marijuana activist born in Brooklyn, New York, he moved to California in 1956 where he operated a head shop with his partner, "Captain Ed" Adair. He is best known as the author of the pro-hemp, scrapbook-style manifesto, *The Emperor Wears No Clothes*, published in 1985 and now in its eleventh printing. He also wrote *GRASS: The Official Guide for Assessing the Quality of Marijuana on the 1 to 10 Scale* (1973). The documentary *Emperor of Hemp* (1999), narrated by Peter

Hemp guru Jack Herer in 1994

Coyote, chronicles his life. In 2000 he suffered a stroke and heart attack. He lives with his wife Jeannie in northern California. 2. A mostly sativa strain named after the activist, created in 1995 by the Dutch company Sensi Seeds. It flowers in sixty to eighty days and has 14 percent THC content. ALSO SEE: CANNABIS CUP STRAINS (P. 31); STONER LEGENDS (P. 194).

HIGH / *hi* / *adj. or n.* 1. The most common word used to describe the effect of marijuana, alcohol, or other drugs on the brain, as in, "I'm so high, dude." Originally, the term was attributed to the euphoric effect of alcohol, dating back to 1627. It was attributed to drugs in the 1930s. 2. Title of a

of unconventional blues melodies and psychedelic riffs not only inspired the counterculture but also impacted the mainstream. By the time he had headlined Woodstock in 1969, featuring his crack-of-dawn performance of "The Star-Spangled Banner," the guitarist was a household name, one affiliated with a variety of mind-altering substances, from

racy 1967 film by Canadian director Larry Kent about a drug-addicted Bonnie-and-Clyde-like couple whose sexual and criminal exploits brought a new perspective to the Summer of Love experience. Just prior to its Canadian premiere, the film was banned from the Montreal Film Festival, which prompted actors Warren Beatty, Jean Renoir, and Fritz Lang to come out in support of the film. ALSO SEE: BAKED; BLASTED; BLAZED; BURNT; BUZZED; CRISPY; FRIED; LIT; LOADED; RIPPED; STONED; TOASTED; WASTED; ZONKED; ZOOTED.

HIGHLIFE Dutch-language marijuana magazine founded by Boy Ramsahai in 1991. Since 1998 the magazine has hosted the Highlife Fair and Cup in Amsterdam every February.

HIGH TIMES Since 1974, the lone American publication to focus on marijuana and the drug war that prohibits it. Founded by political activist/marijuana smuggler Thomas King Forçade, the magazine survived the "Just Say No" propaganda of the 1980s and, embraced by musicians, celebrities, and activists, experienced a rebirth in the 1990s. After Forçade committed suicide in 1978, much of the original staff dispersed. Owned by the privately held Trans-High Corporation (THC), it is operated by a small, dedicated staff based in New York. In addition to publishing twelve issues a year and two best-of collections, the magazine produces special events such as the Cannabis Cup, the Stony Awards, the Doobie Awards, and the Miss High Times Pageant. ALSO SEE: CANNABIS CUP; TOM FORÇADE; HEMPILATION; THE STONYS.

HIPPIE / hip-pee / n. Term originating in the 1960s used to describe people affiliated with the counter-culture movement of the time. It is believed to be derived from the word *hipster*, which itself comes from the jive-era word *hip*, meaning sophisticated or fashionable, and was later used in books authored by Beat-generation writers of the 1940s and 1950s. The word appeared in various forms throughout that decade and into the

Hippie

1960s (for example, the song "Hippy, Hippy Shake," originally written and recorded by Chan Romero in 1959, was a hit for the Swinging Blue Jeans in 1964), but was officially coined in a 1965 article by San Francisco writer Michael Fallon to describe the migration of young bohemians taking up residence in the city's Haight-Ashbury district. By 1968 the word was practically universal, describing an international association of like-minded young people seeking peace, love, and equality in a society torn apart by war and race riots. Hippie fashion and style merged with the flower-power ethos characterized by long hair, flow-y skirts, tie-dyed shirts, sandals, accessories made of natural materials, organic foods and, of course, marijuana. Today, many of these traits still apply to new generations of Deadheads and the hippie name lives on with their successors.

HIPPIE CHICK / hip-pee chik / n. A female hippie.

HIT / hitt / n. A single draw of marijuana, the term applies to any smoking device, as in, "Can I get a hit off that, dude?" ALSO SEE: DRAW; INHALE; PULL; PUFF; SMOKE; TOKE.

HOFMANN, ALBERT (B. 1906) The creator of LSD was born in Switzerland and, at 101 years old, is living proof that the psychedelic drug has special life-extending benefits. In 1938 he synthesized LSD-25 while working as a chemist for Sandoz Laboratories. However, he didn't consume the drug until five years later, when he dosed himself with 250 micrograms and took his now-famous bicycle ride (the first "trip") under the influence. His interest in natural hallucinogens led him to conduct research on psilocybin, *Salvia divinorum*, and morning glory seeds. He wrote about his experience with acid in *LSD: My Problem Child* (1980). ALSO SEE: ENTHEOGENS; LSD; PSILOCYBIN; PSYCHEDELICS; SALVIA DIVINORUM; TRIP.

HOLY ROLLER / hole-ee-role-urr / n. 1. Joint rolled using Bible paper, the closest paper in thinness to your average rolling paper. 2. Term used to describe a devout Pentecostal Christian.

HOMEGROWN / home-groan / adj. 1. Colloquial term used to describe marijuana cultivated in one's personal

Highlife

LSD inventor Albert Hofmann in 1976

"I've never seen two people on pot get into a fight, because it's fucking impossible!"

—Bill Hicks, comedian

residence, be it indoors or outdoors. 2. Stoner movie from 1998 directed by Stephen Gyllenhaal, starring Billy Bob Thornton, Ryan Phillippe, and John Lithgow, about bumbling growers and criminals in the marijuana trade. 3. Song on Neil Young's *American Stars 'n Bars* (1977): "Homegrown is alright with me / Homegrown is the way it should be / Homegrown is a good thing / Plant that bell and let it ring."

HONEY BONG / *hun-ee-bhang* / *n.* A homemade smoking device made out of a supermarket-bought bear-shaped honey bottle. It is also sometimes called a "honey slide." Brad Pitt's character Floyd made it famous in *True Romance* (1993).

HOOKAH / *hoo-kuh* / *n.* An old-world water pipe containing all the parts of a contemporary bong—a chamber, bowl, and stem—but using a hose (one or multiple) as the puffing mechanism for long, steady draws as opposed to one gargantuan hit, and a piece of charcoal for heat. Dating back to India in the 1600s, when it was used primarily to smoke hashish, it is still popular today in the Middle East, especially in countries like Turkey, where locals puff away on tobacco (regular or flavored) at sidewalk cafés and restaurants. It is also known as a narghile. Hookah bars have become popular in the U.S.

Bear-shaped honey bottle

Hookah smokers in Dahab, Egypt

Dennis Hopper in *Easy Rider*

HOPPER, DENNIS (B. 1936) Born in Dodge City, Kansas, he began his career as a TV and movie actor in 1955, appearing in *Rebel Without a Cause*. He directed and costarred in *Easy Rider* (1969) and *The Last Movie* (1971), a major debacle that almost short-circuited his career. He reemerged in *Apocalypse Now* (1979) and since has appeared in *Blue Velvet* (1986), *River's Edge* (1986), and *True Romance* (1993), among his more than one hundred films. ALSO SEE: A BRIEF HISTORY OF DRUGGY DRAMAS (P. 154); EASY RIDER; EASY RIDERS, RAGING BEATS (P. 54).

HOT BOX / *hot-box* / *n.* Cloud that envelops you when smoking in a parked, unventilated vehicle (most commonly a car or van) with the windows rolled up.

HUMBOLDT COUNTY Located on California's North Coast, bordering the Pacific Ocean to the west, it's a land

Hot box

Music to Smoke to

BY MAROON 5'S ADAM LEVINE

Adam Levine likes nothing more than to chill out, literally. A hit off an ice bong and some stony tunes are all this Hollywood homebody needs. Here, the Maroon 5 singer discusses his stony favorites.

Adam Levine
in 2007

Phish: "People scoff at smoking and listening to Phish, but I used to listen to *Junta* a lot. When I saw Phish live, they fell into an amazing groove and it was mind-blowing. They had this funky way they would lock into things. It's very ornate. When I watched Phish, I was studying them because they could do everything. There wasn't one musical trick that they couldn't execute. And that was what was astonishing to me. So I'd go to their shows, smoke a ton of weed, eat mushrooms, and watch and think, 'I'm not that good yet.' We used to listen in disbelief."

Herbie Hancock: "*Head Hunters* [1973] is great, especially if you're smoking when 'Chameleon' comes on. At almost sixteen minutes long, it's a pot-smoker's dream, because there are all these funky little sounds and no vocals to mess it up."

Stevie Wonder: "Sitting in the sun, smoking a joint, and listening to the first disc of *Songs in the Key of Life* [1976] is pretty unbeatable. The minute that album starts, you puff, listen, and it's as if the world makes complete sense. You take a deep breath, and you kind of sigh and realize everything is really OK. That's one of the most comforting records I can think of."

Lauryn Hill: "*The Miseducation of Lauryn Hill* [1998] is a no-brainer. She's the embodiment of true soulfulness. She can rap and she doesn't sound like she's rapping. She can sing and she doesn't sound like she's singing. Her voice is full of pain and it's inspiring at the same time. You feel everything all over. She does it all in a very organic way."

> "If I was playing jazz or in a jam band, then I would be smoking twenty-four hours a day."

Notorious B.I.G.: "Who doesn't like to get high and listen to 'Going Back to Cali' on *Life After Death* [1997]? Smoking a joint in L.A. with the top down, blasting that song is the best thing you can do. I highly recommend it."

Bob Marley and the Wailers: "'Trenchtown Rock' on *Live!* [1975] is another favorite of mine. Listen to it and everything makes sense for a few minutes. When you're high, some records, even if there's an off-key moment, even if someone flubs a groove, nothing is wrong. Everything is right with this one."

Miles Davis: "*Kind of Blue* [1959] is interesting, emotional music, but it numbs you at the same time. When I listen to Herbie Hancock, I'm listening for all the intricacies and musical fanciness, but when you put on Miles, you want to be having sex or doing something sensual that distracts you from the music. It's like a sound track. It's the perfect thing to ignore."

The Seven Stoner Wonders of the World

1 Amsterdam, the Netherlands: The unequivocal stoner capital of the world, due to its relaxed and progressive drug laws, Amsterdam draws thousands of international pot-smoking tourists to the many coffeeshops that line its canal streets. You can get some of the world's best weed and hash in this city, which also hosts the annual Cannabis Cup every November.

TOURIST TIP: Most people buy in moderation (it's a shame to have to throw out entire bags of buds at the end of a trip) and don't take it with them across international borders.

2 Vancouver, Canada: North America's version of Amsterdam (also known as Vansterdam), this bayside city in British Columbia allows legal pot bars and seed shops to exist (mostly on Hastings Street) with its police essentially not enforcing the city's pot possession laws. It's doubtful the dozens of weed-related retailers and street merchants will be going away any time soon.

TOURIST TIP: Travelers advise not to carry cannabis in or out of Canada.

3 California, United States: There's always been good weed in Cali, but thanks to Proposition 215, which legalized marijuana for medical use statewide, it's now easier to get and more potent than ever. From the Bay Area, the one-time hub of hippie culture, to Joshua Tree, Humboldt Country, Los Angeles, and "the O.C.," surfers, skaters, and rock and rollers have kept stoner culture alive throughout the Golden State.

TOURIST TIP: Patrons are required to have medical cards to enter any of California's cannabis dispensaries. Call ahead and ask about the procedure rather than just walking in off the street, or go to the California NORML website (canorml.org) for more info; take note of the difference in climate from southern (hot) and northern (cool) California.

4 Jamaica: The birthplace of Bob Marley and spiritual hub of Rastafarianism—the only religion to espouse the use of marijuana as a way to gain wisdom and be closer to Jah (God)—this Caribbean island ripe with lush scenery and picture-perfect beaches is ideal for traveling stoners. Within five minutes of exiting the airport—before you even have a chance to say "hello"—you'll likely be asked if you want to buy some ganja.

TOURIST TIP: Though it's hard to get busted in tourist-heavy cities like Negril and Montego Bay, don't completely drop your guard. A night in a Jamaican jail will certainly kill your buzz.

5 Nimbin, Australia: This Down Under counterculture hub in the appropriately named "rainbow" region, sits on the base of an extinct volcano fifty miles inland from Byron Beach and hosts the annual MardiGrass festival in May. When stoner running back Ricky Williams took his sojourn to

Negril, Jamaica

Australia, this is where he went. Known for its vibrant music and art scene, and the native Aboriginal community, Nimbin is a hippie enclave worth visiting.

TOURIST TIP: Check out the sacred rock formations; at the 2007 MardiGrass there were more than 100 arrests, so be careful if you attend the event.

6 Morocco: This North African country provides half of the world's hash supply, so it's no surprise that, in virtually every tourist-friendly city, it is easy to find. Anyone who looks like they're traveling through (or carrying a backpack, a dead giveaway) will inevitably be approached by young men offering *kif*, the Moroccan word for hashish. Local men also smoke it in sidewalk cafés out of pipes (called *sipsi*) or hookahs, but because hash is technically illegal (punishable by up to ten years in jail), it is uncommon to see it being sold or smoked out in the open. Still, areas like Ketama in the Rif Mountains region, where much of the country's cannabis is cultivated and hash is made, are worth visiting, though negotiating a deal can be an adventure.

TOURIST TIP: Travel inside Morocco usually involves police checkpoints at major intersections. Those who have been caught with hash recommend asking to pay a fine in lieu of an arrest.

7 Spain: The mellow vibes of Galicia and Ibiza along with the seed shops of Barcelona make Spain and its vague, somewhat lax personal consumption laws the latest stop on the European stoner trail. Both pot and hash are fairly easy to find throughout the Spanish provinces and islands, though the quality tends to be unimpressive, despite

the country's proximity to Morocco. The "soap-bar," a popular form of low-grade hash, and outdoor-grown mid-grade weed, usually mixed with tobacco, are the basics of Spanish stoner life, as are all-night raves and raging beachside parties.

TOURIST TIP: For the ultimate route, consider crossing the Sea of Gibraltar to Morocco. Regular and high-speed ferries from Tarifa and Algeciras

in Spain to Tangier (Morocco) and Ceuta, (Spanish Morocco) run year-round.

Venice Beach, California

Amsterdam, the Netherlands

Essaouira, Morocco

of rugged beauty noted for mountains, redwood trees, and plenty of outdoor-grown marijuana. Adjacent to Mendocino County to the south and Trinity County to the east, the three counties are known as "The Emerald Triangle." Humboldt State University in Arcata is home to 7,500 students and such events as the Mushroom Fair and the Harvest Bash. It's been estimated that as many as 10 percent of the county's 125,000 residents cultivate cannabis. In 2004, in accordance with the state's Proposition 215 medical marijuana law, Ordinance 2328 was passed, allowing registered patients to produce a maximum of three pounds of "cannabis bud" per year. ALSO SEE: EMERALD TRIANGLE; MENDOCINO COUNTY; STONER COLLEGES (P. 206); TRINITY COUNTY.

HYDRO / *hi-dro* / *n.* Shortened term and slang for hydroponically grown marijuana, often further shortened to 'dro. It is not a strain but a general term for marijuana grown in water. ALSO SEE: INDOORS.

HYDROPONIC / *hi-dro-pon-ik* / *adj.* Term to describe an indoor growing process by which marijuana is rooted in a nutrient-rich water system rather than in soil. ALSO SEE: INDOORS.

> "One's condition on marijuana is always existential. One can feel the importance of each moment."
> —**Norman Mailer,** writer

mains one of the few pure indicas. ALSO SEE: CANNABIS; SATIVA; POT COMPARISON (P. 120).

INDOORS / *in-dohwrs* / *adj.* As opposed to outdoors, the term used to describe the closets, basements, attics, enclosed rooms, and greenhouses in which marijuana is grown in dirt or with hydroponic systems. ALSO SEE: GET GROWING (P. 64); GREENHOUSE; HYDROPONIC; OUTDOORS.

INHALE / *inn-hail* / *v.* To draw oxygen or smoke into your lungs. Referenced in Cypress Hill's "Insane in the Brain" (1993): "Inhale, exhale, I just got a pound in the mail." ALSO SEE: DRAW; HIT; PUFF; PULL; RIP; SMOKE; TOKE.

IRIE / *eye-ree* / *adj.* Jamaican term for peace of mind and well being, as in, "Everyt'ing is irie, mon."

ISOLATOR HASH / *ice-o-late-ur-hash* / *n.* SEE BUBBLE HASH.

ITAL / *eye-tail* / *adj.* Word used to describe the Jamaican diet adhered to by Rastafarians eschewing pork, red meat, and shellfish (similar to Kosher and Halal diets). Fish should be no longer than one foot long and food is prepared in clay pots, without salt. Ingredients are fresh and natural; while tobacco, alcohol, and drugs are not allowed, ganja is.

I

Ice bong

ICE BONG / *ice-bahng* / *n.* A water pipe with ice cubes inserted into the tube, which cool down the hit for extra impact. Beware of melting ice flooding the stem.

INDICA / *in-di-ka* / *n.* Also known as *Cannabis indica* (as opposed to *Cannabis sativa*), this cold-weather species is characterized by short, dense plants with wide, dark leaves and is prized in the tropics, where you might hear the request, "Got some indica, mon?" Plants mature in six to eight weeks and produce an extremely potent high. Indicas are generally hybridized with taller sativas. Northern Lights re-

J

JAMAICA Caribbean island noted for cannabis production, reggae music, and ganja use by its Rastafarian inhabitants. Originally colonized by Christopher Columbus, who landed there in 1494, it was seized by William Penn, Sr., in 1655. England imported African slaves to work the sugar plantations. Slavery was abolished in 1838. Jamaica gained independence from England in 1962. It is now one of the four countries (along with Mexico, Canada, and Colombia) that supply the United States with imported marijuana, and total production exceeds 200 tons per year. Its tropical climate produces sativa crops with low THC levels. Penalties

How to Make a Carrot Pipe
🌿 BY WHITESTARR'S RAINBOW

Rainbow, Whitestarr's 'fro-sporting guitarist, has the magic touch when it comes to on-the-fly pipes. Here he explains how he makes a carrot pipe.

CAUTION: DON'T CRACK THE CARROT

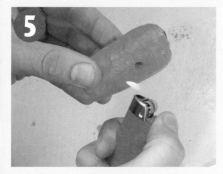

Step 1: "Take a long carrot and cut it in half so that the thicker part remains. Hold it up to your mouth and measure where a bowl could go without scorching your nose or mouth upon being lit."

Step 2: "Take a metal rod, screwdriver, or even a pencil, and drill down about halfway through the carrot."

Step 3: "Then slowly drill your way lengthwise through the center."

Step 4: "If you go too fast you will crack the carrot. You want the hole that goes through the top to meet the one that goes through the length."

Step 5: "Once the two holes connect, the pipe is ready to use. First dry out your 'bowl' with a lighter."

Step 6: "Then pack it up, light it, and puff. A carrot really doesn't burn, so it will be a smooth hit. In the event that your carrot is too small or short, you can take a pen apart and stick the hollowed shell into the center hole so that your 'pipe' is elongated and you don't burn your nose."

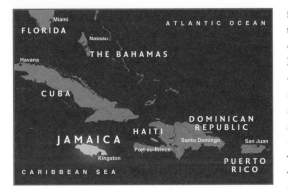

for possession of marijuana there can be severe. However, efforts to "legalize it," as Peter Tosh famously sang, are ongoing, despite U.S. opposition to any change to current ganja prohibition. ALSO SEE: GANJA REGGAE CLASSICS (P. 186); THE SEVEN WONDERS OF THE STONER WORLD (P. 76) STONER BEACHES (P. 202).

JAMES, RICK (1948–2004) Funk pioneer and ganja enthusiast born in Buffalo, New York, who exhorted fans to smoke "Mary Jane" (1978) before his career eventually went up in smoke due to cocaine abuse and legal problems. He moved to Toronto and performed with Neil Young in the Mynah Birds in Toronto in 1965. Seven years later he founded the Stone City Band in Los Angeles, and finally in 1978 released his first hit album, *Come Get It*, which included

Rick James in 1979

"Mary Jane" ("You are my main thing"), followed by *Fire It Up* (1979). "Super Freak" (1981) established him as a top-selling artist. However, convicted for abduction and assault, he spent two years in jail (from 1993 to 1995). In 2005 Dave Chappelle portrayed the R & B singer in a *Chappelle's Show* skit and in joking about his drug use, popularized the oft-repeated phrase, "I'm Rick James, bitch!" ALSO SEE: THE GREATEST POT-THEMED ALBUM COVERS (P. 182).

JAY / *jey* / n. Short for joint, the term is sometimes abbreviated further to just the letter "J."

JEFFERSON AIRPLANE Though they steadfastly claim to have been named after 1920s blues man Blind Lemon Jefferson, these psychedelic rock pioneers were variously rumored to have taken their moniker from a $2 bag of buds (think Thomas Jefferson) or a roach clip made out of a paper match. Whatever the truth is, Grace Slick (vocals), Marty Balin (vocals), Paul Kantner (guitar/vocals), Jorma Kaukonen (lead guitar), Jack Casady (bass), and Spencer Dryden (drums) were never shy about their opinions of drug use. "White Rabbit," their 1967 trip through the looking glass, found them channeling Lewis Carroll's *Alice in Wonderland*; it culminates in Slick's famous incantation, "Feed your head." Three years later, they released a protest single, "Mexico," decrying the Nixon Administration's efforts to stem the flow of marijuana from south of the border. (Slick also reportedly attempted to spike Richard Nixon's tea with LSD during a visit to the White House.) Their album *Long John Silver* (1972) features cigars on the cover and brown Mexican pot on the inside, and literally can be converted into a stash box. Joining placid folk-blues passages, aggressive guitar noise eruptions, and unique male-female harmonies, the band captured the zeitgeist of 1960s San Francisco with such albums as *Surrealistic Pillow* (1967), *Crown of Creation* (1968), and *Volunteers* (1969), and remained influential even as band personnel turnover in the mid-1970s resulted in a name change to Jefferson Starship, and later to just Starship, purveyors of the unfortunate "We Built This City" in 1985.

JOB / *jhawb* / n. French rolling paper company founded in 1830 by Jean Bardoun and named for his initials. The company logo includes a diamond between the J and B, which visually connects the two with an O-like form, creating the word JOB. Made from rice paper, these papers are available in multiple sizes. The company's latest product is Crystal, clear cellulose-based papers similar to Aleda papers. ALSO SEE: GUIDE TO ROLLING PAPERS (P. 116).

JOINT / joynt / n. 1. Term for a marijuana cigarette, it was first used to describe a betting parlor (1870) and later an opium den (1890). In the early twentieth century it became associated with a hypodermic needle used to inject heroin or cocaine. By the 1960s it had evolved to its current definition. Tom Petty sang about it on the hit single "You Don't Know How It Feels" (1994): "So let's get to the point, let's roll another joint." 2. Slang for prison. 3. Hip-hop slang for a song, as in, "Check out my new joint." 4. Hip-hop slang for good, as in, "That's da joint." 5. A place or establishment, as in, "Let's split this joint." 6. Slang for a man's penis. 7. Poker term for a full house in Texas Hold'em. ALSO SEE: HOW TO ROLL A JOINT (P. 119).

K

KAYA Title of and song from Bob Marley album (1978), referring to marijuana or ganja: "Got to have kaya now / For the rain is falling." ALSO SEE: GANJA REGGAE CLASSICS (P. 186); BOB MARLEY.

KEROUAC, JACK (1922–1969) Leading author of the Beat-generation, he was born in Lowell, Massachusetts, to French-Canadian parents. In the 1950s and early 1960s he shook up the writing establishment with his free-form, jazz-inspired prose. His most well-known novel, *On the Road* (1957), written on a long scroll (as opposed to individual sheets of paper) about his free-spirited friends, was famously fueled by Benzedrine, pot, and coffee. Fourteen other books established him as the greatest of all the Beat writers. However, he became an alcoholic and eventually

Jefferson Airplane—(clockwise from bottom left) Grace Slick, Paul Kantner, Marty Balin, Jorma Kaukonen, Spencer Dryden, and Jack Casady—circa 1970

died of cirrhosis of the liver in 1969. ALSO SEE: WILLIAM S. BURROUGHS; EASY RIDERS, RAGING BEATS (P. 54); ALLEN GINSBERG.

KESEY, KEN (1935–2001) Author and counterculture legend, he founded the Merry Pranksters and wrote *One Flew Over the Cuckoo's Nest* (1962), *Sometimes a Great Notion* (1964), and five other books. Born in Colorado, he attended the University of Oregon and Stanford University where, in 1959, he volunteered for a CIA-funded experimental drug study that introduced him to LSD, psilocybin (magic mushrooms), mescaline, and DMT. He moved to La Honda and began his own experiments, which he called "Acid Tests," with friends and colleagues. The Grateful Dead, then known as the Warlocks, performed at the Acid Tests. In 1964 he and the Merry Pranksters embarked on a road trip to New York in a psychedelically painted bus they dubbed "Further." This journey is chronicled in Tom Wolfe's *The Electric Kool-Aid Acid Test* (1968). In 1966 he was arrested for marijuana possession. After faking his suicide and fleeing to Mexico, he returned to the U.S. and spent five months in jail. In 1975 the film adaptation of *One Flew Over the Cuckoo's Nest*, starring Jack Nicholson, won the Academy Award for Best

"Marijuana tends to not kill ya, unless you get high and operate heavy machinery."
—**Kevin Smith,** director

🌿 Stoner Code 🌿

Chances are the cops are not listening in on your phone conversations or monitoring your text messages, but just in case, here are some commonly used code words for weed.

Music: Come up with a band or artist that you associate with pot and ask if you can drop by to borrow or download some of their music, as in, "Got any Al Green CDs?"

Time: Use some breakdown of an hour to convey your order. For example, "Can I come over for fifteen minutes?" means you're looking to pick up a quarter, or "Can we hang out for a couple of hours?" means you're talking about two ounces.

Color: You can incorporate the color green into practically anything, like, "Did you get that *green* bike? How much was it? Can I come check it out?"

Names: A popular first name like Jay, or the less commonly used Bud or Herb, can be an easy way to drop a hint. "Were you able to see Jay today? How is he?" It's a little silly, but it works.

Food: Pizza terminology is a good way to communicate your stony message, using slices as a quantity predetermined by you and your dealer, as in, "Save me two slices." Or you can always go with any variation of "pot pie," as in, "Dude, you gotta come over and taste this chicken pot pie."

YOU BRING THE GREEN VEGGIES FOR DINNER

Marijuana resin glands, a.k.a. kif

Picture. He spent the latter portion of his life in Oregon with his wife, Faye, and his children, Jed, Zane, and Shannon. He died on November 10, 2001, from liver cancer. ALSO SEE: STONER LEGENDS (P. 194).

KIF / *keef* / *n.* 1. Powdered glands of marijuana, also known as resin or trichomes, collected by sifting the marijuana through a screen. 2. Pre-hash traditionally mixed with tobacco in Morocco and smoked in pipes or hookahs. These days, kif is most often used as a condiment, sprinkled on top of a bowl or prerolled joint. ALSO SEE: HASH; RESIN GLANDS; TRICHOMES.

KILO / *key-low* / *n.* Usually packaged in brick form and coming from Mexico, 2.2 pounds of marijuana. The term is often shortened to "key." Arlo Guthrie, in his song "Coming into Los Angeles" (1969), sings about "bringing in a couple of keys." ALSO SEE: FAVORITE STONY LYRICS (P. 180).

KIND / *kind* / *n.* 1. Stoner slang for high-quality marijuana, also referred to as kind bud or K.B., as in, "Who's got the kind?" it evolved from the Grateful Dead lyric in "Uncle John's Band": "Woh–oh, what I want to know is, are you kind?" (1970). As the quality of marijuana improved in the 1980s and the Dead toured the country, Deadheads created the term in order to be able to describe marijuana without having to refer to the illicit substance by name. 2. Virginia-based Grateful Dead cover band The Kind founded in 1987. ALSO SEE: GREAT STONER INNOVATIONS (P. 137); POT COMPARISON (P. 120).

KNIFE HITS / *nife-hits* / *pl. n.* An old-school makeshift smoking technique, wherein two butter knives are wedged into the coils of a medium heat-burner until their tips turn red-hot. Then, hash is pressed between the two touching tips, and the smoke that runs off is inhaled through the mouth, which shouldn't be positioned too close to the surface of the knives, which can burn your lips. This method is similar to heating hash oil on a burning coal. ALSO SEE: HASH OIL.

KONA / *cone-ah* / *n.* Hawaii's coffee-growing region on the "Big Island," the area is also known for marijuana cultivation, hence the term *kona buds.*

KOTTONMOUTH KINGS Founded in Southern California in 1994, the septet combine hip-hop, punk rock, and a love of all things related to marijuana. Their albums include *Royal Highness* (1998), *Hidden Stash* (1999), *Rollin' Stoned* (2002), *Fire It Up* (2004), *Joint Venture* (2005), and *Cloud Nine* (2007). The group is composed of three rappers—Daddy X, D-Loc, and Johnny Richter—and DJ Bobby B, drummer Lou Dog, backup singer Tax Man, and "Visual Assassin" Pakelika, who never speaks onstage, dances robotically, and inhales from a vaporizer during live performances. ALSO SEE: STONER BANDS (P. 177); WHY I LOVE TO VAPE (P. 135).

KRASSNER, PAUL (B. 1932) Born in New York, Krassner cofounded the Yippies in 1967, joined Ken Kesey's Merry Pranksters, and edited Lenny Bruce's autobiography, *How* *to Talk Dirty and Influence People* (1966). He published *The Realist* from 1958 to 2001 (146 issues), and is the author of twelve books, including *Pot Stories for the Soul* (1999). He was inducted into the Counterculture Hall of Fame in 2001. ALSO SEE: YIPPIES.

KRUPA, GENE (1909–1973) Swing jazz drummer born in Chicago, he moved to New York and joined the Benny Goodman Quartet in 1934. He is noted for his propulsive, animated style on such classics as "Sing, Sing, Sing," which featured the first extended drum solo in jazz. Arrested in San Francisco for marijuana possession in 1943 on trumped-up charges, which included contributing to the delinquency of a minor, he spent eighty-four days in jail. As a solo bandleader, he performed the song "I'm Feelin' High and Happy" with Helen Moore on vocals. *The Gene Krupa Story* (1959) stars Sal Mineo. Krupa suffered from emphysema and leukemia, and died of a heart attack on October 16, 1973.

KRYPTO / *krip-toe* / *n.* 1. Generic term for high-grade weed and short for kryptonite. It is sometimes confused with crippy, which means a creeping high, when used in its short form, kryppie. 2. The name of Superman's dog in the comic book series.

KUSH / *kuhsh* / *n.* A highly potent indica strain originally from the Hindu Kush region of Central Asia, which borders northeastern Afghanistan and southern Pakistan. Often crossed with other strains (such as Skunk #1, resulting in Master Kush), it is known for its pungent and sweet smell, tight buds, and strong high, and it is a favorite among rappers like Snoop Dogg, The Game, and B-Real, who've name-checked it on many tracks. Mutations of the strain include Chocolate Kush,

Sugar Kush

Purple Kush, Sugar Kush, Blueberry Kush, and the L.A. favorite: OG Kush. ALSO SEE: OG KUSH.

KUTCHIE / *cooch-ee* / *n.* Jamaican for a marijuana pipe, the term was popularized in the Mighty Diamonds' song "Pass the Kutchie" (1982): "Pass the kutchie pon the lefthand side." The British group Musical Youth changed the word "kutchie" to "dutchie" for their rendition of the song, "Pass the Dutchie," which was a Top 10 single in 1983. ALSO SEE: A BRIEF HISTORY OF THE GREATEST MARIJUANA SONGS (P. 178); GANJA REGGAE CLASSICS (P. 186); PASS THE DUTCHIE."

L

LACED / *laysd* / *adj.* To be contaminated or spiked with some sort of harmful substance. In terms of marijuana, it could mean that some cocaine or other smokeable drug has been sprinkled on top of a bowl or into a joint.

LAMB'S BREAD / *lambz-bred* / *n.* 1. Classic Jamaican strain grown in Westmoreland Parish and enjoyed by Bob Marley, it is named for colas as large as a loaf of bread and/or resembling a lamb's tail. The name relates to sacramental use of ganja by Rastafarians; bread refers to the communion of the body of Christ, and when ganja is inhaled, its smokers are thought to become closer to Jah (God). Though the original strain is no longer available, it is obtainable as a hybrid strain—also known as Lamb's Breath—from various Dutch seed companies. 2. Song title, recorded variously by Sylford Walker and Welton Irie (1977), Dillinger and Sugar Minott (1979), and UB40 (1988). ALSO SEE: CLASSIC STRAINS (P. 11).

LAVA LAMP / *la-vuh-lambp* / *n.* Hippie accessory invented by Edward Craven Walker in England in 1963, it was originally named the Astro Lamp. U.S. rights were sold in 1965 to Adolph Wertheimer and Hy Spector, whose Chicago-based company Haggerty Enterprises continues to manufacture the conical-shaped, color-changing lighting device. Inside the device, oil and wax, when heated (turned on), swirl around, creating psychedelic "blobs." Stoners stare

Acid king Timothy Leary
in 1967

Led Zeppelin Live: Robert Plant
backed by John Paul Jones
(left), Jimmy Page (right), and
John Bonham (obscured)

at these blobs for hours at a time, a practice known as "spacing out."

LEAF / leif / n. Green foliage extending from the stem of a plant and also known as shake. In the case of cannabis, it features five to nine points and is similar to a maple leaf. Along with the stems, it is the most expendable part of the marijuana plant and generally not smoked. It is, however, used to make cannabis butter and isolator hash.

LEARY, TIMOTHY (1920– 1996) Former Harvard professor who instructed the 1960s generation to "turn on, tune in, drop out," primarily by taking LSD. After being fired by Harvard in 1963, he moved to Millbrook, New York, where he and Ram Dass (Richard Alpert) established a "drug scene" that attracted the New York cognoscenti. In 1964 he wrote *The Psychedelic Experience* with Ralph Metzner. He was arrested for marijuana in 1965 and 1968. The latter arrest led to a jail sentence and prison escape engineered by the Weather Underground, followed by exile in Algeria, Switzerland, and Afghanistan, where he was caught and returned to the U.S. and jailed again. He was pardoned by California governor Jerry Brown in 1976. His autobiography, *Flashbacks*, was published in 1983, and in his later years, he toured the world giving speeches. He died on May 31, 1996, of inoperable prostate cancer. Paul Davids's documentary *Timothy Leary's Dead* chronicles the last year of Leary's life. The film's title was taken from the first line of the Moody Blues song, "Legend of a Mind" (1968): "Timothy Leary's dead / No, no, no, no, he's outside looking in." *Timothy Leary: A Biography* by Robert Greenfield was published in 2006. Leary is godfather to Winona Ryder, Uma Thurman, and Miranda July. ALSO SEE: RAM DASS; STONER LEGENDS (P. 194).

LED ZEPPELIN Iconic British heavy blues/hard rock band featuring Robert Plant (vocals), Jimmy Page (guitar), John Paul Jones (bass), and John Bonham (drums), along with mystical lyrics and enigmatic album-cover artwork. Formed by Yardbirds guitarist Page, the band released eight studio albums from 1969 to 1979, including the groundbreaking *Led Zeppelin, Led Zeppelin II* (both in 1969), and *Led Zeppelin IV* (1971), which includes their eight-minute-long rock anthem, "Stairway to Heaven." They are known for their debauched rock-god excesses (Bonham died in 1980 by choking on his own vomit), epic songs with elaborate

Pot Joking Around

WITH DOUG BENSON, ARJ BARKER & TONY CAMIN

The Marijuana-Logues play, written by and costarring Doug Benson, Arj Barker, and Tony Camin, opened in New York in 2004 and still tours around the U.S. *Pot Culture* asked these three stony comics to discuss their favorite pot jokes. Here's a transcription of their conversation.

Doug Benson: So, do either of you guys have a favorite pot joke? I can't really remember any, other than my own. Actually, I can barely remember my own.

Arj Barker: My favorite pot movie moment is in *Dazed and Confused* when Matthew McConaughey says, "It'd be a lot cooler if you did."

Benson: But what's your favorite pot joke, Arj?

Barker: Why did the pot cross the road?

Benson: I don't know.

Barker: Because the hippie crossed the road.

Tony Camin: Did you just come up with that?

Barker: Yeah. [Laughs] But that is my favorite joke.

Benson: OK, but what is your favorite already existing pot joke?

Barker: Tommy Rhodes has a good one. It's about how he doesn't want to smoke pot after he has kids. Because they'd be like, "Daddy, there's a ghost in our room," and he'd be like, "Shit, don't bring it in here!" I might be getting it a little bit wrong.

Benson: I like Marc Maron's bit about how people should have to take the driver's test under the influence of whatever their drug of choice is, and if they pass they get a special license that they can show to the cops when they get pulled over. I don't remember exactly how it goes, but that's the basic idea.

Barker: That's good, that's gonna be really entertaining reading.

Camin: Oh, how about Mitch Hedberg's joke, "I used to do drugs. I still do, but I also used to."

Barker: No, it's "I still do, but I used to, too."

Benson: Let's look it up on the Internet.

Camin: Look up pot jokes on Wikipedia. [Benson looks up pot jokes on Wikipedia.]

Benson: It says, "No page with that title exists."

Camin: Try Google-ing pot jokes.

Barker: What are you guys doing? You are wasting your time. "Why did the pot cross the road" is the best pot joke ever written. Because of its simplicity and elegance. Get it? Hippies have weed, so when the hippie crosses the road, the pot goes with him!

Camin: I thought it meant that the pot was crossing the road to get away from the hippie, because the hippie was gonna smoke it.

Barker: Well, you're stupid.

Cannabis Comics: (left to right) Arj Barker, Doug Benson, and Tony Camin in 2004

🌿 Lighter Etiquette 🌿

When it comes to stealing lighters, stoners, when stoned, are the worst offenders. We've all seen the following scenario before.

Stoner #1: Dude, who's got my lighter?
Stoners #2, 3, and 4: [in unison] Not me, dude.
Stoner #1: Dudes … [A minute passes as everyone stares helplessly at the bowl. Suddenly, there's a confession.]
Stoner #4: Shit, it was in my pocket.
Stoners #1, 2, and 3: [in unison] Busted, dude!

Here are a few things to keep in mind about lighters.

They are not community property:
Even if they are shared, lighters are proprietary. Keep an eye on yours and always return it to the place where you usually keep it.

Bics are best: To make using it easier on the thumb, flick out the little metal child-protection doodad with something pointy. It takes two seconds and is a sure sign of a courteous stoner.

Avoid the cheap see-through kind:
They require you to spin the metal wheel in order to get a light and callus your thumbs worse than any other kind.

Zippos are cool but smell and taste like a gas station:
Inhaling butane is nasty. Keep your Zippo as a souvenir or memento.

Matchbooks are cool: Though they're the healthiest option (no lighter fumes) and fun to collect, matches take too much time to use and are especially difficult to manage when lighting a pipe.

---

arrangements, and over-the-top concerts. Their live album/movie, *The Song Remains the Same* (1976), set the gold standard for documenting pot-smoke-laden 1970s arena rock. A midnight movie favorite, the psychedelic fantasy sequences for each band member barely make sense even when you're stoned.

LEGALIZATION / *lee-gull-eye-zay-shun* / *n.* The complete repeal of marijuana prohibition and removal of all criminal penalties for its use, sale, transport, and cultivation. The Netherlands is the only country in the world with such a policy. ALSO SEE: DECRIMINALIZATION; DEPRIORITIZATION; PROHIBITION.

LENNON, JOHN (1940–1980) SEE THE BEATLES (P. 16).

LID / *lydd* / *n.* 1. Slang for approximately one ounce of marijuana, the term was first used in the 1950s and popularized in the 1960s, as in, "Let's go score a lid." Alternately, it is thought to have evolved from the tin packages used to ship opium in the early twentieth century, and is the amount of the drug that could fit into a Prince Albert tobacco can. Literally, the metal lids of the cans were used to cook opium before injection. 2. Head or brain, as in to "flip one's lid." 3. Hat or chapeau. 4. Toupee or hairpiece.

LIGHTER / *lie-tur* / *n.* Device used to ignite a joint, pipe, blunt, or bong. The most popular brand among stoners is Bic. ALSO SEE: LIGHTER ETIQUETTE (P. 86).

LIGHT UP / *lite-upp* / *v.* 1. To smoke a joint, pipe, bong, or blunt. 2. "Light Up or Leave Me Alone" (1971) is a song by Traffic. 3. "Light Another" (1992) is a song by Cypress Hill. ALSO SEE: POT (OR NOT?) SONGS (P. 99).

LIT / *litt* / *adj. or n.* 1. To be high or stoned, as in, "I'm really lit, dude." 2. Short for literature class. ALSO SEE: BAKED; BLASTED; BLAZED; BURNT; BUZZED; CRISPY; FRIED; HIGH; LOADED; RIPPED; STONED; TOASTED; WASTED; ZONKED; ZOOTED.

LOADED / *low-ded* / *adj.* 1. The feeling or look of being wasted, usually fueled by alcohol, but the term can also be used to describe any person on a mood-altering substance, as in, "Dude, that guy is loaded!" 2. A U.K. laddie magazine. 3. "I Got Loaded" written by Bob Camille and recorded by Robert Cray (1983) and Los Lobos (1984). ALSO SEE: BAKED; BLASTED; BLAZED; BURNT; BUZZED; CRISPY, FRIED; HIGH; LIT; RIPPED; STONED; TOASTED; WASTED; ZONKED; ZOOTED.

LSD / *el-ess-dee* / *n.* Short for lysergic acid diethylamide, a synthetic hallucinogen typically taken orally in either tab form (from a small piece of absorbent blotter paper) or sugar-cube form; it can also be delivered as a liquid (using an eyedropper). It was discovered by Swiss chemist Albert

Blotter tabs of LSD

MAGIC MUSHROOMS SEE PSILOCYBIN.

MAHER, BILL (B. 1956) TV talk-show host and comedian noted for his marijuana advocacy, he was born in New York on January 20, 1956, and raised in New Jersey, and graduated from Cornell University in 1978. A stand-up comedy career and series of HBO specials led to his first talk show, *Politically Incorrect*, which originally aired on Comedy Central in 1994 and later on ABC. His contract was not renewed in 2002 after he made insensitive comments regarding the 9/11 attacks. ("Staying in the airplane when it hits the building, say what you want about it, it's not cowardly.") HBO launched *Real Time with Bill Maher* in 2003. A member of NORML's Advisory Board, he gave the keynote speech at the NORML Conference in 2002 and hosted the NORML benefit in Los Angeles in 2003. He has also hosted Marijuana Policy Project events. He is known for saying, "The worst thing about marijuana is that it makes you eat cookie dough," and that "Marijuana has never killed anyone." SEE ALSO: STONY COMEDIANS (P. 35).

Bill Maher in 2006

Hofmann in 1938 while he worked for Sandoz Laboratories. In 1943 Hofmann took the world's first "acid trip" while riding his bicycle. When acid is ingested, psychedelic properties take over: Visuals turn extra-vivid, perception of time is warped, and other sensory functions, such as smell and touch, are intensified. This effect is known as "tripping." Acid was often "dropped" at Grateful Dead shows to accentuate the band's notoriously long and winding jams. Dead sound engineer Stanley "Bear" Owsley was infamous for his "Owsley acid." Undercover operations on the Dead scene made LSD scarce in the 1990s. Arrests of major manufacturers William Leonard Pickard and Clyde Apperson—both are serving long sentences in federal prison—have significantly reduced availability. ALSO SEE: THE GRATEFUL DEAD; ALBERT HOFMANN; TRIP.

LUDLOW, FITZ HUGH (1836–1870) New York–based author of the first marijuana book, *The Hasheesh Eater* (1857), who experimented with Tilden's extract, a cannabis medicine used for tetanus, an experience that led to the writing of this book (his first) at the age of twenty-one. He later worked for *Vanity Fair* and published his last book, *The Heart of the Continent*, the year he died. Winona Ryder's parents, Michael Horowitz and Cynthia Palmer, created the Fitz Hugh Ludlow Memorial Library for drug-related literature.

MARDIGRASS SEE THE SEVEN STONER WONDERS OF THE WORLD (P. 76).

MARIJUANA / *mare-a-wan-na* / *n.* 1. Mexican term for cannabis, originally spelled marihuana (alternately spelled

M

Bob Marley

"Herb is the healing of a nation."
—Bob Marley

Bob Marley, with spliff, in Kingston, Jamaica, in 1976

The greatest reggae musician of all time, Bob Marley was born Robert Nesta Marley in Nine Mile, Jamaica, and moved to Kingston where he began his recording career with the Wailers (with Peter Tosh and Bunny Livingston). After *Catch a Fire* and *Burnin'* (both released in 1973), he became the group's official frontman. Their next six albums, from *Natty Dread* (1974) to *Uprising* (1980), established him as the most influential artist to come out of Jamaica's burgeoning music scene. A prodigious ganja smoker, he sang about the herb on "Rebel Music (3 O' Clock Roadblock)" on *Natty Dread* (1974), and *Kaya* (1978). He survived an assassination attempt in 1976 but developed cancer in 1977 and died on May 11, 1981. He fathered eleven children with nine different women.

SEE ALSO: KAYA; MARLEY; THE MARLEY FAMILY TREE (P. 89); THE GREATEST POT-THEMED ALBUM COVERS (P. 184); GANJA REGGAE CLASSICS (P. 188); STONER LEGENDS (P. 196); WEARING THE WEED (P. 133).

The Marley Family Tree

Bob Marley, né Robert Nesta Marley, was born on February 6, 1945. He was the son of **Norval St. Clair Marley**, a white Jamaican naval captain, and **Cedella Booker**, a black Jamaican eighteen-year-old girl. Bob had three step-siblings, **Richard**, **Anthony**, and **Constance**. He fathered a total of eleven children. He married **Rita Anderson** on February 10, 1966. They each already had one child from previous relationships: Bob's daughter **Imani Carole**, born May 22, 1963, to **Cheryl Murray**, and Rita's daughter **Sharon**, born November 23, 1964, whom Bob adopted.

Bob and Rita had three children together:
- **Cedella**, born August 23, 1967
- **David "Ziggy,"** born October 17, 1968
- **Stephen**, born April 20, 1972

In 1972, Bob had children with two other women:
- **Robert "Robbie,"** born May 16, 1972, to **Pat Williams**
- **Rohan**, born May 19, 1972, to **Janet Hunt**

Bob had six more children before he died on May 11, 1981:
- **Karen**, born in 1973 to **Janet Bowen**
- **Julian**, born June 4, 1975, to **Lucy Pounder**
- **Ky-Mani**, born February 26, 1976, to **Anita Belnavis**
- **Damian**, born July 21, 1978, to **Cindy Breakspeare**
- **Makeda Jahnesta**, born May 30, 1981, to **Yvette Crichton**

Rita had a fifth child, **Stephanie**, born in 1974.

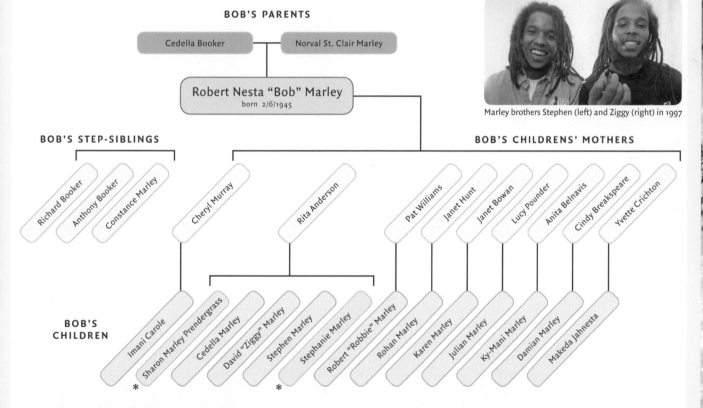

BOB'S PARENTS

Cedella Booker — Norval St. Clair Marley

Robert Nesta "Bob" Marley
born 2/6/1945

Marley brothers Stephen (left) and Ziggy (right) in 1997

BOB'S STEP-SIBLINGS

Richard Booker · Anthony Booker · Constance Marley

BOB'S CHILDRENS' MOTHERS

Cheryl Murray · Rita Anderson · Pat Williams · Janet Hunt · Janet Bowan · Lucy Pounder · Anita Belnavis · Cindy Breakspeare · Yvette Crichton

BOB'S CHILDREN

Imani Carole · Sharon Marley Prendergrass · Cedella Marley · David "Ziggy" Marley · Stephen Marley · Stephanie Marley · Robert "Robbie" Marley · Rohan Marley · Karen Marley · Julian Marley · Ky-Mani Marley · Damian Marley · Makeda Jahnesta

* Children born to Rita Marley whose fathers were not Bob Marley

mariguana) and dating back to the turn of the twentieth century when the substance arrived in the U.S. from Mexico. It was also nicknamed locoweed, because it supposedly made users crazy. Another Mexican term for cannabis is *mota*. When smoked, eaten, or vaporized, it produces a high, due to the plant's cannabinoids, primarily THC (tetrahydrocannabinol). 2. Title of songs by Country Joe & the Fish (1967), the Fugs (1968), Bette Midler ("Marahuana," 1976), Sly & the Revolutionaries (1980), and Reverend Horton Heat (1991). ALSO SEE: GANJA; GRASS; HEMP; HERB; POT; SMOKE; TREES; WEED.

MARIJUANA-LOGUES, THE Off-off Broadway play about the humorous aspects of pot culture, it opened at New York's Actors Playhouse in March 2004 and closed nearly one year later. The show, based on *The Vagina Monologues*, and written and performed by comedians Arj Barker, Doug Benson, and Tony Camin (Tommy Chong has also appeared in the production), continues to tour the U.S. A live-performance CD of the play, *The Marijuana-Logues* (2004), and a book, *The Marijuana-Logues: Everything About Pot That We Could Remember* (2005), are available. ALSO SEE: POT JOKING AROUND (P. 85).

MARIJUANA POLICY PROJECT (MPP) Washington, D.C., advocacy organization founded by former NORML employees Rob Kampia and Chuck Thomas in 1995. It primarily focuses on statewide medical-marijuana ballot initiatives and legislation. It boasts 21,000 members and support from such celebrities as Montel Williams, Bill Maher, and Jack Black. Kampia is its executive director.

MARIJUANA REVIEW The original pot publication founded in 1968 by Michael Aldrich and Ed Sanders, and published by LeMar International and Amorphia. Only nine issues were printed, through 1972, and contributors included Allen Ginsberg, John Sinclair, and Rosemary Leary.

MARIN, RICHARD "CHEECH" (B. 1946) SEE: CHEECH & CHONG (P. 36).

MARINOL / *mare-in-all* / n. Synthetic THC (dronabinol) sold since 1987 in gelcap form by prescription for numerous medical conditions. The drug was developed by Solvay Pharmaceuticals and marketed by Unimed Pharmacueticals

in the U.S., and by Sanofi-Synthelabo Canada in Canada since 2000. A similar product, Cesamet, originally manufactured by Eli Lilly and Company in 1985, has been available in Canada from Valeant Pharmaceuticals since 2001 and in the U.S. since 2006. Unlike smoked or vaporized marijuana, pills require forty-five minutes to an hour to take effect. ALSO SEE: MEDICAL MARIJUANA; SATIVEX.

MARKS, HOWARD (B. 1945) International marijuana smuggler born in Wales who spent seven years in a U.S. prison (from 1988 to 1995) and wrote about it in his autobiography, *Mr Nice* (1996). He followed this work with *The Howard Marks Book of Dope Stories* (2001) and *Señor Nice: Straight Life from Wales to Latin America* (2006). He operates the Mr. Nice Seed Bank with Shantibaba, and lives with his wife Judy in Mallorca, Spain.

MARLEY / *mar-lee* / n. An exceptionally large fatty, as in, "Dude, that's one Marley-size joint!" ALSO SEE: CONE; BOB MARLEY; SPLIFF.

MARLEY, BOB (1945–1981) SEE PAGE 88.

MARY JANE / *mare-ee-jayne* / n. 1. Colloquial name for marijuana based on the letters "M" and "J" corresponding with the first and third syllables of the name. Usage of the term dates back to the 1920s. It is often referred to in song lyrics, as in, "I love you Mary Jane," by Cypress Hill (*Hits from the Bong*, 1994). 2. Title of songs by Janis Joplin (1975), Rick James (1978), Mary J. Blige (1994), Alanis Morissette (1995), Coolio (1998), and The Vines (2002). 3. Other usages: Mary Jane Girls, a singing group produced by Rick James (1983–1986); and "Mary Jane's Last Dance" by Tom Petty (1993). 4. Peter Parker's girlfriend in the *Spiderman* comic book and movie series, played by Kirsten Dunst. ALSO SEE: A BRIEF HISTORY OF THE GREATEST MARIJUANA SONGS (P. 178).

MASON JAR / *may-sen-jahr* / n. The perfect airtight glass container for storing buds. It can be bought in any hardware store or dollar store. ALSO SEE: CURING; KEEPING YOUR BUDS FRESH (P. 25).

MAUI Second-largest Hawaiian island, it has a stable climate (seventy-three to seventy-eight degrees year round), stunning topography, and picture-perfect beaches, making it a tropical paradise. As an added bonus, the island's nutrient-rich soil makes for prime growing conditions and yields sought-after strains like Maui Wowie. Beach bums and celebrities have flocked to the island for the past forty years. While there, keep an ear out for locals asking, "Do you smoke?" Just in case, the Hawaiian term for weed is *pakalolo* (meaning crazy tobacco). The price is reflected in the quality, with the average eighth going for around $60. ALSO SEE: STONER BEACHES (P. 202).

MAUI WOWIE / *mow-ee-wow-ee* / *n.* 1. Classic sativa strain, alternately spelled Maui Wowee, grown on the Hawaiian island of Maui. Tall, resinous, and hash-smelling with a hint of tropical fruit flavor (due to compost fertilization), the strain has been mixed with Skunk to create Original Hawaiian Maui Skunk, which is available from many seed banks. 2. Generic product name for blunt wraps (watermelon flavor), snack foods (Skinny Sticks Maui Wowie Spicy Tropical Crunch), drink mixes (Maui Wowie Punch—coconut rum, melon liquor, and orange and pineapple juices), a video game, and even a guitar model (Gibson Custom J-45 Maui Wowie Koa Acoustic Guitar). ALSO SEE: CLASSIC STRAINS (P. 11).

MCCARTNEY, PAUL (B. 1942) SEE THE BEATLES (P.16); FAMOUS POT BUSTS (P. 194).

MEDICAL MARIJUANA / *med-ick-al-mare-i-wan-ah* / *n.* Though the medical marijuana movement—which aims to legalize the use of cannabis in any form for the relief of a variety of ailments and diseases—is considered controversial, up until seventy years ago, pot was used like aspirin in many parts of the world. The Marihuana Tax Act of 1937 put a stop to that in the U.S. and in effect criminalized the sale of cannabis on the grounds that it caused "murder, insanity and death." The only person to object to the bill at the time represented the American Medical Association. In 1969 after being arrested at the Mexican border, Timothy Leary successfully challenged the law on the basis that it was unconstitutional. However, in its place came the Controlled Substances Act of 1970, which reclassified marijuana as a Schedule I drug alongside heroin. Since then, anecdotal evidence has shown that marijuana is a viable form of medicine for people suffering from glaucoma (it relieves pressure on the eyes), cancer (it helps lessen the nausea resulting from chemotherapy), AIDS (it stimulates the appetite), multiple sclerosis (it stops spasms), and many other afflictions. This eventually led to the passage of California's Proposition 215 or the Compassionate Use Act of 1996. Supported by a 55 percent majority, the law allows a person to possess or cultivate marijuana for personal consumption or on the recommendation of a doctor. Similar laws have passed in eleven other states: Alaska, Colorado, Hawaii, Maine, Montana, New Mexico, Nevada, Oregon, Rhode Island, Vermont, and Washington. In California, hundreds of dispensaries have opened their doors, but the Drug Enforcement Administration, under federal jurisdiction, continues to periodically raid and harass these stores and patients who depend upon them. ALSO SEE: COMPASSION CLUB; DISPENSARY; MELISSA ETHERIDGE (P. 92); MARINOL; MEDICAL EDIBLES (P. 57); SATIVEX.

MENDOCINO CIGAR SEE BUBBLE ROLL.

MENDOCINO COUNTY The area located directly south of Humboldt County and part of California's cannabis-centric Emerald Triangle (Trinity County is the third part of that triumvirate). In 1999 residents voted to decriminalize marijuana. Registered medical patients are allowed to cultivate twenty-five plants at one time. Such towns as Willits, Ukiah, and Laytonville are longtime havens for marijuana growers. Mendocino is also known for its dramatic coastline and boutique wineries.

Pacific Sour Diesel—one of the many strains available at California medical-marijuana dispensaries

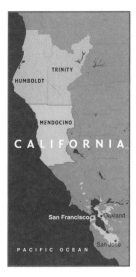

"I support decriminalization. People are smoking pot anyway and to make them criminals is wrong."
—Paul McCartney, musician

M

Melissa Etheridge

ON MEDICAL MARIJUANA

She's sold almost thirty million albums, shared the stage with Bruce Springsteen, won two Grammy awards and even an Oscar (for the theme song to the documentary *An Inconvenient Truth*), but when Melissa Etheridge was diagnosed with breast cancer in 2004, her future as a rock star suddenly seemed uncertain. What followed were weeks of difficult treatment to rid her body first of the tumor, then of any lingering cancerous elements. But there was one thing that helped her deal with it: medical marijuana. Now cancer-free, Etheridge tells *Pot Culture* how alternative therapy got her back on her feet again.

Pot Culture: What does chemotherapy do to your body?
Melissa Etheridge: When I was first diagnosed, I thought chemotherapy was a drug that kills cancer and makes you lose your hair. But when you enter the huge medical community, you realize what chemotherapy really is. It's a poison that they put in your body—they hope it kills the cancer before it kills you. It brings your whole body this close to death. It's extremely barbaric and there's a lot of pain and discomfort. They give you steroids, heavy-duty painkillers, and antacids, all with long lists of side effects. I thought, why would I want to take all that when I could smoke cannabis or eat cannabis or vaporize cannabis about every two hours and have no side effects?

PC: How did you learn that marijuana was an option?
ME: Sometimes you make choices where options might not have been formally presented, but you are aware of them. When I went into chemotherapy, close friends told me that they'd had other friends who said marijuana was the only way they could get through it. And when I was diagnosed, I'd never been sick before. I've always been kind of a natural gal. Being in rock and roll I'd certainly seen my share of drugs, but I was never drawn into heavy usage of anything, ever. But when I was facing chemotherapy, I just heard from many people that marijuana was the way to go.

PC: How did it help?
ME: It immediately helped with the nausea. That's the biggest thing it does—it takes away the nausea.

It gives you back your appetite, and I had to eat to keep up my weight and strength. It kept me in a place where I could get through it and not totally lose my body. But I realized that the pain comes back about every two hours and that I was going to be smoking this about every couple hours. I'd never done that before and it was intense. But I realized that when you're sick, your body needs balancing. Then when you smoke cannabis, it takes you to a place of "normal." You don't get high. When you're healthy and you smoke, you go to other places higher than your own consciousness, but when you're in physical distress, it takes you to a place of peace within your body.

PC: Was it difficult to get?
ME: No. I live in California and a fella who has one of

the medicinal clubs delivered it to me. My personal favorite was called Church, but it's hard to get. I found that indicas worked best—Bubble Kush, Sno-Cap, it was all good ...

"We all know the truth about pot but are afraid to speak it."

PC: What method did you use to inhale?

ME: I'm not a smoker so having to smoke something every two hours and to be so nauseous that when I coughed it would make me throw up, I got to a point where I went with better water pipes, like the three-chambered kind. Then I discovered the ROOR bong, which is absolutely the greatest ever. Then I heard about vaporizers and the genius of the Volcano. Sometimes when you smoke and burn pot at too high of a level, the smoke gets to your brain cells and gives you that sort of dizzy high. When you just inhale the THC from a vaporizer, you get all the effects and get more of a clear high sensation than the foggy high. I also ate it. The thing about cannabis is that to get the healing agent, THC, you have to put it in a fatty substance like butter—that's why you've got your brownies and cookies. When even the vaporizer was making me sick, I would put the butter on potatoes or anything. It's not very tasty, but it's medicinal and you get longer relief when you eat it.

PC: What do you say about a government that won't let people legally medicate themselves with marijuana?

ME: It makes me sad that this is something so beneficial to so many people and there are those who would do it if it was legal, but they don't want to break the law. They're good citizens who are afraid. And it saddens me to see these people struggle with drugs that do more damage to them and even get them hooked.

PC: What should every American know about marijuana and its place in our society?

ME: This is an herb that the Earth gives us. It's been around forever, but just like homosexuality and sex in general, it has been conveniently removed from the history that we're taught. So we don't understand that there has been a huge culture and understanding of cannabis forever. It was used in wonderful ways, for clarity and peace. Bring me two enemies, make them smoke, and then let them fight. They're not going to fight. There's a big spiritual aspect to pot, too. And as we move into this new age of thought—understanding that the Earth is a living thing that we need to take care of—then we start realizing what we can take back from it. And these synthetic things that we keep shoving into our bodies, maybe people will start to reject them and look to herbs like marijuana. So just keep your eyes open and feel your own truth about things. We all know the truth about pot but are afraid to speak it. It's don't ask, don't tell. Our whole culture seems to be like, "OK, you can do it, just don't let me see." We're so afraid of the truth.

PC: Do you still partake?

ME: I smoke occasionally.

"The only effect that I ever noticed from smoking marijuana was a sort of mild sedative, a release of tension when I was overworking. It never made me boisterous or quarrelsome. If anything, it calmed me and reduced my activity."

—Robert Mitchum,
actor

MEZZROW, MEZZ (1899–1972) Chicago-born jazz musician/pot dealer, who brought marijuana to Harlem. Arrested for possessing sixty reefers, or joints, at the New York World's Fair in 1940, he spent seventeen months in Riker's Island prison. The term "mezz" is jazz slang for marijuana. He published his autobiography, *Really the Blues* (written with Bernard Wolfe), in 1946. ALSO SEE: REEFER JAZZ CLASSICS (P. 190)

MIDGRADE / *midd-grayed* / *adj.* Term for average-quality marijuana (unmanicured, weaker, and/or leafier) that is not quite kind bud but a notch up from schwag. Also known as middies.

MIDNIGHT EXPRESS 1. The title of 1978 film (di-

Brad Davis as Billy Hayes is searched by Turkish authorities in *Midnight Express*

rected by Alan Parker with a screenplay by Oliver Stone) based on a book of the same name written by Billy Hayes, an American student who was caught trying to smuggle almost two kilos of hashish taped to his body out of Turkey. The Turkish high court handed Hayes a thirty-year sentence, and he was subjected to torturous conditions in a Turkish prison. He escaped to Greece in 1975 and, upon his return to the U.S., penned the book about his experiences. Turkey's tourism industry suffered greatly after the release of the hit movie. 2. Name of a passenger train line in Turkey that ran from Istanbul to the Turkish town of Edirne (it left at 10:10 p.m. and arrived the following morning at 8:01 a.m.) and briefly traveled through Greek territory. In the 1960s

and 1970s, when American pressure on Turkey to curb drug trafficking was at an all-time high, the Turks came up with a somewhat diplomatic way of dealing with foreign offenders: After a court judgment, they would allow the accused to appeal and walk out on their own recognizance, but stripped of their passport. These "convicts" would then board the Midnight Express—which was technically a domestic train and didn't require a passport—and when it cut across a corner of Greece, would jump off and head to their respective embassies claiming their passport had been lost. Once in Greece with new papers, they were pretty much free to travel anywhere. ALSO SEE: STONER MOVIES TO AVOID (P. 159).

Actor Robert Mitchum mops up in jail in 1949

MITCHUM, ROBERT (1917–1997) A Hollywood star, he appeared in film noir classics such as *The Night of the Hunter* (1955) and the original *Cape Fear* (1962). He and actress Lila Leeds were arrested for marijuana possession in 1948 in a

Smart Munchies

Perhaps the one drawback to smoking pot is those unhealthy munchies you'll inevitably crave. Instead of packing on the pounds, try these alternatives to the stoner snacks of the past.

Instead of **Nachos Supreme** (though chips and salsa won't kill you), try some carrots or broccoli with dip instead.

Instead of **cookie dough** or **ice cream**, go for frozen yogurt, which has come a long way in terms of flavors. Many brands (or the soft-serve style) taste as good as ice cream, but with half the calories.

Instead of **cheese puffs**, forget those toxic, processed snacks and give Pirate's Booty a try. It's the all-natural alternative and comes in more than twenty flavors, several of which are vegan varieties. Or if Pirate's Booty is too "crunchy," there's always good old-fashioned popcorn. Without the butter, it's practically good for you.

Instead of **potato chips** or **Doritos**, try the baked variety of either, which will lower your calorie intake by up to 50 percent. They are easily found at most supermarkets.

Instead of a **burger**, have the vegetarian kind with all the fixings. Certain brands (like Morningstar Farms and Boca) come pretty close to the taste of real meat, but are better for you.

Instead of **chocolate** or a **rich dessert**, fruit is a good choice. Then again, dark chocolate is good for you. Just don't eat the whole bar in one sitting.

How to Make a Mute

🍁 BY 311's P-NUT

The bubbler-loving, head-banging bass player of 311 is a respectful stoner, so much so that he and several other members of the band's pot posse began constructing a smoke-filtering device called "The Third Lung." Here, P-Nut describes the process and importance of this updated mute.

"The Third Lung was made by some guy in California, but the company went out of business, so when we couldn't get them anymore, we took one apart and figured out that we could probably make it ourselves. A mute is used in many different situations, such as in a dorm room or some sort of shared living space, like a tour bus. The last thing you want is to get pulled over and have it be like Spicoli's van spilling out smoke when the door opens. And I love that it's called a mute, because it functions like it would on a trumpet mute when you put it up to your mouth. It's a long way from the toilet paper roll, but almost as easy to make."

Step 1: "Take fifteen dollars to a local hardware store, the kind of place that sells paint and painting supplies. Buy a piece of PVC [plastic tubing] that fits around your mouth—about one inch in diameter. Use a thin saw to cut it down to three inches in length or you can often buy it in the right size—it costs about 46¢. This will be what you blow into."

Step 2: "Look for a replacement cartridge for a standard paint or dust mask, nothing too fancy—a two-pack costs $20. This is the filter."

Step 3: "Attach the PVC tube to the filter and seal the two together."

Step 4: "We use a glue gun, but almost any tube of adhesive will work."

Step 5: "Once the glue dries, your mute's ready to use. Make three or four at a time. When the mute collects so much residue and tar that you can see it, or when you can no longer blow through the mute, it means it's time for a new one."

Step 6: "Take a hit. Exhale into the mute. Look, no smoke!"

sting operation intended to snag Hollywood celebrities. He spent sixty days in jail, but the conviction was overturned in 1951. *L.A. Confidential* (1997) fictionalizes the arrest in a subplot involving Kevin Spacey's Jack Vincennes character. Leeds starred in the exploitation film *Wild Weed* (a.k.a. *She Shoulda Said "No"!*) in 1949. Mitchum recorded several albums, including *Calypso—Is Like So . . .* and *That Man, Robert Mitchum, Sings*. He died from lung cancer and emphysema on July 1, 1997. ALSO SEE: FAMOUS POT BUSTS (P. 192).

MOLD / *mould* / *n.* Plant disease or fungus—also known as bud rot, plant rot, and botrytis—caused by humidity and lack of air circulation and ventilation in a growroom. White powderlike spores (a.k.a. powdery mildew) eventually turn brown, rotting affected areas. Treat with 5 percent bleach solution and 10 percent baking soda solution. If mold persists, remove the plant from the room. Mold can also occur during curing, when the container (glass jar, plastic bag, or Tupperware) holding the buds is too tight and moisture remains. An ammonia smell is the telltale sign. Molded buds should not be smoked. However, they can be used to make water hash.

MOTA / *moe-tah* / *n.* 1. Mexican slang for marijuana. 2. A fleck or speck. 3. Song title by the Offspring (1997): "Hearing Jimmy Buffett never sounded so good."

MOTHER PLANT / *muh-ther-plant* / *n.* Female marijuana plant grown in the vegetative state, from which multiple cuttings are taken to make clones to create future uniform crops.

MUNCHIES, THE / *mun-cheez-the* / *pl. n.* 1. Hippie term from the 1960s for the hunger pangs generally felt after smoking marijuana, which stimulates the appetite. The tendency is to impulsively eat junk food, hence pot-smokers' reputation for loving cookie dough and Doritos. 2. Numerous food companies have adopted the name for their products: Munchies Snack Mix (Frito-Lay), Milky Bar Munchies (Nestlé), and Almond Munchies (Sunkist). 3. Title of a film, *Munchies* (1987), starring Harvey Korman. The sequel is titled *Munchie* (1992). 4. Title of a syndicated comic strip by Jason Gluskin. 5. A song titled "Munchies for Your Love" by Bootsy's Rubber Band (1977). 6. "Munchies for Your

Bass" song title and album by Nemesis (1991). ALSO SEE: SMART MUNCHIES (P. 95).

MUSIKKA, ELVY (B. 1939) The first woman to receive medical marijuana from the federal government's Compassionate Investigational New Drug program (usually called the Compassionate IND program), she remains among the handful of patients prescribed three-hundred joints per month. A glaucoma sufferer born in Colombia on August 10, 1939, she was arrested for marijuana cultivation in Florida, won the case, and then petitioned the FDA for pot in 1988. She has spoken at countless rallies and events, and claims marijuana has improved her vision from 20/400 to 20/200. ALSO SEE: MEDICAL MARIJUANA.

MUTE / *myoot* / *n.* Name for a homemade device that catches and filters exhaled pot smoke. It conceals the smell and cuts down on the emission of smoke particles into the air. It is constructed by attaching the pouring end of a two-liter soda bottle (cut about five inches below the opening) to a breathing filter—similar to one you'd find in a gas or paint mask—and sealing it off. After you take a hit, you exhale into the spout. Nothing comes out the other side. ALSO SEE: HOW TO MAKE A MUTE (P. 96); POPE; THIRD LUNG.

MYSPACE / *mai-spase* / *n.* A hugely popular social networking Web site and youth-driven phenomenon that contains literally millions of proud potheads looking to (anonymously) congregate online with their stoner brethren. ALSO SEE: YOUTUBE.

N

NARC / *nahrk* / *n. or v.* 1. Short for police officer who works undercover as a narcotics agent to bust drug dealers and users. They dress and look the part of the person

> "I think people need to be educated to the fact that marijuana is not a drug. Marijuana is an herb and a flower. God put it here. If He put it here and He wants it to grow, what gives the government the right to say that God is wrong?"
>
> **—Willie Nelson,** musician

narc someone out" means to tell or snitch on someone, as in, "You totally narced me out, dude!" 3. Title of a 2002 movie directed by Joe Carnahan, starring Ray Liotta and Jason Patric. 4. Name of an arcade video game (1988). ALSO SEE: DRUG ENFORCEMENT ADMINISTRATION.

NEDERHASH / *ned-ur-haash* / *n.* Hash made from Dutch marijuana. It is often green in color.

NEGRIL Jamaica's famous beach town was discovered by Christopher Columbus in 1494 and was originally named Negrillo for its black cliffs. A popular destination for stoner travelers, it's located at the westernmost tip of the island in two parishes, Westmoreland and Hanover. Negril is known for snorkeling, scuba diving, nude bathing, ganja, and expensive resorts such as Sandals and Hedonism II. The West End is cheaper; the East End is more expensive. The town's lengthy coastline, called Seven Mile Beach, and cliffs are its main attractions. Ganja is readily available and sold as colas, for between $5 and $20. ALSO SEE: COLA; STONER BEACHES (P. 202).

NELSON, WILLIE (B. 1933) Grammy-winning singer-songwriter, musician, actor, and longtime advocate of marijuana legalization, he was born in Abbott, Texas, on April 29, 1933. He first came onto the American music scene in the 1960s as a Nashville-based songwriter and later in the 1970s as a member of "The Outlaws," a name derived from the title of Waylon Jennings's 1972 album *Ladies Love Outlaws* and used to describe rabble-rousing country singers who wouldn't conform to the popular Nashville sound.

Willie Nelson, with joint, aboard his famous bus in 2005

they're trying to nab and, by way of blending in, are able to collect information on illegal activities for future prosecution. They are difficult to recognize since they're allowed to partake in drug activity to a certain extent (this varies by municipality and the scope of the crime being investigated). The term also refers to drug informants, who turn in other drug users or dealers in order to have charges against themselves dropped. 2. When used as a verb, "to narc" or "to

From the 1960s to the 1980s, Nelson had a string of hits, including "Crazy," "On the Road Again," and "Always on My Mind." Simultaneously, his burgeoning film career grew. He appeared in the movies *The Electric Horseman* (1979), *Barbarosa* (1982), *The Redheaded Stranger* (1986), and *Wag the Dog* (1997) and he played the "Historian Smoker" in *Half Baked* (1998), Uncle Jesse in the movie adaptation of *The Dukes of Hazzard* (2005), and a guy searching for teammates to compete in a world-championship marijuana-smoking contest in Amsterdam in *Beerfest* (2006). He smoked pot on the roof of the White House in 1978 and is cochairman of the NORML Advisory Board. His ultra-potent pot, famously known as "Willie Weed," is the subject of Toby Keith's song, "Weed with Willie" (2003) in which Keith swears he'll "never smoke weed with Willie again." In addition to his pro-pot stance, Nelson champions hemp farming, biodiesel fuel, and humane treatment of horses. His benefit organization Farm Aid has produced a yearly concert since 1985. He's been arrested several times for marijuana: in 1995 in Texas and in 2006 in Louisiana, when he pleaded guilty to possessing 1.5 pounds of pot and 3.2 ounces of magic mushrooms and was fined $1,024 and placed on six months' probation. ALSO SEE: CANNABIS COUNTRY CLASSICS (P. 188); FAMOUS POT BUSTS (P. 192); GREATEST POT-THEMED ALBUM COVERS (P. 182); GREATEST SMOKING SONGS (P. 125); STONER LEGENDS (P. 194).

NEW ORLEANS JAZZ & HERITAGE FESTIVAL The most diverse music festival (a.k.a. Jazzfest) in the U.S., it was founded in 1970 by Quint Davis and takes place at the Racetrack Fair Grounds in the Gentilly section of New Orleans. The musical menu includes jazz, blues, R & B, Cajun, zydeco, brass bands, Dixieland, and Mardi Gras Indians chanting and drumming. National headliners and regional artists perform on eleven stages simultaneously during the last weekend of April and the first weekend of May (six days total). Local food delicacies (no hot dogs, burgers, or pizza) are a major attraction. Despite damage to the site caused by Hurricane Katrina in 2005, the event took place in 2006 and 2007. ALSO SEE: STONER FESTIVALS (P. 196).

Pot (or Not?) Songs

"Puff the Magic Dragon"
Peter, Paul & Mary

This nursery-rhyme song was a Top 10 hit for the folk trio in 1963. It's about a magic dragon named Puff and his friend Little Jackie Paper, who "loved that rascal Puff." You can draw your own conclusions, just as Ben Stiller (as Gaylord Focker) did in *Meet the Parents* (2000) when he told his father-in-law-to-be, Jack (Robert De Niro), that the song was about marijuana while they listened to it on the car radio. The conservative Jack took this as another reason why Gaylord was not suitable for his daughter.

"Along Comes Mary"
The Association

These Los Angeles folk-rockers bolted into the Top 10 in 1966 with this early psychedelic hit. It's the first song to reference "Mary" as a metaphor for marijuana: "And then along comes Mary / And does she want to set them free, and let them see reality / From where she got her name."

"Rainy Day Women #12 & 35"
Bob Dylan

This 1966 Top 10 hit contains twenty-five references to getting and being "stoned," but never mentions marijuana. When Dylan sings, "They'll stone you when you're riding in your car / They'll stone you when you're playing your guitar / Yes, but I would not feel so all alone / Everybody must get stoned," it's a reaction to being told by authority figures what you can't do. The solution is to "get stoned," which we now know means to get high, but in 1966 that was not very clear. Also, when multiplied, the numbers in the title add up to 420.

"Light Up or Leave Me Alone"
Traffic

Drummer Jim Capaldi wrote and sang the lyrics to this stony song on their 1971 rock classic *The Low Spark of High Heeled Boys*: "You're up all night preaching your mind / Come home in the morning with your latest find / I'm gonna have to lay it to you straight on the line / Either light up or leave me alone."

"Rocky Mountain High"
John Denver

Named Colorado's second state song in 2007, some legislators objected to the lyric, "Friends around the campfire and everybody's high." It was a Top 10 hit for Denver in 1973. The folkie singer was not noted for advocating marijuana use, but the song clearly indicates that a joint will help you get in touch with the power of nature: "And they say that he got crazy once and he tried to touch the sun / I've seen it rainin' fire in the sky / You can talk to God and listen to the casual reply / Rocky Mountain high."

NICHOLSON, JACK (B. 1937) Oscar-winning actor best known for starring roles in *Chinatown* (1974), *One Flew Over the Cuckoo's Nest* (1975), and *The Shining* (1980), he came to Hollywood from New Jersey, where he was born on April 22, 1937, in Neptune. He began his movie career behind the scenes as a writer in the 1960s with credits in psychedelic movies like *The Trip* (1967) and *Head* (1968). This work led to his breakthrough supporting role, with Peter Fonda and Dennis Hopper in *Easy Rider* (1969), for which he received his first Oscar nomination. In recent years, Nicholson has expanded his acting scope to romantic comedies (*As Good As It Gets*, 1997), superhero action flicks (*Batman*, 1989), and intense dramas (*A Few Good Men*, 1992, and *The Departed*, 2006). He also has gained notoriety for being quite the playboy and the life of many a Hollywood party, including the annual Golden Globe Awards, where he is known to hold court at a boozy table surrounded by friends and peers. ALSO SEE: A BRIEF HISTORY OF DRUGGY DRAMAS (P. 154); CLASSIC STONER DIALOGUES (P. 152); EASY RIDER; EASY RIDERS, RAGING BEATS (P. 54); JACK NICHOLSON'S STONIEST MOVIES (P. 101).

NICKEL BAG / *nik-al-bhag* / *n.* 1. Five dollars' worth of marijuana, the smallest amount one can buy. Its popularity peaked in the 1970s when good pot was still affordable, but this quantity is rarely offered as a purchase option today.

NIMBIN Australian hippie haven nearly 500 miles north of Sydney and fifty miles west of the beach town Byron Bay in New South Wales. It is home to the aboriginal Bundjalung people and located on the eastern slope of Mt. Warning (or Wollumbin), an extinct volcano noted for its sacred rock formations. Since 1993 the annual MardiGrass and Drug Reform Rally has taken place here during the second weekend of May. The event includes a Cannabis Cup, Hemp Trade Fair, and Hemp Olympics, and attendance exceeds 10,000. Though cannabis is tolerated, it is still illegal, as it is throughout Australia. ALSO SEE: THE SEVEN STONER WONDERS OF THE WORLD (P. 76); STONER BEACHES (P. 202).

NORML / *nor-mull* / *n.* The National Organization for the Reform of Marijuana Laws, a marijuana-legalization organization based in Washington, D.C., was founded by Keith Stroup in 1970. Its major accomplishments include decriminalization of marijuana in twelve states in the 1970s, and more recently, medical marijuana and deprioritization initiatives and legislation. The organization supports "responsible use" and elimination of criminal and civil penalties for marijuana. Advisory Board members include Willie Nelson, Woody Harrelson, Bill Maher, Tommy Chong, Dan Stern, Kary Mullis, Ron Mann, Rick Steves, and Dr. Lester Grinspoon. Allen St. Pierre is the current executive director. ALSO SEE: WEED SITES ON THE WEB (P. 220).

NORTHERN LIGHTS #5 / *nor-thurn-lites-num-burr-feyev* / *n.* 1. One of the original marijuana strains, it was created in the 1970s in the Seattle, Washington, area. A pure indica of Afghani heritage, it is now available from every seed bank as a mostly indica hybrid crossed with Haze and other sativas. Noted for its deep green color, wide leaves, exceptional resin production, compact buds, and powerful high, it flowers in sixty to sixty-five weeks and has 14 to 16 percent THC content. 2. A dazzling display in the sky caused by the collision of solar particles and gas particles in the earth's atmosphere, creating photons, or light particles, that appear as red, blue, and violet streaks of light in northern latitudes. Known as the northern lights, they are usually seen in early spring and late autumn at twenty-seven-day intervals. The term was coined by Galileo in the seventeenth century. The effect is also known as the aurora borealis. 3. The name of music festivals in Aurora, Minnesota; Ajijio, Mexico; Saskatoon, Canada; and Tromso, Norway. 4. Title of a TV movie (1997) starring Diane Keaton. 5. Title of a movie (*The Northern Lights*, 1978). ALSO SEE: ALL-TIME GREATEST STRAINS (P. 124).

Jack Nicholson's Stoniest Movies

Emerging from the 1960s drug-dazed Hollywood underground, Jack Nicholson established himself as an actor to watch when he strapped on a football helmet and rode with Peter Fonda in *Easy Rider*. Here are a few of his highest movie moments.

The Trip (1967): Under the guidance of mentor and B-movie director Roger Corman, Nicholson penned the script for this rambling exploration of LSD starring Peter Fonda, Dennis Hopper, and Bruce Dern. Nicholson's experimental writing style steers this cult classic through the typical period acid trip—replete with writhing naked ladies covered in psychedelic body paint and colored lighting. Subtitled "A Lovely Sort of Death" (get it?), the film was one of the first on-screen meditations on 1960s drug culture.

Head (1968): Written and produced by Nicholson, *Head* changed the clean-cut Monkees' image forever. In one of the strangest psychedelic movies of the decade, Nicholson makes a cameo appearance along with Hopper and Frank Zappa.

Psych-Out (1968): Susan Strasberg and Bruce Dern play sister and brother in this psychedelic romp set in Haight-Ashbury. Nicholson, with prosthetic ponytail and perfectly glazed eyes, is a band member appropriately named "Stoney." Just beginning to hone his on-screen stoner chops, Nicholson spends the bulk of the movie helming the band's van, miming renditions of "Purple Haze" on his electric guitar, and delivering the line "out of sight" numerous times.

Easy Rider (1969): Nicholson comes fully into his own with a now-legendary performance as George Hanson, the small-town lawyer and alcoholic who joins the easy riders (Hopper and Fonda) on their quest to find the true America. Given his first joint by his biker cohorts, Hanson bursts forth with some deeply poignant philosophical comments. With a script penned by Fonda, Hopper (he directed), and gonzo scribe Terry Southern, this is the film that blew out the doors on 1960s cinema and ultimately made Nicholson and his friends the icons they are today.

Tommy (1975): The height of both 1970s rock-and-roll excess and the genius insanity of director Ken Russell is captured in this cinematic adaptation of the Who's classic-rock opera. Nicholson makes his singing debut as "The Specialist," a medical quack who tries to cure Tommy's woes. The film also features Tina Turner as the Acid Queen.

Jack Nicholson (left) and Dean Stockwell (right) share a joint in *Psych-Out*

☘ One-Hitter Guide ☘

If you're a stoner on the go, you know the importance of carrying a one-hitter so you can sneak a toke. Here are four options for the sly, solo smoker.

Dugout: This classic wooden container with one compartment for granulated buds and another for your piece (usually a metal oneie) is a relic of the 1960s and 1970s that has remained popular to this day.

Fake Cigarette: The ultimate sneak-a-smoke tool, it looks like a cigarette, but certainly doesn't smell like one. Still, anyone standing nearby would have a hard time figuring out who the culprit is. Most often sold in metal form, it is also available in ceramic, which tastes and hits better, but can break if knocked against a hard surface.

Glass: Smaller handblown pieces usually pack way more than a single hit, but they're still considered one-hitters because of their shape and the absence of a carb. While glass oneies taste great and are easy to clean, they are also fragile.

Bullet: Another device that packs a powerful hit, this combination metal-plastic tube pipe, which resembles a bullet, has a twist-off cone top with a lighter hole, which minimizes the smoke and stashes the weed.

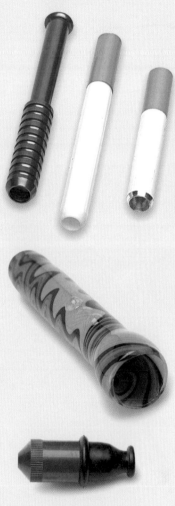

NUDIE / *noo-dee* / *n.* 1. Slang for a single sheet of clear cellulose rolling paper. 2. A suit created by Ukranian-American tailor Nudie Cohn, whose North Hollywood, California, store specialized in outlandish, bold, rhinestone-encrusted stage outfits for entertainers like Elvis Presley, Hank Williams, and Roy Rogers. Nudie's most famous suit was worn by country-rock pioneer Gram Parsons for his band the Flying Burrito Brothers' 1969 album, *Gilded Palace of Sin*. It was emblazoned with pot leaves, pill bottles, and a cross on the back. 3. An adult or X-rated film. ALSO SEE: ALEDA; CLEAR; GRAM PARSONS; SWAYZE.

Tightly manicured nug buds

NUG / *nuhgg* / *n.* 1. Short for nugget, this term refers to high-quality, properly cured and tight marijuana buds (a.k.a. nugs)—the opposite of leafy, loose weed. It was popularized by Deadheads at concerts in the 1980s, where hippies would stroll the parking lot looking to score "kind nugs." 2. What is stashed in glass-blown jars called nug jugs. 3. Hip-hop slang for a friend or homie, as in, "for my nugz," from Twista's "Stories" (2001). ALSO SEE: BUD; KIND.

O

OG KUSH / *oh-gee-koosch* / *n.* 1. Popular Southern California indica strain available only as a clone. The name refers to the abbreviation of the term "Original Gangsta" and the Hindu Kush mountain range in Pakistan and Afghanistan. It is believed to be a cross between Chemdog and Afghani strains. The strain's heavily resinated buds with 20 percent THC content cost $600 per ounce. Dutch company TH Seeds bred it with G-13 to create its MK Ultra strain.

Other hybrids include Bubba Kush, Master Kush, Purple Kush, and Sour Kush. **2.** The name of a reggae band based in Vancouver, Canada. ALSO SEE: ALL-TIME GREATEST STRAINS (P. 124).

ONE-HITTER / *won-hit-urr* / *n.* A pipe (a.k.a. a oneie) made out of glass, metal, or ceramic and designed for single use, during which the smoker can and should clear his or her own hit. It comes in a variety of shapes, themes, and sizes, from fake markers to the most popular kind, the pseudo-cigarette. ALSO SEE: BAT; DUGOUT; ONE-HITTER GUIDE (P. 102); ONEIE.

ONEIE / *won-ee* / *n.* **1.** Shortened from one-hitter, as in, "Dude, load me up a oneie." It's intended for discreet personal use in public spaces. ALSO SEE: BAT; DUGOUT; ONE-HITTER; ONE-HITTER GUIDE (P. 102).

"ONE TOKE OVER THE LINE" Top 10 single by Brewer & Shipley in 1970 on the *Tarkio Road* album on the Kama Sutra label, it was written and performed by Missouri natives Mike Brewer and Tom Shipley. The lyrics ("One toke over the line, sweet Jesus / One toke over the line / Sitting downtown in the railway station / One toke over the line") refer to being high on marijuana—perhaps a tad too high. The duo's debut album *Weeds* was released in 1969. They recorded an update of "One Toke" with the Rainmakers for *Hempilation 2: Free the Weed* (1998). They still live in Missouri, where Brewer continues to perform as a solo artist and Shipley works for the University of Missouri. ALSO SEE: A BRIEF HISTORY OF THE GREATEST MARIJUANA SONGS (P. 178).

OPERATION GREEN MERCHANT DEA campaign in 1989 against U.S. garden-supply shops (nineteen were shut down) and Dutch seed companies that resulted in hundreds of arrests over a two-year period. The magazine *Sinsemilla Tips* was forced to suspend operations due to loss of advertisements from the raided companies. ALSO SEE: OPERATION PIPE DREAMS.

OPERATION PIPE DREAMS DEA campaign against paraphernalia manufacturers, head shops, and Web sites netted fifty people, including Tommy Chong, and shut down numerous bong companies (such as Chong Glass) in 2003. While Chong went to jail for nine months, most of the others arrested paid fines or had charges dropped. The documentary *a/k/a Tommy Chong* (2006) tells the story of then-Attorney General John Ashcroft's overzealous efforts to wipe out the paraphernalia industry. ALSO SEE: TOMMY CHONG; DOCUMENTARIES (P. 166); OPERATION GREEN MERCHANT; PARAPHERNALIA.

OUTDOORS / *owt-doors* / *n.* Where marijuana is grown when it is not grown indoors. Locations include personal property, backyards, porches, fire escapes, window boxes, rooftops, and various properties owned by others or the government. Dangers include police detection, weather conditions, animals, pests, and thieves (a.k.a. rippers). ALSO SEE: GET GROWING (P. 64); GREENHOUSE; INDOORS; RIPPERS.

O.Z. / *oh-zee* / *n.* **1.** Short for one ounce of marijuana, as in, "I need an o.z., dude." **2.** Spelled as Oz: where the Wizard is from. **3.** One-hour HBO drama about prisoners (1997–2003). ALSO SEE: EIGHTH; GRAM; Q.P.; QUARTER; STONER SYNCHRONICITY (P. 128).

P

PACK / *pak* / *v.* The act of filling a bowl (bong or pipe) and pressing the weed into place, not too tightly or you'll scorch your buds faster and waste valuable THC. ALSO SEE: BLUNTED HIP-HOP CLASSICS (P. 184).

PAKALOLO / *pok-a-low-low* / *n.* Hawaiian term for kind buds found on the island. The word originates in the island's native language and means "crazy tobacco." ALSO SEE: KONA; MAUI; MAUI WOWIE.

PANAMA RED / *pan-a-mah-read* / *n.* **1.** Classic sativa strain from the Central American country known best for its forty-eight-mile canal connecting the Atlantic and Pacific oceans. The strain was grown in the mountains north of the Canal Zone in the 1960s and 1970s. Noted for its rusty,

"I highly approve of stoners... I tend to get high in the evenings to unwind."
—**Isaac Brock,** singer, Modest Mouse

reddish color and top-grade quality, it fetched high prices at the time ($40 per ounce compared to $10 Mexican), and is no longer available. 2. Song written by Peter Rowan in 1973 and recorded by the New Riders of the Purple Sage and Old and In the Way, featuring Jerry Garcia. Lead song on the New Riders' *The Adventures of Panama Red* (1973). 3. Singer-songwriter based in Nashville (formerly with Kinky Friedman & the Texas Jewboys) whose albums are titled *Homegrown* (2000) and *Choice Buds* (2005). 4. A rock band from Wales. 5. The title of a movie about a pot dealer, directed by Bob Chinn (1976). ALSO SEE: CLASSIC STRAINS (P. 11); A BRIEF HISTORY OF THE GREATEST MARIJUANA SONGS (P. 178).

PAPERS / *pay-purrs* / *pl. n.* 1. Shorthand for rolling papers, often used in a question, as in, "Dude, do you have any papers?" Sometimes the term is further abbreviated to papes. 2. International identification documents, such as a passport or visa. ALSO SEE: GUIDE TO ROLLING PAPERS (P. 116); ROLLING PAPERS.

PARAPHERNALIA / *pear-ah-fur-nail-ya* / *n.* Oft-misspelled catchall word for items used to aide and abet the smoking and storing of marijuana and other drugs. It includes pipes, rolling papers, bongs, blunts, screens, grinders, roach clips, filter tips, vaporizers, stash containers, nug jugs, and lighters.

PARSONS, GRAM (1946–1973) American singer-songwriter credited with popularizing country rock through his own music as a solo artist, as frontman for the International Submarine Band and the Flying Burrito Brothers, as well as with the Byrds. Born Cecil Ingram Connor into a wealthy family who made their fortune in citrus fruits, he went to boarding school in Florida, attended Harvard University for a semester, and lived in New York City for a stint before finally moving to Los Angeles in 1967. He joined the Byrds in 1968 and greatly influenced the sound of *Sweethearts of the Rodeo*, thought to be one of the first mainstream country-rock records. He and Chris Hillman left the Byrds to form the Flying Burrito Brothers. Their first album, *Gilded Palace of Sin* (1969), featured Parsons wearing his famous Nudie suit with pot leaves and pills embroidered on it. He became friends with Keith Richards and was a constant presence during the Rolling Stones' *Exile on Main Street* sessions (many believe he had a hand in writing "Honky Tonk Woman"). After several solo albums, his hard-drug use eventually lead to his death (he overdosed on morphine and alcohol) in Joshua Tree, California, on September 19, 1973. In a strange, final twist to his short life, tour manager Phil Kaufmann stole the coffin from LAX airport, drove it to the Joshua Tree National Monument and, according to Parsons's wishes, burned it in a spot called Cap Rock. Years later, fans still pay homage by visiting Cap Rock. ALSO SEE: THE BYRDS; NUDIE; WEARING THE WEED (P.133).

PARTAKE / *pahr-taik* / *v.* 1. To join in, as in, "Mind if I partake, dude?" 2. The question, "Do you partake?" is a common way of asking whether someone smokes pot.

PARTY / *par-dee* / *n. or v.* 1. A social gathering where guests are encouraged to have a good time. 2. When used as a verb, the term describes a call for fun, as in, "Let's party!" It was popularized by Mike Myers and Dana Carvey in the *Saturday Night Live* skit "Wayne's World," and the subsequent feature films (1992 and 1993) about a cable-access show run by two Illinois stoners out of their basement. Myers's Wayne and Carvey's Garth often use the catchphrase, "Party on." 3. Southern U.S. term for smoking pot.

PASS / *pas* / *v.* To hand off a joint, bowl, bong, or vaporizer balloon to the next smoker so he or she can take a hit. Stoner etiquette dictates that puff, puff, pass is OK, but more than two hits on a single turn is a no-no. It's also preferred to pass to the left, as in, "Pass the dutchie pon the left-hand side." ALSO SEE: BLUNTED HIP-HOP CLASSICS (P. 186); STONER ETIQUETTE 101 (P. 10).

"PASS THE DUTCHIE" Top 10 single by British reggae group Musical Youth in 1982, the song was recorded earlier that year by the Jamaican group the Mighty Diamonds as "Pass the Kutchie." Written by Leroy Stibble and Jackie Mittoo, it extols the virtues of smoking ganja and instructs listeners to hand the spliff to the person to your left ("pon the left-hand side"). Since Musical Youth members—singer Dennis Seaton, and brothers Kelvin and Michael Grant, and

> "The war on drugs has been an utter failure. We need to rethink and decriminalize our marijuana laws."
> —**Barack Obama**, politician

Patrick and Junior Waite—were in their teens, it was decided to change the word "kutchie" (synonym for ganja) to "dutchie" (slang for a Dutch oven). The group disbanded in 1985. Bassist Patrick Waite died in 1993 while in police custody on a drug charge. Seaton and Michael Grant still occasionally perform as Musical Youth. ALSO SEE: A BRIEF HISTORY OF THE GREATEST MARIJUANA SONGS (P. 178); GANJA REGGAE CLASSICS (P. 186).

PEACE PIPE / *peece-pype* / *n.* 1. Smoking device traditionally made by Native Americans out of pipestone (catlinite) of various colors (red, blue, green, black, and salmon) and wood-carved stems. It is used ceremoniously to help mediate problems, as in "to pass the peace pipe." 2. Top 40 hit by Brooklyn-based funk band BT Express in 1975 ("Put it in your peace pipe / Smoke it on out").

David Peel in 2000

PEEL, DAVID (B. 1942) New York–based folk singer born in Brooklyn on August 1, 1942, and best known for pot songs, such as "I Like Marijuana" (1968). His albums include *Have a Marijuana* (1968), *American Revolution* (1970), and *The Pope Smokes Dope*, produced by John Lennon and Yoko Ono and released on Apple Records in 1972. He was originally managed by *High Times'* founder Tom Forçade, and has appeared in several movies, including *Medicine Ball Caravan* (1971) with Forçade; *Please Stand By* (1972); *Rude Awakening* (1989); and *High Times' Potluck* (2003). He continues to record on his label, Orange Records. ALSO SEE: A BRIEF HISTORY OF THE GREATEST MARIJUANA SONGS (P. 178); THE GREATEST POT-THEMED ALBUM COVERS (P. 182).

PERMAGRIN / *purr-muh-grin* / *n.* Short for "permanent grin," a stoned facial expression consisting of a wide and virtually unmovable smile.

PERON, DENNIS (B. 1949) Gay activist who led the campaign to legalize medical marijuana in California. Born in New York, Peron moved to San Francisco where he operated the "Big Top" pot supermarket in the 1970s. He co-wrote Proposition 215 and opened the first pot dispensary, the Cannabis Buyers' Club, in 1993. ALSO SEE: STONER LEGENDS (P. 194).

PEYOTE / *pay-oh-tee* / *n.* Cactus plant that, when ingested, produces lengthy hallucinogenic experiences. It was originally used by North Mexican Indian tribes such as the Tarahumara, Huichol, and Cora, and then adopted by southwestern Native American tribes such as the Kiowa, Comanche, and Kickapoo. The top portion of the cactus (*Lophophora williamsii*), known as the mescal button, is ground and generally consumed in tea form. The buttons contain mescaline. Approximately one dozen buttons are required for a peyote trip, which lasts ten to twelve hours, and is characterized by deep introspection and insight, and possible nausea. Though illegal, religious use under the aegis of the Native American Church is permitted in the U.S.

PHILLIES / *phil-leaze* / *n.* Popular brand of cigar that can be hollowed out and used to make marijuana blunts. Product of the nineteenth century Philadelphia company Bayuk Cigar, the brand was sold to Hav-a-Tampa in 1982 and has since been acquired by Altadis, U.S.A., the largest cigar company in the world (it also owns the Dutch Masters and El Producto brands). Available in eighteen flavors, from banana to watermelon, they are sold

Blunt cigar and a dime bag

five to a pack for less than $3. ALSO SEE: BLUNT; BLUNTED HIP-HOP CLASSICS (P. 184); HOW TO ROLL A BLUNT (P. 20).

PHISH SEE P. 106.

PIECE / *peese* / *n.* A term of respect for a high-quality handblown glass pipe, as in, "Dude, that's a beautiful piece."

Phish

Band formed in 1983 by guitarist Trey Anastasio, bassist Mike Gordon, keyboardist Page McConnell, and drummer Jon Fishman when they were all students in various Vermont universities. They made their first appearance at local Burlington bar Nectar's (used in the title of their third album, 1992's *A Picture of Nectar*). Commonly referred to as one of the originators of the "jam band" sound, their music offers a unique blend of jazz, rock, and psychedelia, often with multiple melodies and complex arrangements. From 1988 to 2004 they recorded ten studio albums, including *Hoist* (1994) and *Billy Breathes* (1996). Their large hippie following reached stadium proportions after the demise of the Grateful Dead in 1995, whose audience they ostensibly inherited. Known for lengthy live shows and mini-festivals, their career highlights include annual Halloween and New Year's Eve blowouts, full-set album covers like the Who's *Quadrophenia*, and campout festivals in New York (Clifford Ball), Maine (The Great Went, It, Lemonwheel), Florida (Big Cypress), and Vermont (Coventry). In 2000 the band began a two-year hiatus. After reuniting in 2002, they broke up in 2004. Group members have gone on to many solo projects.

Phish—(left to right) Page McConnell, Jon Fishman, Mike Gordon, and Trey Anastasio—in 1996

More Jam Bands

Allman Brothers Band

The Southern blues-rock alternative to the Dead has gone through band changes over the years, but still puts on a solid show, thanks to guitarists Warren Haynes and Derek Trucks, and the always-engaging band cofounder Greg Allman.

Blues Traveler

One of the original jam bands had commercial success in 1994 with the hit single "Run-Around" and the album *Four*. Since then, and following the death of bassist Bobby Sheehan in 1999, the band has declined. But frontman John Popper can always be proud of their accomplishment, which included creating the 1990s HORDE Tour. Together with fellow New Yorkers the Spin Doctors they helped define the early funky stylings of the jam-band movement.

Disco Biscuits

Merging traditional rock and electronica, this Philadelphia ensemble excites fans with its long-distance jams. Since 2002 their Camp Bisco summer fest has moved around the Northeast.

Gov't Mule

Guitarist Warren Haynes and bassist Allen Woody's side project has taken on a life of its own, with Haynes alternating between Mule, the Allman Brothers, and Phil Lesh and Friends (Woody died in 2001). Haynes is the jam-band scene's most prolific player, sitting with virtually everyone at one time or another, and organizing benefit concerts.

Medeski Martin & Wood

Representing the jazzy wing of the jam-band universe (also including Galactic, Greyboy AllStars, Karl Denson's Tiny Universe, Soulive, and Robert Walter's 20th Congress), vocal-less concerts by this New York–based trio have never been so much fun.

moe.

Jam-band stalwarts from upstate New York follow the Phish formula, but offer lengthier instrumental sections to turn on the twirling fans. Since 2000, on Labor Day weekend, they've hosted the moe.down festival in Turin, New York.

String Cheese Incident

Probably the most influential jam band after Phish, this Colorado-based sextet provided an eclectic mix of rock, bluegrass, jazz, world beat, and reggae. Multi-band summer tours kept SCI's live profile extremely high before lead singer Billy Nershi split the group in 2007, leaving their future plans in doubt.

Widespread Panic

This jam-band followed in the Southern-rock footsteps of the Allman Brothers, even recording on the Capricorn Records label through the 1990s. The Athens, Georgia–based six-piece remains a touring favorite, despite the loss of guitarist Mike Houser to cancer in 2002. Jimmy Herring has since replaced Houser.

Disco Biscuits' Marc Brownstein (left) and Jon Gutwillig (right) at Camp Bisco in 2007

PINCH / pinch / v. The act of stealing a small amount of weed (just enough to fit between your thumb and index finger) from a bag that does not belong to you. Some dealers consider it a service charge, as if they're entitled to a little bit of your stash for having scored it in the first place. Either way, it's not cool.

Pinching some weed

PINK FLOYD British progressive-rock band that reached international fame in the 1970s. Formed by guitarist Syd Barrett in 1966, the band originally included bassist Roger Waters, keyboardist Rick Wright, and drummer Nick Mason. After the release of their psychedelic masterpiece, *The Piper at the Gates of Dawn* (1967), Barrett was replaced by guitarist David Gilmour. But it wasn't until the *Dark Side of the Moon* (1973), *Wish You Were Here* (1975), and *The Wall* (1979) that they established themselves as one of the great rock bands of all time. When Waters left the band in 1985, Gilmour continued performing and recording under the band's name. In 2005 at London's Live 8 concert, Waters joined Gilmour onstage for the first time in twenty-four years. Waters and Gilmour continue to tour separately. Barrett died of natural causes on July 7, 2006. ALSO SEE: STONER SYNCHRONICITY: DARK SIDE OF THE RAINBOW (P. 128); THE WALL.

PINNER / pin-urr / n. Joint rolled superthin so that it's easy to hide and makes for a faster burn with less smoke.

PIPE / phighp / n. Device used to smoke marijuana. It can be made out of glass, metal, wood, stone, ceramic, cans, pens, fruits, and vegetables. ALSO SEE: BOWL; HOW TO MAKE A CAN PIPE (P. 29); HOW TO MAKE A CARROT PIPE (P. 79); HOW TO MAKE AN APPLE PIPE (P. 12); PARAPHERNALIA; PEACE PIPE; PIPE OPTIONS (P. 110); PROTO PIPE.

PLANT / plant / n. or v. 1. A living, vegetative organism that grows in dirt or water. 2. As a verb, to start the life cycle of the vegetative organism by placing a seed or cutting in dirt or a rockwool cube. 3. Also as a verb, to place something somewhere. In the case of marijuana, police have been known to "plant" pot on a person in order to make a bust.

POKER / poak-urr / n. 1. Long, slim utensil used to clear a blocked bowl, stem, or carb openings by "poking" built-up resin through the hole. It can be a toothpick, a thin piece of metal (like a paper clip), or an actual pipe cleaner. 2. Extremely popular card game. ALSO SEE: CLEAR; POKERS IN A PINCH (P. 109).

POLLEN / paul-len / n. Male reproductive cells in powder form that release when the sac containing them bursts. These cells go on to inseminate female plants—the main reason to separate males from females. In Holland, *pollem* refers to the initial screening of trichomes or resin glands.

POPE / poap / n. A homemade device that masks odors. It is constructed by attaching a sheet of fabric softener to one end of an emptied toilet paper or paper towel roll. By blowing the smoke through the open end, the marijuana smell is disguised and diminished somewhat, but not completely. ALSO SEE: HOW TO MAKE A MUTE (P. 96); MUTE; THIRD LUNG.

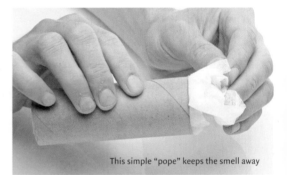

This simple "pope" keeps the smell away

POT / paht / n. The most common term for marijuana, the word is believed to derive from the Spanish or Portuguese *potaguaya* or *potiguaya*, meaning "drink of grief." It may also refer to the container that plants and flowers are grown in. ALSO SEE: GANJA; GRASS; HEMP; HERB; MARIJUANA; SMOKE; TREES; WEED.

POTENCY / poe-ten-see / n. The strength of an intoxicating agent, measured by the amount that is required to produce an effect. With marijuana, the effect is derived primarily from THC content, determined as percentages from 1 percent to as high as 30 percent. Kind bud is stronger (15

The standard seven-pointed pot leaf

to 20 percent THC) and more potent than schwag (3 to 5 percent THC).

POTENT / *poe-tent* / *adj.* Term used to describe particularly strong pot, as in, "Dude, that chronic is potent!"

POTHEAD / *paht-hed* / *n.* Someone who smokes marijuana on a regular basis. The term tends to be used in a derogatory fashion, as in, "He's such a pothead." ALSO SEE: STONER; VIPER.

POT LEAF / *paht leef* / *n.* Green-colored five- to seven-pointed extension from the branch of a cannabis plant. It has very little THC content and is either disposed of or is used to make hash or to cook with. It is the enduring and iconic symbol for marijuana.

POTLUCK / *paht-luck* / *n.* 1. Meal consisting of dishes provided by many friends in a communal fashion. 2. Title of a movie coproduced by *High Times* (2003).

PROHIBITION / *pro-uh-bih-shun* / *n.* General term for the ban of anything, such as marijuana, alcohol, or other drugs. The Harrison Narcotics Tax Act banned cocaine, opium, and heroin in 1914. The Volstead Act banned alcohol from 1919 to 1933. The Marihuana Tax Act in effect banned cannabis in 1937. LSD was banned in 1966 and Ecstasy in 1985.

PROPOSITION 215 The statewide voter initiative (a.k.a. Compassionate Use Act of 1996, or Prop 215), primarily written and championed by Dennis Peron, that legalized the use of medical marijuana in California. It reads: "Exempts patients and defined caregivers who possess or cultivate marijuana for medical treatment recommended by a physician from criminal laws which otherwise prohibit possession or cultivation of marijuana." The law allows for the establishment of cannabis dispensaries in California and generally ushered in the modern medical-marijuana movement. ALSO

The multi-purpose Proto Pipe

🍁 Pokers in a Pinch 🍁

For dedicated stoners, the dreaded bong clog or bowl block happens way too often. Here are your best bets for clearing the resin logjam.

Pro Poker: You can find these slim metal spikes that do wonders for one-hitters at most head shops for less than $2. If you're an everyday smoker, keep one in your stash box at all times.

Pipe Cleaner: These soft, fuzzy, and colorful devices contain thin wire strips that enable you to poke them through and clean out the sticky black stuff. A pack of twenty-five or fifty will cost you less than $2.

Paper Clip: The large-size ones are the perfect width for a clogged stem or bowl. Still, be forewarned: The abrasive texture may scratch or crack your glass.

Toothpick: The standard restaurant variety is a handy and cheap way to remove resin buildup. However, they're usually not long enough to clear a one-hitter. For longer stems, a wooden skewer does the trick.

Twig: Outdoors, you can find a perfectly sized branch or stick practically anywhere. All you have to do is snap it to the right length. This old-fashioned method never fails and is biodegradable.

SEE: DISPENSARY; MEDICAL MARIJUANA; DENNIS PERON.

PROTO PIPE / *pro-toe-pype* / *n.* A brass smoking device, patented in 1981, which includes a lid, storage chamber, poker, rubber mouthpiece, and removable parts that allow for cleaning.

PSILOCYBIN / *sill-oh-sigh-been* / *pl. n.* Hallucinogenic fungi (a.k.a. *Psilobye Cubensis*, *Psilocye Semilanceata*, or more commonly, magic mushrooms) containing tryptomine alkaloid that were discovered by R. Gordon Wasson among

P

Pipe Options

Glass

Price Range: $10 to $250 and up. **Description:** Pretty to look at and smoother on the intake, glass is the preferred way to puff. Pipes range from simple one-hitters to elaborate art pieces. They are available in many sizes, color schemes, themes, and shapes, including the spoon, the hammer, the bubbler, and the sidecar. **Pros:** Better draw, doesn't require a screen, easy to clean. **Cons:** Fragile, expensive.

Metal

Price Range: $7 to $20. **Description:** From the staple pull-apart aluminum-plastic model to the fake-outs (lipstick, magic marker, or cigarette lighter), metal offers the most variety at the lowest price. **Pros:** Cheap. **Cons:** Harsh hits, requires a screen, may set off a metal detector.

Wood

Price Range: $8 to $70. **Description:** A perennial material since the dawn of tobacco smoking, wood offers a cheap, natural way to toke with options ranging from the traditional Sherlock Holmes model of pipe to the more stoner-friendly, easy-to-conceal flat pipe. Another popular option is the wood pipe with the twist top, such as Jack Herer's Double Barrel Venturi Effect pipe, which minimizes smoke leakage when sealed immediately after toking. **Pros:** Natural material, cheap. **Cons:** Wears down with repeated use, often clogs due to heat, prone to burn marks, requires a screen.

Stone

Price Range: $5 to $15. **Description:** Whether rectangular or spoon-shaped, stone pipes are often made of travertine or marble, allowing for a no-nonsense hit. They have a longer shelf life than most other pipes because they don't break or wear as easily. **Pros:** Natural material, cheap, durable. **Cons:** Heavy in weight.

Corn

Price Range: $2 to $10. **Description:** One of the oldest smoking devices, the classic corncob pipe is constructed from a portion of a hollowed-out ear of corn attached to a plastic mouthpiece. Once popular in the Southern U.S. (where it was widely used by farmers) and in Cuba, it is still available at urban bodegas and head shops. **Pros:** Easy to clean, natural material, low price. **Cons:** Wears down with repeated use, requires a screen.

Nut

Price Range: $5 to $10. **Description:** Made out of a reinforced shell from a hard nut (like an acorn), the smooth "skin" of the nut pipe is pleasant to hold and smoke out of. However, its popularity is waning. **Pros:** Texture, cheap. **Cons:** Bulkiness.

Mexico's Mazatec Indians in 1957 and defined by LSD founder Albert Hofmann in 1959. A mushroom trip lasts two to six hours, depending on the amount ingested (two to five grams either eaten or drunk as a tea) and potency. Though nontoxic compared to their cousin, *Amanita Muscaria* (toadstools), which can be poisonous, use is prohibited and generally punishable by a felony charge.

PSYCHEDELIC / *sigh-cuh-del-ick* / *adj.* 1. This broad term for all things physically colorful was coined by psychiatrist Humphry Osmond in 1957. It refers to the effect of music, movies, art, fashion and style on the mind (psyche in Greek). 2. Synonymous with hallucinogenic, its first popular culture reference was in the album title *The Psychedelic Sounds of the 13th Floor Elevators* (1966). 3. Psychedelics, the plural form of the term, refer to drugs such as LSD, psilocybin, DMT, peyote, and mescaline. 4. Psychedelia refers to all things psychedelic. ALSO SEE: DMT; ENTHEOGEN; LSD; MUSIC TO SMOKE TO (P. 112); PEYOTE; PSILOCYBIN.

PUFF / *pughff* / *n. or v.* A hit off a joint, pipe, or bong containing marijuana. Also the term used to describe the act of smoking, as in, "Let's puff, dude." ALSO SEE: DRAW; HIT; INHALE; POT (OR NOT?) SONGS (P. 99); RIP; SMOKE; TOKE.

PULL / *puhl* / *v. or n.* Releasing the smoke from a bong chamber by lifting the stem from the base. It can also be used as a noun, as in, "Can I get a pull, dude?" ALSO SEE: BONG HIT; DRAW; HIT; INHALE; PUFF; RIP; SMOKE; TOKE.

Pulling a hit

PURPLE / *purr-pul* / *adj.* Coveted color for marijuana caused by genetics, anthocyanin pigments, and seasonal temperature changes, usually expressed in the leaves. Mostly sativa strains include Purple Haze, Purple Power, Purple Passion, and Grandaddy Purps.

The Merry Pranksters' psychedelic bus, Further, in 1966

Music to Smoke to

BY BOB POLLARD

The Guided By Voices frontman is about as prolific as they come, not just in the hundreds of songs he writes on a yearly basis, but also in his encyclopedic knowledge of music, no matter how obscure. Here Pollard sifts through his record collection—vinyl, naturally—for his ten favorite albums to smoke to.

Bob Pollard, with cigarette, in 2005

Sea Shanties (1969)
High Tide

"For maximum effect, play this album extremely loud and look at the original gatefold sleeve. Violin, guitar, bass, and drums are fast and furious."

CQ (1968)
The Outsiders

"The greatest Dutch band ever are crazy with layers of experimental sounds over great songs."

Vincebus Eruptum (1968)
Blue Cheer

"Ultraheavy stoner stuff—including their hit 'Summertime Blues'—with great fuzz guitar by Leigh Stephens."

Pretties for You (1969)
Alice Cooper

"The illustrated cover disturbed me when I was a kid, but now I understand."

The Gordons (1981)
The Gordons

"The heaviest of the late 1970s and early 1980s bands on the Flying Nun label, the Gordons later became Bailter Space."

Godz 2 (1967)
Godz

"Studio experiments with minimal instrumentation on the New York–based ESP label. It's what the Beatles and Stones would like to have recorded in 1967."

Orgasm (1969)
Cromagnon

"Their 1969 album on ESP features a guy who somehow screams and whispers simultaneously for about four minutes."

The Plateau Phase (1982)
Crispy Ambulance

"British post-punk band's weird, moody, and I think some sort of post-death, metaphysical-journey concept, which is different from their earlier records."

Paradieswärts Düül (1970)
Amon Düül

"It's a German hippie drum/chant communal glorification of whatever."

In Search of Space (1972)
Hawkwind

"It has a glorious foldout cover and Hawkwind logo to examine as you listen to this album that opens with the sixteen-minute 'You Shouldn't Do That.'"

"PURPLE HAZE" 1. A popular song by the Jimi Hendrix Experience on *Are You Experienced?* (1967), the title refers to LSD created by Owsley Stanley: "Purple haze all around / Don't know if I'm coming up or down." 2. Raspberry-flavored wheat beer manufactured by Abita Brewing Company in Abita Springs, Louisiana. 3. Title of an album by hip-hop artist Cam'ron (2004).

"PUSHERMAN" Title of a Curtis Mayfield song on the *Superfly* sound track (1972): "I'm your doctor when in need / Want some coke, have some weed."

"PUSHER, THE" Lead song by Steppenwolf on the *Easy Rider* sound track (1969): "You know I've smoked a lot of grass / Oh Lord, I've popped a lot of pills." ALSO SEE: EASY RIDER.

Q

Q.P. / *kyoo-pee* / *n.* Weight measurement denoting a quarter pound (four ounces) of marijuana. ALSO SEE: EIGHTH; GRAM; O.Z.; QUARTER.

Q.T. / *kyoo-tee* / *n.* Like the saying "on the d.l.," this term also means something done in secret. Its origin is commonly believed to be from the word *quiet*, abbreviated down to the first and last letters.

QUALITY / *kwal-eh-tee* / *adj.* Word used to describe general excellence. With marijuana, the term refers to high-end strains, like kind or chronic, as in, "I only buy quality." ALSO SEE: CHRONIC; KIND.

QUANTITY / *kwan-tah-tee* / *n.* Denotes a large size or amount of marijuana (an ounce and up) available for purchase, as in, "Does your dealer have quantity?"

QUARTER / *kwar-tur* / *n.* 1. Denotes weight often used for the commonly purchased quarter ounce, which is two-eighths, or quarter pound, which is four ounces. 2. Twenty-five U.S. cents. ALSO SEE: EIGHTH; GRAM; O.Z.; Q.P.

R

RAICH, ANGEL (B. 1965) Fearing arrest and prosecution, this medical-marijuana patient born in Stockton, California, sued the Justice Department and the DEA in 2002. She, along with Diane Monson, took the case to the U.S. Supreme Court, which ruled against them in 2005. A mother of two, she suffers from an inoperable brain tumor, life-threatening wasting syndrome, seizure disorder, scoliosis, nausea, and severe chronic pain. Both Raich and her doctor claim she wouldn't be alive without marijuana. ALSO SEE: MEDICAL MARIJUANA.

RALLY / *ral-lee* / *n.* A marijuana legalization event that includes speeches, bands, and information tables, and usually occurs in a city park or on a college campus. Rallies first took place in the late 1960s when pot culture started to take hold in the U.S. and around the world. ALSO SEE: BOSTON FREEDOM RALLY; HASH BASH; SEATTLE HEMPFEST; SMOKE-IN; U.S. POT RALLIES (P. 200).

RAM DASS (B. 1931) An associate of Timothy Leary, he was born in Newton, Massachusetts, in 1931 as Richard Alpert, but changed his name during a trip to India in 1967. He taught at Harvard with Leary, was a major player in the Millbrook, New York, psychedelic scene from 1963 to 1966, is the author of more than a dozen books, including *Be Here Now* (1971), and is the subject of Mickey Lemle's documentary *Ram Dass, Fierce Grace* (2001). He suffered a stroke in 1997. ALSO SEE: TIMOTHY LEARY.

RASTA / *rah-stah* / *n.* A way of life and religious belief system founded by Leonard Howell and promoted by Marcus Garvey in Jamaica in the 1930s and

Rasta smokes chalice in Jamaica

adopted by Bob Marley and other reggae musicians in the 1960s. Devotees, known as Rastas or Rastafarians, worship Haile Selassie I, the emperor of Ethiopia and first black leader of an African nation, born in 1892, as Jah, or the black Messiah. Before Selassie's coronation, his name was Ras Tafari Makonnen, hence the term. Lifestyle traits include wearing dreadlocks, smoking ganja, eating Ital (also spelled I-tal) food, speaking patois, and engaging in spiritual "nyabinghi" drum ceremonies and generally peaceful behavior.

RECREATIONAL USE / *wrech-ree-ay-shu-nul-yuce* / *n.* Marijuana consumed for pure enjoyment and for the benefits associated with smoking, including levity, creativity, and spontaneity. Nonrecreational uses are medical, industrial (hemp), and spiritual or religious. ALSO SEE: HEMP; MEDICAL MARIJUANA.

RED EYE / *rehd-I* / *n.* 1. Another way of describing the bloodshot eyes caused by irritation, illness, or the intake of drugs or alcohol. With marijuana, blood vessels in the eyes expand as THC enters the bloodstream, a temporary condition that can be treated with a vasoconstrictor—or eye-drops—like Visine. 2. Widely used word for overnight air travel, such as a flight from Los Angeles to New York that leaves Los Angeles at 10 p.m. and arrives in New York at 6 a.m. the next morning. 3. The name of a North Carolina–based music distribution company with a stable of critically acclaimed indie artists on its label roster, including the Polyphonic Spree, Robyn Hitchcock, Widespread Panic, Little Feat, Sloan, and the Apples in Stereo. 4. Title of a marijuana magazine published in England. ALSO SEE: VISINE

REEFER / *ree-pher* / *n.* Slang for marijuana or a joint, this term dates back to the 1920s though its derivation is unclear. A midshipman is also known as a reefer. A rolled sail is a reef. A double-breasted jacket, such as a pea coat, worn by a midshipman is called a reefer. A refrigerated compartment on a ship—or in a trailer or van—is also known as a reefer. Drugs might have been smuggled in reefers. Some say the Spanish word *grifa*, or *greefa*, translates to marijuana or a drug addict. The rolled sail appears to be the closest explanation for the term. ALSO SEE: REEFER JAZZ CLASSICS (P. 190).

REEFER MADNESS 1. The granddaddy of all marijuana exploitation movies, it was directed by Louis Gasnier and was originally named *Tell Your Children.* Dwain Espers, who also directed *Marihuana: The Weed with Roots in Hell* (1936), purchased *Tell Your Children*, added exploitation elements, and renamed it *Reefer Madness* (1936). Viewed as comical today, the lurid story of a naive teenager drawn into an adult pot-smokers' clique was a major factor in the enactment of the 1937 Marihuana Tax Act. The film was rediscovered in 1971 by NORML founder, Keith Stroup, who paid $297 for the copyright to the film, which was released by New Line Cinema for college screenings and midnight showings. A theatrical musical version of the film was adapted for cable television, starring Neve and Christian Campbell and Alan Cumming in 2005. 2. Term concocted in the 1930s to scare people into believing that marijuana caused users to engage in abhorrent behavior. It is still in use today. ALSO SEE: A BRIEF HISTORY OF STONER MOVIES (P. 146).

RESIN / *reh-zin* / *n.* Dark, greasy substance that accumulates inside pipes and bongs as a result of smoking mari-

Warren McCollum as Jimmy Lane is introduced to marijuana in *Reefer Madness*

juana. It's not recommended to "scrape resin" and smoke it. 2. Caustic Resin: Boise, Idaho–based stoner-rock band. 3. Resin Music: California-based reggae label.

RESIN GLANDS / *rez-in-glandz* / *pl. n.* SEE TRICHOMES.

RESIN HEAVEN / *rez-in-hev-in* / *n.* SEE GREAT STONER INNOVATIONS (P. 137).

RIGHT ON / *rite-on* / *interj.* Slang that implies being in agreement or solidarity with someone. It can also be used as a positive exclamation, as in, "You scored some weed? Right on!" The phrase originates in early 1960s African-American slang. It is also a shortening of the military term, "right on target," and the theatrical term, "right on cue."

RIP, RIPPED / *ripp, rippt* / *n., v., or adj.* 1. Slang for a bong hit, as in, "That was a huge rip, dude." 2. Alternately used as a way of signaling getting something started, as in, "Let her rip!" 3. To illustrate ultimate stoniness, as in, "No thanks, dude. I'm ripped." ALSO SEE: BAKED; BLASTED; BLAZED; BONG HIT; BURNT; BUZZED; CRISPY; FRIED; HIGH; HIT; LIT; LOADED; STONED; TOASTED; WASTED; ZONKED; ZOOTED.

RIPPERS / *ri-pas* / *pl. n.* Unscrupulous, petty criminals who steal marijuana plants, usually from outdoor gardens.

RIZLA+ / *riz-lah-kwa* / *n.* French rolling paper company founded in 1532 by the Lacroix family. The company switched from pulp paper to rice paper in 1865. Their name stands for rice (Riz), Lacroix (La), and cross (croix in French) (+). The company added menthol and strawberry flavors in 1906 and patented their gum edge in 1942. They sold the company to Imperial Tobacco in 1997 who in 2003 added king-size papers for spliff smokers. ALSO SEE: GUIDE TO ROLLING PAPERS (P. 116).

ROACH / *rowch* / *n.* The tail end of a joint, it is usually shorter than an inch in length and good for only three to four hits. The term derives from the Mexican slang for marijuana, *la cucaracha*, which means "the cockroach." ALSO SEE: ROACH CLIP.

The remainder of a smoked joint, a.k.a. a "roach"

ROACH CLIP / *rowch-klip* / *n.* Device used to hold and pass a roach so that it doesn't burn the user's fingertips or lips. The most common is an alligator clip much like the one a dentist uses to fasten a bib in place. Another popular medical utensil smokers use is a hemostat, which resembles a pair of pliers. Tweezers, paper clips, clothespins, keys, and twigs are alternatives. This particular stoner tool saw its heyday in the late 1960s, when *Rolling Stone* promised potential readers "a roach clip with every subscription." However, in the 1980s, the magazine switched its focus with a two-page ad promoting a money clip ("now") versus a roach clip ("then"). ALSO SEE: ROACH.

The alligator roach clip

ROCKWOOL / *rawk-wuhl* / *n.* Substrate for starting seedlings from cuttings or clones. It's most commonly used in hydroponic systems, though it can also be placed directly in soil. A Danish product, it was discovered in the 1970s and is made from basalt salt and chalk and spun into a cube shape. ALSO SEE: GET GROWING (P. 64); HYDROPONIC; INDOORS.

ROLL / *role* / *v.* The act of forming a joint or blunt by placing marijuana on a piece of smokeable paper and twisting it into a proper shape (without seeds, stems, or air pockets), as in, "Roll another, dude!" ALSO SEE: GUIDE TO ROLLING PAPERS (P. 116); HOW TO ROLL A BLUNT (P. 20); HOW TO ROLL A JOINT (P. 119); VINTAGE VINYL FOR ROLLING & LISTENING (P. 48).

ROLLING MACHINE / *role-ing-mah-sheen* / *n.* Device containing two spools, or rollers, that catch ground marijuana or loose tobacco. To use, place a sheet of rolling paper into the spools, load the pot or tobacco onto the paper, and rotate the spools with your thumbs to form a perfectly shaped joint or cigarette. Most rolling paper companies, such as Zig-Zag and Rizla+, manufacture these machines. They generally retail for about $6 apiece. An even cheaper option is the "rolling mat," which is made

A rolling machine

Guide to Rolling Papers

Aleda

Established: 2005 **Country of Origin:** Brazil **Signature Paper:** King-size transparent wrap (made of natural cellulose) **Sizes Available:** King Size, Double Wide, Mini **URL:** www.aledausa.com

Bambu

Established: 1764 **Country of Origin:** Spain **Signature Papers:** Bambu 1 ¼ (made of chemical-free, naturally gummed pulp paper) and Big Bambu (both sizes are available as hemp papers) **Sizes Available:** 1 ¼, Big Bambu, Double Wide, Half Extra **Flavors:** Strawberry, Banana, Peach, Mint, Chocolate, Coconut, Grape, Cherry, Vanilla **URL:** www.bambu.com

e-z wider

Established: 1971 **Country of Origin:** U.S. **Signature Paper:** e-z wider Double Wide **Sizes Available:** Original 1 ¼, Pure Hemp 1 ¼, Pure Hemp, 1 ½, Double Wide, Slow Burning, Lights 1 ½, Ultra Lights 1 ½, French 1 ¼ **Flavors:** Wild Berry **URL:** www.ezwider.com

RAW

Established: 2005 **Country of Origin:** U.S. **Signature Paper:** Created by HBI International, a Phoenix, Arizona–based company founded in 1960, RAW is the company's most popular brand. It is made from unbleached rice and flax fibers, is light brown and translucent, and the custom-designed watermark prevents bad burns. **Sizes Available:** RAW comes in 1 ¼ and King Size Slim sizes. **URL:** www.rollingsupreme.com

Randy's

Established: 1975 **Country of Origin:** U.S. **Signature Paper:** All Randy's papers contain a thin imbedded surgical stainless steel wire that you can grasp from the burned end of a joint to allow you to smoke down to nothing. **Sizes Available:** Classic 1 ¼, Randy's USA Hemp 1 ¼, King Randy's Hemp 1 ½ **URL:** www.randys.com

Rizla+

Established: 1532 **Country of Origin:** France **Signature Paper:** Green King Size (the most popular rolling paper in the UK and common all over Europe) **Sizes Available:** Regular green (medium weight, cut corners), red (medium), white (perforated), silver (ultra-thin); King Size green, red (medium), blue (thin); King Size Slim blue (thin), silver (ultra-thin) **Flavors:** Licorice **URL:** www.rizla.com

Smoking

Established: 1879 **Country of Origin:** Spain **Signature Paper:** King Size Green (extra-long papers made of hemp) **Sizes Available:** Small (red, blue, green, hemp), Medium (arroz, maiz, de luxe, master, green, eco, 200, 300), King Size (red, blue, slim, de luxe, master, green, eco) **Flavors:** Orange, Licorice **URL:** www.smokingpaper.com

Zig-Zag

Established: 1879 **Country of Origin:** France **Signature paper:** Zig-Zag Orange (among the most popular papers in the U.S.) **Sizes available:** 1 ¼, (orange) 1 ½, King Size **URL:** www.zigzagpapers.com

R

The Rolling Stones—(left to right) Mick Jagger, Keith Richards, Charlie Watts, Bill Wyman, and Brian Jones—in 1968

out of bamboo and sells for $2. ALSO SEE: HOW TO ROLL A JOINT (P. 119).

ROLLING PAPERS / *role-ing-pay-purrs* / *pl. n.* Small, ultrathin sheets of paper made out of wood pulp, rice, flax, or hemp and used to form marijuana into a joint or tobacco into a cigarette. They also come in roll form, so smokers can custom cut a size to their preference. They are produced by dozens of manufacturers all over the world, primarily in Europe. The most popular brands sold in America are Zig-Zag, Bambu, and e-z wider. Other perennial favorites are Rizla+—which outside the U.S. is the world's best-selling brand—and the Club. The latest trend—clear papers made from cellulose—was started by the Brazilian company Aleda, who introduced their product to the U.S. market in 2006. ALSO SEE: ALEDA, BAMBU, CLUB; E-Z WIDER; GUIDE TO ROLLING PAPERS (P. 116); JOB; NUDIE; RIZLA+; SMOKING; SWAYZE; ZIG-ZAG.

ROLLING STONE Magazine dedicated to covering music, politics, and popular culture, it was founded in 1967 by Jann Wenner at the height of the San Francisco flower-power era and celebrated its fortieth anniversary in 2007. Its stable of writers initially included Hunter S. Thompson (whose *Fear*

and Loathing in Las Vegas was printed as a two-part series in 1971), Cameron Crowe (*Almost Famous* and *Fast Times at Ridgemont High*), and Ben Fong-Torres. In addition to *Rolling Stone*, Wenner Media publishes *Us Weekly* and *Men's Journal*.

ROLLING STONES, THE The second greatest rock-and-roll band of all time (after the Beatles), they continue to release albums (more than thirty-five overall) and tour—some four decades after they were founded by Brian Jones (guitar), Mick Jagger (vocals), and Keith Richards (guitar) in 1962 in London. Bill Wyman (bass) and Charlie Watts (drums) subsequently joined the group. In 1965 the band had their breakout international hit with "(I Can't Get No) Satisfaction." By 1967, like the Beatles, they steered in a psychedelic direction with a string of influential albums—*Their Satanic Majesties Request* and *Beggars Banquet* (featuring "Sympathy for the Devil")—culminating with their greatest album of the period, *Let It Bleed* (1969). Also, in 1967, Richards and Jagger were arrested for marijuana possession at Richards's home in a highly publicized bust. They were both convicted and sentenced to jail time, but the convictions were dismissed on appeal. One month after Jones left the group in 1969, he drowned in his pool. (Director Stephen Wolley told the story of Jones's life and death in 2006's *Stoned*.) Also, in 1969, the band headlined the Altamont festival east of San Francisco during which a concertgoer was knifed to death by a member of the Hell's Angels. (All of the graphic footage was captured by the Maysles brothers in their 1970 documentary, *Gimme Shelter*.) Jones was replaced by Mick Taylor, and later by Ron Wood. The band's commercial success continued with *Sticky Fingers* (1971); the country-crossover classic, *Exile on Main Street* (1972); and the disco-influenced *Tattoo You* (1981). In 1977 Richards was arrested for possessing heroin in Toronto. (He was sentenced to perform several benefit concerts.) Richards's bouts with heroin and other hard drugs over the years remain legendary. In 2007 he claimed he had snorted his recently deceased father's ashes.

ROOR / *roar* / *n.* German company that engineered a line of water pipes known for their beaker-like shapes and utilitarian design. Sandblasted glass fittings—called

✻ How to Roll a Joint ✻

OPTIONAL

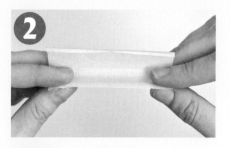

Step 1: Break off a bud and grind it into a chunky, green powder.

Step 2: Make a crease in the rolling paper by folding it over at about a third of the width from the gummed line. Sprinkle the pot onto the paper so the fold holds it in place.

OPTIONAL (shown): Add a filter by cutting a strip of rolling paper cardboard or use actual filter paper and roll it into a tight tube. Insert the filter at the left or right tip of the joint.

Step 3: Spread out the bud so that it's evenly distributed along the entire length of the paper.

Step 4: Pinching the folded paper at both ends, begin tucking and rolling the paper with your thumb and forefinger so that the weed is enveloped by the paper but does not fall out the ends.

Step 5: Continuing to grip both ends, tighten the shape more, and twist it toward the gum.

Step 6: Lick the gum and finish rolling by sealing the joint.

Step 7: Make sure there are no dry gaps in the gum line or breaches in the paper and you're ready to go.

OPTIONAL: Use a dollar bill to roll a tight and perfectly shaped joint. Place the paper a third of the way from the bottom of the bill, fold it over, and roll up and down with your thumb and forefinger. Or use a rolling machine.

glass-on-glass—allow for the ultimate in suction through high-quality thickness. Its bongs retail for $145 and up and are considered high-end pieces. The ice pinch feature costs an additional $25 to $30. ALSO SEE: ANATOMY OF A BONG (P. 23); BONG; GLASS VS. PLASTIC (P. 59).

ROSENTHAL, ED (B. 1944) The marijuana activist, cultivation expert, and writer known as the "guru of ganja" was born in the Bronx, New York, and resides in Oakland, California. He is the author of more than a dozen books, including the *Marijuana Grower's Guide* (1978, with Mel Frank), and since 1980 his "Ask Ed" column has appeared in *High Times*, *Cannabis Culture*, and *Heads.* He was convicted in 2003 for growing marijuana for medical use, fined $1,000, and sentenced to one day in jail. The federal government retried and convicted him again in 2007.

> "I would like to see all fifty states and the federal government decriminalize medical marijuana."
> **—Montel Williams,**
> talk-show host

S

SACK / *sak* / *n.* 1. Slang for a bag of weed. 2. Satchel for your stash, this popular hippie accessory usually made of cotton, hemp, or burlap can be carried in a pocket or in a bag or purse, and is commonly used to transport weed and/or a glass pipe (the cloth cushions the contents in case of an accidental drop).

SALAD / *sal-ed* / *n.* A mix of two or more strains of marijuana used for any type of hit (bong, bowl, joint, or vaporizer). It is made when

Mixing a salad

Pot Comparison

	SCHWAG	VS. KIND
TEXTURE:	DRY	CURED
STEMS:	LOTS	SOME
SEEDS:	LOTS	NONE
THC:	2%–5%	10%–20%
TASTE:	HARSH	SMOOTH
	SATIVA	VS. INDICA
SIZE:	TALL	BUSHY
LEAVES:	THIN	WIDE
HIGH:	ENERGETIC	LETHARGIC
STRAIN:	HAZE	NORTHERN LIGHTS
THC:	10%–15%	15%–20%

there are several stoners who want to contribute to the session, or when someone has built up tolerance to a particular strain.

SALVIA DIVINORUM / *sal-vee-ya-dih-vih-nor-umm* / *n.* Hallucinogenic plant native to Oaxaca, Mexico, and known as the "sage of the seers." It was first discovered in 1939 by Jean Basset Johnson and later rediscovered by R. Gordon Wasson among Mazatec Indians, who either chew the leaves or squeeze them, then mix the liquid substance with water and drink the concoction. Popularized in the 1990s as a smokeable substance, it creates a trancelike effect with visuals characterized by colorful fractal patterns and geometric shapes. A trip lasts less than ten minutes. It is available on the Internet and in Dutch "smart shops" and is sold in a range of strengths (5x, 10x, 20x). It is legal in the U.S. but banned in Australia.

SATIVA / sah-teeve-ah / n. Also known as *Cannabis sativa* (as opposed to *Cannabis indica*), this warm-weather species is characterized by tall plants and thin leaves. Noted for producing a cerebral high, plants mature in ten to fourteen weeks and have lower THC content than indicas. Sativas are generally hybridized with shorter indicas, and Haze remains one of the few pure sativas. ALSO SEE: CANNABIS; INDICA; POT COMPARISON (P. 120).

SATIVEX / saa-taa-vecks / n. Prescription mouth spray made from actual marijuana by England's GW Pharmaceuticals and distributed by Bayer Healthcare. It has been available in Canada and Spain since 2005 and is primarily used for neuropathic pain and spasticity caused by ailments like multiple sclerosis. In 2006 the FDA approved trials for its use in the U.S.

SCHWAG / shwag / n. Low-grade marijuana, most often imported from Mexico. Generally dry, leafy, and brown-colored, it frequently contains seeds and produces a very weak high. ALSO SEE: BRICK WEED; DITCH WEED; POT COMPARISON (P. 120).

SCORE / skoar / v. To purchase drugs from a dealer. ALSO SEE: THE ART OF SCORING (P. 32); POT ON TOUR (P. 122).

SCREEN / screen / n. or v. 1. A circular piece of thin metal-wire mesh that is placed in the bowl of a pipe or bong to prevent marijuana from being sucked into the stem or chamber prematurely. Available at smoke and head shops, they usually come in packs of five or ten and sell for less than 25¢ each. 2. To screen a call is to let the answering machine or voicemail pick up when you're avoiding a certain call or person or to pretend

Screens

that you're someone else when receiving a phone call intended for you.

SEATTLE HEMPFEST The largest annual marijuana event held in the U.S., it was founded in 1991 by Vivian McPeak and the Peace Heathens. This rally takes place during the third weekend of August in Myrtle Edwards Park along Puget Sound. More than 100,000 people attend the two-day, multi-stage extravaganza featuring speakers, bands, and vendors. *No Prison for Peace*, a documentary of the event, was released in 2003. ALSO SEE: BOSTON FREEDOM RALLY; RALLY; SMOKE-IN; U.S. POT RALLIES (P. 200).

SECOND-GENERATION JOINT / seck-end-gen-ur-ra-shun-joynt / n. A joint rolled with marijuana collected from leftover roaches.

SEED / cede / n. The result of the pollination of a female plant by a male plant, it is used to start a new plant. Extremely valuable, marijuana seeds are sold in packs of ten by companies based in Holland, Great Britain, and Canada, for a range of $5 to $50 per seed. It is illegal to sell them in the U.S. and most other countries. ALSO SEE: OPERATION GREEN MERCHANT.

SENSI SEEDS Holland's oldest seed company, it was founded by Ben Dronkers in 1988 and merged with the Seed Bank in 1990. Its trademarked strains include Jack Herer, Silver Pearl, Shiva Skunk, Jack Flash, and their latest, Ed Rosenthal Super Bud. It was the first company to grow and market hemp industrially in Holland. Dronkers, with his son Alan, also founded the Hash, Marihuana & Hemp Museum in Amsterdam's red-light district.

SESSION / sesh-un / n. Gathering of several stoners whose main objective is to get everybody in the room high, as in, "Let's have a session." Often the term is shortened to "sesh."

SHAKE / sheyk / n. Remnants or leafy leftovers of a bag of pot often sold at a discount since they are devoid of buds. It

"There's not another drug in life that I'm glad I took but grass."
—George Michael, singer

A session in progress

Pot on Tour

BY FALL OUT BOY'S JOE TROHMAN

Fall Out Boy's guitarist Joe Trohman is a daily toker, so flying and driving from gig to gig present a persistent problem: buying buds in strange cities. Here he explains the fundamentals of hooking up on the road.

Joe Trohman rocks out in 2007

"When it comes to touring, I usually try to bring a stash with me. I try to never fly with any weed. One friend of mine will just put it in his bag, but I think that's crazy (though I have pondered getting a vacuum sealer). If we're on a bus, two ounces will last me a while (I bring my Volcano vaporizer on U.S. tours). Still, I have run out on occasion and, since I get a little cranky after two days of not smoking, I have been forced to figure out ways to find that hookup."

"All of our fans know I smoke. Why should I hide it?"

Look for the sound guy: "At any venue, there are local crew or people who work there. Talk to them. Or find the house sound guy, or better yet, the onstage monitor guy, and he'll probably know how to get weed or will have someone he can call. A metalhead dude is always a good sign because a lot of us metal guys like smoking and listening to Sabbath all day."

Talk to people: "Especially if you're in a smaller band, it's good to talk to everybody that comes to your show because you'll inevitably meet people who can hook you up. You can even find a regular dealer that way, and then you'll have someone you know every time you come through that town."

Take fan offerings: "All of our fans know I smoke. Why should I hide it? So people occasionally come up and ask, 'Wanna smoke?' and I'm like, 'All right!' I like to have people to smoke with. But generally, I try not to smoke before a show. When I do play high, I have to really pay attention and I don't want to have to concentrate that hard. But I'll smoke right after."

Secure your stash in a major hub: "After six years of touring, I've gotten to know somebody in every major city, so what I'll do is buy in the major hubs and have enough to get through the smaller, weirder places in the Midwest where it's harder to get."

Sometimes you have to settle for schwag: "When you're out in the middle of nowhere, you may have to smoke crappy weed. Like our first time in Mexico City, I didn't know anybody. Then this one guy in a band brought by a ton of weed, but it was all really bad, the kind that gives you a headache. I'm spoiled by California, but when you're on the road and you've gone a day without, you just want to smoke something."

can be used for cooking or added to a pipe or joint containing fresher weed to stretch out your stash.

SHOTGUN / *shot-gun* / *n.* A unique delivery method whereby one person places his or her mouth over the lit end of a joint and blows the smoke through the other end of the joint into the mouth of another person. This technique (a.k.a. a blowback) is employed to conserve weed (if you don't have enough for two whole hits, you're basically splitting one), to hide the smell of weed (the mouth-to-mouth delivery significantly minimizes the smoke), or as a sometimes sexy, mostly awkward come-on (one not recommended for use on strangers). The famous scene with Willem Dafoe and Charlie Sheen in Oliver Stone's *Platoon* (1986) demonstrates the original method in which an actual rifle is used. ALSO SEE: SHOTGUN ETIQUETTE.

SIFT / *sifpht* / *v.* To separate marijuana buds from seeds and stems. Back in the days when seeds were commonly found with buds, it took quite a bit of work and effort to de-seed. ALSO SEE: DE-SEED.

SINCLAIR, JOHN (B. 1941) Political activist and spoken-word performer born in Flint, Michigan, he is known for managing the MC5 from 1966 to 1969, for his involvement with the White Panther Party, and for being busted for pot in 1969. On his behalf, John Lennon and Yoko Ono performed a benefit concert, Ten for Two (referring to his ten-year sentence for selling two joints to undercover police), in 1971 in Ann Arbor on the same bill with Stevie Wonder, Phil Ochs, Bob Seger, Commander Cody, and David Peel. A *Ten for Two* documentary by Steve Gebhardt was released the same year. Sinclair wrote *Guitar Army* (1972) while in prison. He moved to New Orleans, where he was a DJ at WWOZ and formed John Sinclair & His Blues Scholars, a band that recorded several albums, including *Fattening Frogs for Snakes* (2002). He moved to Amsterdam in 2004. ALSO SEE: DAVID PEEL; FAMOUS POT BUSTS (P. 192).

SINSEMILLA / *sin-sa-meal-ya* / *n.* 1. Spanish term for seedless marijuana, often shortened to sinse or sense. It was originally grown in Mexico in the west coast state of Michuoacan and was imported to the U.S. in the 1970s. Separating female and male plants prevents pollination and

🌿 Shotgun Etiquette 🌿

If you're going to be on the giving or receiving end of a shotgun hit (when one person exhales smoke directly into another person's mouth), follow these simple rules to prevent any awkwardness.

1 **If you don't know the other person well, try to avoid direct lip-to-lip contact:** Form a tight opening with your lips, almost as if you're going to whistle, and, from an inch away, blow the smoke into your partner's open mouth. The receiver should inhale slowly.

2 **If the person is someone you're attracted to or dating, a lip-to-lip seal accentuates the effects of the shotgun technique:** But prep your partner by explaining that as soon as his or her lips hit yours, he or she should be inhaling. Otherwise, he or she will end up coughing directly onto you.

3 **A shotgun is meant to be a dry hit, so swapping spit is not always appropriate:** Be sure you have permission if you plan on using any tongue in the process.

seed production; a seeded female plant is significantly less valuable than a seedless female plant, which contains more THC. 2. Album and song title by Black Uhuru (1980): "I have a stalk of sinsemilla growing in my backyard." 3. Title of a Sublime compilation, *Sinsemilla 86–96* (1996). ALSO SEE: GANJA REGGAE CLASSICS (P. 186).

SINSEMILLA TIPS Oregon-based marijuana magazine published by Tom Alexander from 1980 to 1990. Alexander ceased publication after the DEA's Operation Green Merchant raided the magazine's advertisers. ALSO SEE: OPERATION GREEN MERCHANT.

SKIN / *skinn* / *n. or v.* 1. British slang for one sheet of rolling paper. 2. Also used as a verb, to "skin up," which means to roll a joint or spliff. ALSO SEE: BRITISH POT SLANG (P. 130).

Sinsemilla Tips

S

All-Time Greatest Strains

AK-47

Blueberry

G-13

Hash Plant

Haze

Northern Lights #5

OG Kush

Skunk #1

Sour Diesel

White Widow

Blueberry is an Afghani × Purple Thai strain created by DJ Short

SKUNK #1 / *scunk-numb-ber-won* / *n.* 1. Beloved, mostly indica strain consisting of Colombian, Mexican, and Afghani genetics, it was developed by Skunkman Sam and Sacred Seeds in California in 1978 and taken to Holland in the 1980s. It is noted for its sweet and fruity smell, taste, and flavor. Many hybrids have been introduced, including Hawaiian Skunk, Thaitanic, and California Orange. It flowers in sixty to seventy days and has 8 to 10 percent THC content. 2. Name of a Canadian marijuana magazine, based in Montreal. 3. Name of Sublime's record company. 4. Mammal known for its black-and-white coat and foul odor (which is emitted when it's in danger). ALSO SEE: ALL-TIME GREATEST STRAINS (P. 124); CANNABIS CUP STRAINS (P. 31).

SLIDE / *slide* / *n.* The male part of a bong (glass or metal), which is inserted into the female part (the stem). Pulling it out while inhaling creates a suction effect and assures a full hit. They are available in a variety of widths and lengths depending on the size of the bong. ALSO SEE: ANATOMY OF A BONG (P. 23); STEM.

SMART SHOP Retail store in Holland that sells magic mushrooms, *Salvia divinorum*, marijuana seeds, and other mind-altering delicacies.

SMOKE / *smoak* / *v. or n.* 1. The act of combusting marijuana and inhaling as it burns. 2. Street dealer code word for pot, as in, "Need some smoke?" 3. Slang for tobacco cigarette, as in, "You got a smoke?" 4. Title of a movie directed by Wayne Wang (1995) starring Harvey Keitel, William Hurt, and Forest Whitaker that is set in a smoke shop (for cigar aficionados, not potheads) in Brooklyn, New York. ALSO SEE: DRAW; GRASS; HERB; HIT; POT; PUFF; PULL; RIP; SMOKE; TOKE; WEED.

SMOKE-IN / *smoak-inn* / *n.* The original name for a marijuana rally at which attendees civilly disobey the pot laws by lighting up in public while listening to speeches and bands. The oldest such event is Washington, D.C.'s Fourth of July Smoke-In, which was first held in 1969. New York's Smoke-In, held annually on the first Saturday in May, was expanded and renamed the Global Marijuana March. ALSO SEE: LIGHT UP; RALLY; U.S. POT RALLIES (P. 200).

Greatest Smoking Songs

BY BO BICE

Imagine competing on the fourth season of *American Idol*, making it all the way to the finale (Carrie Underwood won), and being a stoner. Bo Bice was the first and certainly the most outspoken pot-loving *Idol* contestant we'll likely ever see. Here Bo lists his favorite tunes to listen to baked.

Bo Bice

1. **"Don't Bogart Me,"** *Easy Rider* soundtrack, Fraternity of Man (1969): "The THC content in this old recording alone could give you a contact buzz. The sound waves were high as they oozed out of the speakers. Maybe it's not the most popular song on this list, but I'm sure everyone will agree that we've all hummed or sung along ("Don't bogart that joint my friend") with it at some point in time while passing a bong."

2. **"You Don't Know How It Feels,"** *Wildflowers*, Tom Petty (1994): "'Let's get to the point / Roll another joint.' Petty sums it up pretty well. I'd love to sit down with this guy for a few minutes and discuss his views on agricultural indulgence."

3. **"Sweet Emotion,"** *Toys in the Attic*, Aerosmith (1975): "From the very first thump of the bass line to that sloppy swagger of Joe Perry's guitar, the song takes you for a ride and then drops you off at your friend's house wondering, what the hell just happened?"

4. **"The Joker,"** *The Joker*, the Steve Miller Band (1973): "This is the first song that I think I ever smoked to. The entire album is great from beginning to end, but this particular song will resin up your ear canals and you can't help but sing along with its catchy chorus ("I'm a smoker, I'm a midnight toker")."

5. **"Wiser Time,"** *Amorica*, the Black Crowes (1994): "The Black Crowes are one of my all-time favorite bands. The texture on this track makes you feel like you're cruising down the road, smoking a jay in the middle of the desert, and the sun's going down."

6. **"Willin',"** *Little Feat*, Little Feat (1971): "It's undeniable that the raw tone and vibrato of this incredibly talented Southern rock band still continues to inspire bands today."

7. **"Burn One Down,"** *Fight for Your Mind*, Ben Harper (1995): "Harper captured every toker's mantra with this tune. Burn one down, burn two down, burn a fistful."

8. **"Comfortably Numb,"** *The Wall*, Pink Floyd (1982): "You also can't have a list without Pink Floyd. The title of the song lets you know what you're in store for. Flick your lighter and let it burn."

9. **"In Memory of Elizabeth Reed,"** *The Allman Brothers at Fillmore East*, the Allman Brothers (1971): "It is physically impossible to resist sparking up a doobie within the first eight bars of this lengthy instrumental. A smoke-filled room, a couple of beers, and the Allman Brothers ... perfect!"

10. **"Whiskey River,"** *Shotgun Willie*, Willie Nelson (1973): "You can't have a list without including Willie Nelson. He's not only one of the coolest people I have ever had the chance to jam with, he loves the bud."

Bo Bice faces the *Idol* judges in 2005

Seth Rogen

TALKS STONER MOVIES

Thanks to starring roles in *Knocked Up* and *Pineapple Express* (out on DVD in late 2008), not to mention his highly quotable turn as the loveable Cal in *The 40-Year-Old Virgin*, Canadian Seth Rogen has officially become the modern-day-stoner poster boy. Where does his pot sensibility stem from? Rogen fills us in on the stony flicks that influenced him growing up in Vancouver and provides insight into stoner moviemaking today.

Talk about some of the stoner characters you've played and what they lend to the story. "In *Knocked Up*, it was like, who's the worst guy to get a driven businesswoman pregnant? And that's the lazy pothead, I would imagine. But I didn't consider the weed to be a real linchpin of the character, it's one of two hundred things that guy does. With *Pineapple Express*, it's more about people involved in the weed world, and the different customs and rituals that go along with that … It's also about the drug dealer–drug buyer relationship—how [James] Franco

"The single most influential weed movie for me and my friends was *Friday*."

thinks he's my friend, but I don't really like him that much, he's just the guy I buy weed from. It's that fine balance of how quickly can I leave after buying the weed, but not insult him so I can come back and buy more. With *The 40-Year-Old Virgin*, I remember having conversations with [director] Judd [Apatow] about how I hadn't seen guys casually smoking in a lot of movies, so that was like testing the waters

to see if people would freak out [to see] characters nonchalantly passing joints in this mainstream romantic comedy. But no one did, people loved it! I remember the shot of Steve [Carrell] smoking out of an apple pipe. The first time we showed it in a theater, the audience exploded in applause. That's when we thought, maybe we can make *Pineapple Express*."

Is it more challenging to market a stoner movie than your average R-rated comedy? "The rules are so funny. In the trailer [for *Pineapple Express*], I'm clearly smoking weed—you just can't show me sucking it in. But you can show me blowing it out. I'm driving around with smoke coming out of my mouth saying, 'That feels good in my brain!' And James Franco says, 'You smoke all day, that's your job.' But you can't say, 'You smoke weed all day,' as we're clearly baked off our asses. I've actually been pretty impressed with how clear it is that *Pineapple* is a movie about weed—I call it the first-ever weed action comedy—and the name is a type of weed. It seems like they'll be able to market it like *Superbad*, without having to do sneaky promotions and stuff."

Growing up, which stoner movies had an impact on you? "The single most influential weed movie for me and my friends was *Friday*. It came out right when we all started smoking and we would just quote it endlessly. We loved it, and it holds up really well. Also

The Big Lebowski is the end-all, be-all … It's one of my favorite movies of all time, and with any stoner you meet, *Big Lebowski* quotes are like a secret language."

With some stoner movies, the lead character ends up giving up pot. Is there pressure in Hollywood to have that kind of messaging? "That was something we did not want [for *Pineapple Express*]. I liked *Half Baked*, but the ending drove me crazy! The whole movie is for potheads, clearly, then at the end he stops smoking weed … A lot of these weed movies shoot their core audience in the foot when they do that."

What's the best and worst thing about being today's stoner poster boy? "There's really nothing bad about it. People don't expect much from me. I can say stupid things and people think, 'He's probably high, don't worry about it.' There's really no major downside to it right now. I guess if I want to one day star in an Atom Egoyan film about Holocaust survivors, it might hurt my chances, but maybe not."

Portions of this interview originally appeared in *Entertainment Weekly*.

SMOKE OUT / smoak-owt / v. To provide a quick toke or a longer session for someone other than yourself, as in, "I owe you one, dude, let me smoke you out this time."

SMOKING / smoa-king / n. Spanish brand of rolling papers manufactured since 1929 by Miquel y Costas & Miquel, S.A. The company dates back to the eighteenth century, and produces rice and hemp papers in various sizes, including king-size, which is popular for spliff rolling. ALSO SEE: GUIDE TO ROLLING PAPERS (P. 116).

SMUGGLE / smuh-gull / v. 1. The act of carrying contraband (a.k.a. illegal drugs) or an undocumented person across an international border. 2. A smuggler is the individual involved in such an act. 3. "Smuggler's Blues": Title of a hit single (No. 12, 1985) by Glenn Frey on *The Allnighter*.

SNOOP DOGG (B.1971) Born Calvin Broadus Jr. in Long Beach, California, on October 20, 1971, and originally known as Snoop Doggy Dogg, hip-hop's leading weed smoker was introduced to the public in 1992 by Dr. Dre on *The Chronic* (1992). He had his own solo breakthrough with *Doggystyle* (1993), featuring the Top 10 hit "Gin and Juice." He's had six solo albums and hit songs since, including the No. 1 hit "Drop It Like It's Hot" (2004). He has appeared in such movies as *The Wash* (2001), *Soul Plane* (2004), and *Starsky & Hutch* (2004) as well as hosted MTV's comedy show, *Doggy Fizzle Televizzle* (2002–2004). He has been arrested numerous times. The first was in 1989 for cocaine possession (when he was sentenced to jail time), he was acquitted of gang-related murder charges in 1996, and he was charged with marijuana and weapon possession in 2006. ALSO SEE: CHRONIC; FAVORITE STONY LYRICS (P. 180).

SOUR DIESEL / sow-er-deez-uhl / n. Coveted, mostly sativa strain also known as East Coast Sour Diesel, it should not be confused with Soma Seeds' NYC Diesel. Like OG Kush, it was originally bred by Chemdog. Now it is available only as clones and hybrid strains, such as Sour Jack and Sage 'n' Sour. Difficult to grow, it is a low yielder that has a grapefruit taste and lemony smell. It flowers in nine to eleven weeks and has 20 percent THC content. ALSO SEE: ALL-TIME GREATEST STRAINS (P. 124).

SPACE CAKE / spase-kayk / n. Any form of noncookie baked good that contains marijuana (in butter form). Popularized in Amsterdam coffeeshops, its physical effect takes thirty to forty-five minutes to kick in, but once it does, it produces a powerful body high that can feel almost trippy in nature. Eating too much, however, may put you to sleep. ALSO SEE: BROWNIE; CANNABUTTER (P. 211); MEDICAL EDIBLES (P. 57).

SPACED / spaisd / past tense of space Slang that, when used as a verb, means to forget, as in, "Was I supposed to be there at ten? Sorry, dude, I spaced."

SPACED OUT / spaisd-owt / adj. or v. The sensation of your mind wandering. In the active form, you are "spacing out." The term is likely derived from "out of space," meaning something extraterrestrial or not from this world.

SPLIFF / spleef / n. Jamaican and European term for a king-size joint rolled in a cone shape with a filter. It often consists of a combination of marijuana and tobacco. ALSO SEE: CONE; FATTY; JOINT.

STASH / stasch / n. or v. 1. Something stored because of its value or preciousness. The term originates from stashes (private reserves) of tea given to captains of clipper ships. As it relates to marijuana, it denotes a quantity of pot (usually an eighth or more) that one possesses, as in, "I only have a joint, my stash is at home." 2. As a verb, it means to hide something. 3. Name of a tea company based in Tigard, Oregon, since 1972. 4. Title of a Phish song on *A Picture of Nectar* (1992): "The sloping companion I cast down the ash / Yanked on my tunic and dangled my stash."

STASH CONTAINER / stasch-cawn-tane-urr / n. Common household object such as a shaving cream can or water bottle that has been fitted with a false bottom and/or hidden compartment that can be used to store marijuana or other drugs. Such items are sold at head shops and online for $10 to $20.

STASH POCKET / stasch-pock-ett / n. A compartment sewed into a piece of clothing such as a hat or a pair of

A space cake with a tart twist

S

Stoner Synchronicity

DARK SIDE OF THE RAINBOW

Pink Floyd's *Dark Side of the Moon* (1973) syncs up perfectly when played simultaneously with *The Wizard of Oz* (1939). Though the band has repeatedly denied that it was intentional, the coincidences continue to boggle even the stoniest mind. Try it yourself and get ready for a serious head trip.

1 Load *The Wizard of Oz* into your DVD player and *Dark Side* (you can also substitute the Easy Star All Stars' *Dub Side of the Moon*) into your CD player or iPod with the repeat option turned on.

2 With *Dark Side* on pause, start the movie. Immediately following the third roar of the MGM lion, press play on your CD player or iPod. If the music kicks in just as producer Mervyn Leroy's credit hits the screen, you're in sync.

3 Take a couple of hits, sit back, and be amazed when the lyric "balanced on the perfect wave" pops up just as Dorothy is balancing atop a fence, or when "Great Gig in the Sky" comes on just as the tornado is spinning with the house in its wake, or when munchkins dance in time to the odd beat of "Money," or when "Brain Damage" is played just as the Scarecrow sings "If I Only Had a Brain." There are actually dozens of these matchups.

More movie-music matchups:

- Radiohead's *The Bends* with *Fight Club* (start after the 20th Century Fox logo fades).
- Radiohead's *OK Computer* with *Fantasia* (start with the first drop of rain).
- Metallica's *And Justice for All* with *The Empire Strikes Back* (start when the last line of the epilogue fades offscreen).
- Public Enemy's *Fear of a Black Planet* with *West Side Story* (start with the first film credit).
- Jane's Addiction's *Ritual de lo Habitual* with *Trainspotting* (start when the Miramax logo appears).
- Rush's *2112* with *Willie Wonka and the Chocolate Factory* (start when the Warner Bros. logo fades to black).

Dorothy (Judy Garland) fast asleep in the poppy field in *The Wizard of Oz*

128

pants and used to store small amounts of marijuana or other drugs.

STEM / *stehm* / *n.* 1. The main vertical shoot of a plant. 2. The smaller shoots that grow out from the main shoot. Marijuana buds are attached to these shoots, which when harvested and dried are not intended to be smoked. 2. The female part of a bong into which the slide is inserted. 3. Title of song "Seed and Stems (Again)" by Commander Cody & His Lost Planet Airmen (1972): "I'm down to seeds and stems again." ALSO SEE: ANATOMY OF A BONG (P. 23); SLIDE.

STICK / *styck* / *n.* Hipster slang for a marijuana joint, as in, "Hey, Daddy-O, let's smoke that stick of tea."

STINKY / *stin-kee* / *adj.* Possessing a pungent odor or scent. For example, kind weed, even in a sealed bag, can give off a strong fruity or skunky smell.

STONED / *stoaned* / *adj.* The most commonly used word to describe the effect of marijuana or hash—whether it has been smoked, eaten, or vaporized—on a person. Some speculate the term originated from a nineteenth century cocktail called the "stone fence," which is a mixture of ale and brandy, while others believe it is somehow derived from the biblical term, "to stone" (stoning is a form of punishment whereby those deemed criminal offenders are pelted with rocks). In pot terms, the word was first popularized with Bob Dylan's "Rainy Day Women #12 & 35," the opening track on, *Blonde on Blonde* (1966), whose title is often mistakenly thought to be "Everybody must get stoned," a line Dylan repeats throughout the song. ALSO SEE: BAKED; BLASTED; BLAZED; BURNT; BUZZED; CRISPY; FRIED; HIGH; LIT; LOADED; RIPPED; TOASTED; WASTED; ZONKED; ZOOTED.

STONER / *stow-nurr* / *n.* 1. Someone who regular smokes marijuana. 2. The readers of this book (a.k.a. you!). ALSO SEE: PLAYING A MOVIE STONER (P. 126); POTHEAD; VIPER.

STONYS, THE *High Times* movie and television awards presented annually since 2000. Best movie winners have included *Blow, Go, How High, Traffic, Road Trip*, and *Harold & Kumar Go to White Castle*.

STRAIN / *strane* / *n.* The name of a type of marijuana, such as Sour Diesel, OG Kush, and Jack Herer. Also called a variety. ALSO SEE: ALL-TIME GREATEST STRAINS (P. 124); CANNABIS CUP STRAINS (P. 31); CLASSIC STRAINS (P. 11).

STRAWBERRY COUGH / *straw-behr-ree-coff* / *n.* East Coast strain acquired by Dutch Passion Seed Company from former *High Times* staffer Kyle Kushman that is a mostly sativa cross between Strawberry Fields and Haze. This fruit-flavored, medium yielder flowers in nine to ten weeks and has 18 percent THC content. It is referred to and smoked several times by Michael Caine's hippie character in *Children of Men* (2006).

STROUP, KEITH (B. 1943) The founder of NORML (his last name is pronounced "Strop") was born on December 27, 1943, in Centralia, Illinois, where he grew up on a 160-acre farm. After graduating from Georgetown Law School in 1968 and inspired by Ralph Nader's original group of "Nader's Raiders," he started NORML (National Organization for the Reform of Marijuana Laws) in 1970 with a $5,000 grant from the Playboy Foundation. The organization, a marijuana smokers' lobby, focuses on decriminalization and what Stroup calls "responsible" marijuana use. Executive director until 1979, he served again from 1995 through 2005 and is currently NORML's legal counsel. ALSO SEE: NORML; STONER LEGENDS (P. 194).

STUDENTS FOR SENSIBLE DRUG POLICY (SSDP) Washington, D.C.—based organization of campus groups opposed to marijuana prohibition and the war on drugs, it was founded in 1998 at the Rochester Institute of Technology by

"Pot was great at the genesis of my becoming a songwriter."
—Tim Delaughter, singer, Polyphonic Spree

Strawberry Cough is a Haze × Strawberry Fields strain

S

🌿 British Pot Slang 🌿

Spliff: The most commonly used term for a joint in Great Britain, as in, "Pass me those Rizlas and let's knock up a spliff."

Skin up: To roll a joint. Skin, another word for a sheet of rolling paper (king-size Rizlas are the most popular brand in the U.K.), also refers to the outer layer of a joint, as in, "Let's get this off the street, mate, and go to your flat to skin up."

Caned: Stoned. The term can be used in the active form, as in, "They've been caning it all night," or a noun, as in, "They're a bunch of caners," or the most common, "I'm really caned."

Cabbage: Schwag. In Europe's ever-growing socially decriminalized scene, low-quality, dry, seedy pot (most likely shipped in from Africa) costs half or less of what high-grade weed costs. Cabbage is the kind of smoke you buy on the street, but even aficionados use it as a substitute for tobacco, as Londoners tend to do when skinning up.

Stone over: Brit speak for a pot hangover.

Draw: Word that describes a personal stash, usually less than an ounce, as in, "Let's head down to Brighton for the weekend—I've got the draw covered, you bring the lager."

Kris Lotlikar, Shawn Heller, Brian Gralnick, Christy Gomez, and Dan Goldman and boasts more than one hundred chapters. Kris Krane is its executive director.

SUBLIME / *suh-blighm* / *n. and adj.* 1. Weed-loving ska-punk-reggae trio from Long Beach, California, who came together in 1988 and rose to mainstream popularity in 1996 with their self-titled album and hit single, "What I've Got." Singer-songwriter-guitarist Brad Nowell died of a heroin overdose on May 25, 1996. Bassist Eric Wilson and drummer Bud Gaugh subsequently formed the Long Beach Dub Allstars. Sublime covered "Smoke Two Joints" on *40 Oz. to Freedom* (1992) and "Legalize It" on *Hempilation: Freedom Is NORML* (1995). They are the subject of a tribute album, *Look at All the Love We Found* (2005). 2. Transcendent excellence.

SUMMER OF LOVE / *sum-mur-ov-luv* / *n.* 1. In 1967 countless young people all over the world began embracing the concept of free love and celebrating a new social order that involved revolutionary ideas, psychedelic drugs, and rock and roll. The movement's epicenter was San Francisco, which drew more than 100,000 out-of-towners looking to be part of the hippie lifestyle to its Haight-Ashbury neighborhood. This period kicked off on January 14, 1967, with the Human Be-In in Golden Gate Park. The flower-power frenzy firmly took hold in June, when the Beatles' *Sgt. Pepper's Lonely Hearts Club Band* was released and the Monterey Pop Festival, featuring the Mamas and the Papas, Jefferson Airplane, Jimi Hendrix, and Janis Joplin, among others, took place one hundred miles south of San Francisco. Weeks later, the Beatles' "All You Need is Love" was broadcast globally and watched by 350 million television viewers. By the time September rolled around, the fashions, music, and liberal behaviors of the burgeoning counterculture had a ripple effect—not just on American youth, but worldwide. 2. Book by San Francisco music journalist Joel Selvin titled *Summer of Love: The Inside Story of LSD, Rock and Roll, Free Love and High Times in the Wild West* (1994).

SWAYZE / *sway-zee* / *n.* Slang for clear rolling papers, that makes reference to Patrick Swayze's starring role in *Ghost* (1990). Swayze was also name-checked in the classic *Saturday Night Live* digital short, "Lazy Sunday" ("Throw the snacks in the bag and I'm ghost like Swayze!"). ALSO SEE: ALEDA.

TALL / *tawhl* / *v. or n.* 1. Obscure 1930's jazz term for getting high. 2. The Tall Brothers: Vancouver, British Columbia-based swing-style jazz band who released the album *Reefer Blues* (2004). 3. *The Lost Sessions* (2006) by the Black Crowes is also known as "The Tall Sessions."

TEA / *tee* / *n.* Jazz and hipster slang for marijuana and a popular term from the 1930s through the 1950s, as in, "Let's smoke some tea, man." The term is referenced in "Texas Tea Party" by Benny Goodman.

THAI STICK / *tie-steek* / *n.* 1. Classic sativa strain popular in the 1960s among soldiers stationed in Southeast Asia and imported to the U.S. through the late 1970s. It is made of buds and leaves grown in Thailand that are compressed and literally tied to a piece of stalk or strip of bamboo four to six inches long with string, hemp fiber, or animal hair. It is occasionally dipped in opium for a more powerful effect. 2. Thai restaurant chain in the San Francisco Bay Area. 3. Thai dish featuring shrimp wrapped in crispy noodles and fried. 4. Drumstick manufactured by Calato.

THAT '70S SHOW Television sitcom that aired on Fox from 1998 to 2006, it was set in a fictional suburb called Point Place, Wisconsin, in the late 1970s and focused on the teenage antics of its six primary characters: high school friends Eric (Topher Grace), Kelso (Ashton Kutcher), Donna (Laura Prepon), Jackie (Mila Kunis), Steven (Danny Masterson), and Fez (Wilmer Valderrama). They are often seen sitting in a circle in a smoky basement and talking nonsensically. In one famous episode, they painted a pot leaf on the town's water tower.

THC / *tea-aych-see* / *n.* Short for tetrahydrocannabinol, the primary psychoactive chemical in the cannabis plant, which, even in low doses, causes a high or euphoric sensation. It was discovered in 1964 when Raphael Mechoulam and Yechiel Gaoni from the Weizmann Institute in Rehovot, Israel, isolated the compound. Further research has shown that cannabinoid receptors in the brain naturally respond to THC and are, in fact, neuroprotective. The physiological effects, meanwhile, are at the center of the medical marijuana movement, which claims that they provide legitimate medicinal relief to people suffering from cancer, AIDS, and a host of other ailments. In its synthetic form, the THC pill Marinol is available by prescription. To date, there has not been a single case of THC overdose, yet cannabis remains on the Schedule I list of controlled substances, alongside heroin. ALSO SEE: CANNABINOIDS; MARINOL.

THIRD LUNG SEE HOW TO MAKE A MUTE (P. 96); MUTE; POPE.

THOMPSON, HUNTER S. (1937–2005) The writer and journalist who invented the term "gonzo journalism" for his particularly aggressive, drug-induced personal writing style, he was born in Louisville, Kentucky, and was hired by *Rolling Stone* to cover events and chronicle the pulse of American life in the late 1960s and early 1970s. He is the author of fifteen books, including the drug-lit classic *Fear and Loathing in Las Vegas* (1972), adapted to the screen by Terry Gilliam in 1998. His biopic *Where the Buffalo Roam* (1980) starred Bill Murray. Thompson committed suicide February 20, 2005. ALSO SEE: STONER LEGENDS (P. 194).

TIE-DYE / *ty-die* / *v.* To create psychedelic patterns on shirts and other articles of clothing by using string to make circles and shapes. Tie-dyed garments are a quintessential style among hippies and Deadheads.

TOASTED, TOASTY / *toe-stead, toe-stee* / *past part. of toast or adj.* Synonym for being high, as in, "I'm toasted, dude." Used as an adjective, as in, "I'm feeling toasty." ALSO SEE: BAKED; BLASTED; BLAZED; BURNT; BUZZED; CRISPY; FRIED; HIGH; LIT; LOADED; RIPPED; STONED; WASTED; ZONKED; ZOOTED.

TOKE / *toak* / *v. or n.* 1. To take a hit off a joint 2. An actual hit off a joint. Popularized in song by Brewer & Shipley's "One Toke Over the Line" (1971). The term possibly evolved from the Spanish verb *tocar*, meaning to touch or play. Chehalis tribe leader Chief Toke hailed from Tokeland, Washington. ALSO SEE: DRAW; HIT; INHALE; PUFF; PULL; RIP; SMOKE.

TOLERANCE / *tall-ur-rinse* / *n.* Diminished effect of a drug after continual use. In the case of marijuana, the more often you smoke, the more you need to attain the desired high. Also, many believe that smoking the same strain will lessen its impact after an extended period of time.

TORCH / *torch* / *v.* The act of overburning or scorching the bowl with an unnecessarily high flame. ALSO SEE: LIGHTER; LIGHTER ETIQUETTE (P. 86).

TOSH, PETER (1944–1987) One of the original members

The THC molecule

131

Peter Tosh, with a ganja-leaf headband, in 1979

of the Wailers—Jamaica's greatest group ever—with Bob Marley and Bunny Livingston. He was born as Winston McIntosh in Kingston's Trenchtown ghetto and joined the group in 1962 when they were known as the Wailing Wailers. He performed on *Catch a Fire* and *Burnin'* (both in 1973) before leaving the group to pursue a solo career that began auspiciously with *Legalize It* (1976) and followed with *Equal Rights* (1977), *Bush Doctor* (1978), and six more albums. One of the most influential champions of marijuana, "Stepping Razor" (his nickname) was famous for always performing with a spliff in his hand. He was killed in a robbery on September 11, 1987, the details of which have never been completely resolved. Nicholas Campbell's *Stepping Razor: Red X* (1993) documents Tosh's illustrious career. ALSO SEE: A BRIEF HISTORY OF THE GREATEST MARIJUANA SONGS (P. 178); GANJA REGGAE CLASSICS (P. 186); THE GREATEST POT-THEMED ALBUM COVERS (P. 182).

TRAILER PARK BOYS Successful Canadian TV mockumentary (since 1999) about two friends—Ricky (Rob Wells) and Julian (John Paul Tremblay)—who, among many of their schemes, devise a plan to grow pot in an Airstream RV and sell the harvest to the guards at the prison in which they were jailed. Their daily travails are entertaining enough, but the antics of their wacky neighbor, the bug-eyed shopping-cart fixer Bubbles (Mike Smith), push this already hilarious show over the top. The series was adapted into a feature-length movie, *The Trailer Park Boys* (2006), by Michael Clattenburg. ALSO SEE: COMEDIES TO WATCH WHILE YOU'RE STONED (P. 156).

TREES / *treez* / *n.* Hip-hop slang for marijuana, as in, "Let's smoke some trees, son." ALSO SEE: GANJA; GRASS; HEMP; HERB; MARIJUANA; SMOKE; WEED.

TRICHOMES / *try-combs* / *pl. n.* The often misunderstood and misspelled term for the resin glands on the marijuana plant containing the vast portion of THC. Microscopic follicles turn from clear to amber when the plant is ready to harvest. In hash-producing countries, resin is screened off the plants, which are then discarded. In the U.S., resin is prized as an essential part of the plant. It is visible as snow-like white crystals on the buds and the leaves closest to

buds. When dried, it appears as a powdery substance in colors ranging from green to tan. Resin can be self-screened with devices like the Resin Heaven. Smoke it by itself in a pipe or sprinkle it in a joint. Do not attempt to inhale it nasally. ALSO SEE: CRYSTALS; GREAT STONER INNOVATIONS (P. 137).

TRINITY COUNTY Along with Humboldt County to the west and Mendocino County to the south, part of northern California's Emerald Triangle, it is noted for marijuana cultivation and liberal laws. Medical patients or caregivers are allowed to have either six mature plants or twelve immature plants and possess half an ounce of marijuana. ALSO SEE: THE EMERALD TRIANGLE; HUMBOLDT COUNTY; MENDOCINO COUNTY.

TRIP / *trihp* / *n. or v.* 1. Term used to describe the effect of being high on a hallucinogen such as LSD or magic mushrooms. To "take a trip" means an experience in which perception of time and the senses (in particular sight, touch, and sound) is altered. 2. To act somewhat irrationally, as in, "You're tripping, dude." 3. A vacation or a long journey by car, as in "road trip." ALSO SEE: ALBERT HOFMANN; LSD.

TRIPPY / *trihp-pee* / *adj.* 1. Term to describe altered visuals and sounds, or hallucinations, spurred by psychedelics like LSD or magic mushrooms, as in, "Dude, that wallpaper pattern is so trippy."

TUBE / *toob* / *n.* 1. Slang for a bong, as in, "Let's go rip a tube, dude." 2. Slang for television, as in, "the boob tube." 3. An underground subway system. 4. The extension of a hookah from which one draws smoke by puffing.

TURN ON / *tern ahn* / *v.* Slang for the act of getting someone high on marijuana or other drugs, as in, "Turn me on, dude." Popularized in the famous Timothy Leary slogan, "Turn on, tune in, drop out."

TWIST / *twihst* / *v. or adj.* 1. To roll a joint, as in, "to twist one up." Term derived from the act of turning the ends of the joint so that it's easier to light. 2. When used as an adjective, it means something strange or screwed up, as in, "That's twisted, dude!" ALSO SEE: HOW TO ROLL A JOINT (P. 119).

Wearing the Weed

CELEBRITY STONERS WHO PUT POT ON DISPLAY

Chris Robinson: The Black Crowes' frontman followed Gram Parsons's lead when he wore pot-leaf adorned pants on the MTV Video Awards in 1992.

Kate Hudson: Robinson's former wife has been photographed wearing a pot-leaf belt buckle (on the cover of *Rolling Stone*) and a pot-leaf patch on her denim shorts.

Helen Hunt: The Academy Award–winning actress was strolling one day with her baby and a friend wearing a huge pot-leaf design on her light-blue sweater.

Brad Pitt: Angelina Jolie's hunky husband donned a similar sweater, this one beige, when he was married to Jennifer Aniston.

Snoop Dogg: Back when he was known as Snoop Doggy Dogg, he wore the pot-leaf hat in Dr. Dre's "Nuthin' But a 'G' Thang" video (1993). Of course, MTV blurred out the leaf. More recently, Snoop has been showing off a diamond-encrusted pot-leaf microphone, which he uses on tour and for TV appearances, as well as a pair of pot-leaf slippers.

Britney Spears: When she was still married to Kevin Federline and before she wigged out, Spears was

seen wearing a sweat jacket with a pot leaf in place of the Adidas logo.

Gram Parsons: Among other things, the Flying Burrito Brother was famous for his custom-made Nudie suit with pot leaves, pills, and other ornaments.

Bob Marley: After his death, Marley merch took off. T-shirts with photos of him blazing spliffs are a must-have for Rasta wannabes.

Snoop Dogg

Gram Parsons

Helen Hunt

Britney Spears

133

U

UP IN SMOKE The greatest marijuana movie of all time, starring Richard "Cheech" Marin and Tommy Chong, it was released in 1978. After Cheech (Pedro) picks up a hitchhiking Chong (Anthony Stoner), they smoke a huge doobie ("Is that a joint, man?"). Hilarity ensues as the duo enters a rock band contest and meets stoner chicks and brainless cops along the way. Follow-up films include *Cheech & Chong's Next Movie* (1980), *Nice Dreams* (1981), and *Still Smokin'* (1983). ALSO SEE: A BRIEF HISTORY OF STONER MOVIES (P. 146); CHEECH & CHONG (P. 36); CLASSIC STONER DIALOGUES (P. 152); TOMMY CHONG; RICHARD "CHEECH" MARIN.

V

The Volcano vaporizer and accompanying turkey bag inhaler

VANCOUVER Capital of British Columbia, Canada's westernmost province noted for marijuana tolerance and dubbed "Vansterdam" and "Dankouver." Named for a British Royal Navy captain George Vancouver (1791), it was settled in the 1860s, incorporated in 1886, and is now home to more than 2.2 million residents and 5,000 grow-ops. Hastings Street in the Eastside section features many head shops. *Cannabis Culture* is based there. "B.C. Bud" strains sell for between C$200 and C$250, and mushrooms are also available. Needle exchange and injection sites cater to hard-drug users. ALSO SEE: THE SEVEN STONER WONDERS OF THE WORLD (P. 76).

VAPORIZER / *vay-pour-eye-zer* / *n.* A device invented in 1990 by the mysterious "Dr. Lunglife," it is used to heat marijuana without combusting it. Marijuana is heated in a metal container and vapor is captured in an enclosed globe or plastic bag. Research indicates that it is safer than smoking combusted marijuana, hence its popularity among medical marijuana patients. The Volcano, manufactured by Storz & Bickel in Germany, sells for as much as $600. Cheaper varieties with tube inhalers sell for between $100 and $500. The term has been shortened to "vape" when used as a verb. ALSO SEE: GREAT STONER INNOVATIONS (P. 137); PARAPHERNALIA; WHY I LOVE TO VAPE (P. 135)

VARIETY / *va-righ-a-tee* / *n.* Term for a marijuana strain, such as AK-47, Northern Lights #5, White Widow. ALSO SEE: STRAIN.

VENICE BEACH, CALIFORNIA Beach community located in West Los Angeles, just south of Santa Monica, it was founded by tobacco millionaire Abbot Kinney in 1905 and modeled after its namesake, Venice, Italy, complete with several working canals. A popular tourist destination, it is famous for its eclectic counterculture and oceanside scene. Cheap rents for run-down bungalows first attracted predominately European immigrants to the area along with young writers and artists. In the 1950s members of the Beat generation hung out at the Gas House on Oceanfront Walk and at Venice West Café on Dudley Street, where they held poetry readings and smoked pot openly. The area became a hippie mecca in the 1960s and also a favorite spot for surfers. In the 1970s the district known as Dogtown became ground zero for the burgeoning skateboarding craze and home to

Why I Love to Vape

BY THE KOTTONMOUTH KINGS' PAKELIKA

The Kottonmouth Kings' masked, robotic-dancing "visual assassin," known only as Pakelika ("Pak" to his friends), is the first band member to use a vaporizer onstage. Here he tells *Pot Culture* why he prefers to "vape" rather than to "smoke."

The masked Pakelika takes a pull off his vaporizer in 2007

The Vaporbrothers vaporizer with plastic tube inhaler

Why vape: "First off, it's the cleanest high. It's healthier than smoking. When you smoke, you burn the plant and the THC. When you vape, the plant isn't burned and you benefit from getting the most THC possible."

Favorite vaporizer: "I prefer the Vaporator. It's glass on glass and the easiest to use. Best results, best taste. This is the one I use on stage."

Other favorites: "My first sponsor was VaporTech. They sponsored the whole band. Then Vaporbrothers sponsored us. Vaporator is our current sponsor. But I own pretty much one of every vape that's worth having."

Tasting the buds: "The most incredible taste is from the vape. It's all in knowing your equipment and using it correctly. Anyone who says otherwise has been using the vape wrong. Send them to me. They will definitely taste the herb."

Vape vs. smoke: "You get higher using the vape than smoking. You get more of the THC because you're not burning the plant. Just vaping the THC, you might not realize how high you are."

Trend or not: "If it's a trend, it's a trend I've been doing for nearly a decade. I think it's looked at or will be looked at like a joint, blunt, or bong. Vape is a personal choice. If you want the cleanest high, best taste, and the healthiest way, then vape is your method."

Who else vapes: "I know B-Real and Sen Dog from Cypress Hill like to vape, and pretty much any band we've played with. Most I can't mention, unfortunately. One day I hope weed won't be an issue that needs to be hidden."

Vape songs: "If you listen, we mention vaping in numerous songs. But I'm dedicating a track or two to it on my next solo album."

California's Kottonmouth Kings—Pakelika (center) surrounded by (clockwise from top left) Brad Daddy X, Lou Dog, DJ Bobby B, Johnny Richter, and D-Loc—in 2004

Classic VW Bus models

time, it works like tears, lubricating dry eyes. It can be used safely as many as three times a day, making it a must-carry for stoners. ALSO SEE: RED EYE.

VW BUS / *vee-duh-bull-you-bus* / n. Volkswagen's high-occupancy passenger van, or bus, manufactured in its first form, the Type 2 from 1950 to 1967 (the Type 1 was the Beetle) was the hippie ride of choice for most of the 1960s and 1970s and lives on today as an enduring symbol of the counterculture. The original model, also called the Splittie (for its split front windows), was marketed specifically for its affordability, cargo room, and horsepower (the engine, like all VWs of the time, was in the back). But what was intended for blue-collar American workers was embraced by an entirely different segment of society. The vehicle's reasonable price—particularly for used models—made it attractive to the school and surf crowd. Its roomy interior offered a way to transport a lot of stoner buddies and was perfect for long road trips, not to mention quick dashes to the Canadian border for anyone wanting to escape the Vietnam War draft. Even the VW logo on the front got the hippie treatment, with many owners painting a peace symbol over it, one of many artful treatments exhibited on buses at the time. The VW bus experienced its first resurgence in popularity in the 1980s in the parking lots of Grateful Dead shows. In movies, it has also been a popular prop over the years such as in *Fast Times at Ridgemont High* (1982) and *Little Miss Sunshine* (2006). Today, old buses are collector's items, and, when sold in good condition, can fetch as much as $100,000.

its forefathers, the Z-Boys, who were documented in Stacey Peralta's *Dogtown and Z-Boys* (2001) and later in Catherine Hardwicke's *Lords of Dogtown* (2005). After a brief period of neglect, it has been experiencing a renaissance with the spread of bars, nightclubs, art galleries, and edgy apparel shops. In the Coen Brothers' *The Big Lebowski* (1998), The Dude, a.k.a. Jeffrey Lebowski, played by Jeff Bridges, lives there. ALSO SEE: A BRIEF HISTORY OF STONER MOVIES (P. 146); STONER BEACHES (P. 202).

VIPER / *vy-purr* / n. 1. Jazz slang for a marijuana smoker, the term was commonly used in the 1930s and 1940s and refers to the hissing sound made when inhaling a joint. Song titles include Fats Waller's "Viper's Drag" (1934) and Stuff Smith's "If You're a Viper" (1936). 2. Name of a New York–based record label owned by Jonathan Stuart. 3. Snake; serpent. ALSO SEE: POTHEAD; REEFER JAZZ CLASSICS (P. 190); STONER.

VISINE / *Veye-zeen* / n. A brand of eye drops manufactured by Johnson & Johnson whose slogan promises "to get the red out" of bloodshot eyes. When one or two drops are applied directly to the eyeball, its active ingredient, tetrahydrozoline hydrochloride, causes blood vessels to constrict, thereby lessening the appearance of red lines. At the same

"I get the munchies, but I don't have a problem with that. That's the best part."
—**Norah Jones,**
singer

Great Stoner Innovations

Kind Bud: The remarkable result of the evolution of marijuana from imported varieties (often schwag) to homegrown strains, kind bud fetches as much as $600 to $800 per ounce because the stuff is just so damn tasty.

Glass: The arrival of handblown glass pipes and bongs, many of which could easily stand alone as art pieces, completely redefined smoking culture. First embraced by Deadheads, and later the rest of the stoner populace, glass eliminated the harsh hit of the metal pipe and the rank aftertaste of the resinated plastic bong.

Grinder: Saving countless smokers from severe cases of green thumb, the grinder, which first came on the scene in wooden form (thanks to Sweetleaf),

prepares pot to perfection with a simple twist of the hand. Today, metal with the optional pollen catcher and wide pegs (as opposed to pointy spikes), is the way to go.

Vaporizer: Why burn your buds when you can vaporize them instead, preventing tars and carbon monoxide from invading your stony space? Invented by the mysterious Dr. Lunglife in 1990, it took a decade for the vaporizer to catch on. Now there are dozens on the market, from the German-made Volcano, which catches vapor in a turkey bag, to the tube-style BC Vaporizer. Prices range from $20 (for the Dominizer) to $600 (for the Volcano).

Resin Heaven: Make your own trichomes (or kif) with this handy product, which screens marijuana when you break it up, leaving a brownish-green powder on the mirror placed strategically below the screen. The Resin Heaven was invented in 1979 by Pat and Don Collins of Pype's Palace, a head shop based in Portland, Oregon.

Formula 420: Finally, a solution for all your cleaning needs, this line of heavy-duty cleaners effectively eliminates a variety of "party fouls,"

as the packaging proclaims. Products include Smog Out (for room odors) and Spill Clean (for those unfortunate accidents), in addition to cleaners

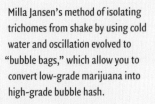

specifically designed for glass and plastic bongs and pipes. Formula 420's all-natural ingredients don't just work on your piece, they can tackle a variety of household spills and stains as well.

Clear papers: The twenty-first century finally caught up to the rolling-paper world with the advent of Aleda, the Brazilian company that first released the see-through, smokeable, cellulose-based sheets in 2005. Still a novelty in the U.S., Aleda papers and other knockoff brands continue to gain in popularity and can be found at most head shops.

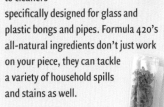

Pollinator: More for growers than for smokers,

Milla Jansen's method of isolating trichomes from shake by using cold water and oscillation evolved to "bubble bags," which allow you to convert low-grade marijuana into high-grade bubble hash.

The Original Buddy: This magnetic device methodically scrubs glass surfaces clean and removes ugly resin buildup. According to the company's Web site, it can be used on "vases, baby bottles, coffee pots, fish bowls, small aquariums, wine decanters, antiques, hookahs, tobacco pipes, and glass art." Combined with rubbing alcohol, detergent, or nail-polish remover, it will wipe out the nastiest brown stains.

Lighter Leash: What stoner hasn't lost his or her lighter about a hundred times? This product from the Indianapolis-based company Fire Essence enables you to strap the lighter to your body, like a key chain. Place a standard or mini Bic in the rubber holster and clip it to your belt loop, pocket, or purse. The nylon cord extends three feet, so you can pass it around in close company. Lighter Leashes retail for $4 to $5 each and come with a lighter, of course.

How to Hide the Smell

BY ADRIANNE CURRY

The first *America's Next Top Model* winner in 2003—she's now married to Christopher Knight, with whom she costars on *My Fair Brady*—smokes at practically every opportunity—before a red carpet appearance, while reality TV cameras are rolling, even on her wedding day. Here, she reveals to *Pot Culture* her foolproof methods for disguising the scent of kind bud.

Left: Adrianne Curry with Doug Benson at the Stonys in 2006
Right: Curry with bong in 2007

What's in her purse: "I carry orange lip gloss, which covers up the pot smell in my mouth for my husband when I tell him I haven't been smoking. My Dolce & Gabbana sunglasses cover my eyes—they're the real big, rock-star ones, where you know that someone's on acid. I have the Body Shop cocoa butter lotion for my hands to get the smoke smell out. My perfume is Dior Pure Poison. For mints, I prefer Icebreakers. They're really strong and burn your tongue, but they cover the smell up in two seconds."

The secret ingredient: "There are these blue drops you can get in France that clear your eyes like *that*. They're like Visine, only brilliant blue. You can't use them in if you have contacts because they stain them."

If you get pulled over: "After eating whatever it is I had in my car, or not wanting to part with it and shoving it into my nether regions, I spray some Ozium, which is like the ultimate freshener that hospitals use to disinfect the air. It will kill the smell of pot and kicks Glade Potpourri's ass. One tiny

> "I normally drop a breath mint, put on some lip gloss, pull down my shirt as low as it'll go, and just pray to God."

spritz is so strong it smells like a bushel of oranges. Then, I normally drop a breath mint, put on some lip gloss, pull down my shirt as low as it'll go, and just pray to God."

W

WACKY TOBACKY / *wah-kee-toe-back-ee* / *n.* 1. Humorous southern U.S. term for marijuana, said best with a thick accent. 2. Title of a song by NRBQ (1979). ALSO SEE: FUNNY CIGARETTE.

WAKE AND BAKE / *waik-and-baik* / *v.* To toke within an hour of arising in the morning and certainly before breakfast. It's a common stoner ritual that is not recommended for those with real jobs. The term may be a play on Shake 'n Bake, a popular brand of breadcrumbs first brought to market in 1965. Or it may have derived from the military term "shake and bake," which was code for the white phosphorus fire bombs used in the Vietnam War. That term was later adopted by Will Ferrell and John C. Reilly in *Talladega Nights: The Ballad of Ricky Bobby* (2006) to describe the duo's method of NASCAR racing. ALSO SEE: WAKE-AND-BAKE BASICS.

WALL, THE 1. A double album by Pink Floyd released in 1979 and regarded by many to be the quintessential rock opera. It spent fifteen consecutive weeks as the No. 1 album in the U.S. and contains the hit single, "Another Brick in the Wall (Part II)." 2. *Pink Floyd The Wall* (1982): Alan Parker's film adaptation of the epic four-sided album incorporating animated imagery into a dark and dense plot. It stars Bob Geldof as Pink, an on-the-edge rock star tormented by his past and slowly retreating into the fantasy world of his mind. The Wall (built and later knocked down) serves as a metaphor for Pink's journey of

Pink Floyd The Wall

🌿 Wake-and-Bake Basics 🌿

While it's not recommended for those with nine-to-five jobs, sometimes there's nothing better than waking up, smoking, and getting on with things. Here are some basics to maximizing productivity on one of those days.

Generally, to wake and bake means to smoke within an hour of getting up: No matter what time you actually wake up, it's recommended that you eat beforehand, just to minimize bingeing later on a high-calorie breakfast.

Lay out everything you might need: In order to exit the house with all your belongings (keys, wallet, cell phone), place everything in a visible, hard-to-miss spot so you don't have to look for it later.

If you have anything to do that day, you might be better off smoking a sativa rather than an indica: The latter tends to be a heavy high that may send you into a stupor (or back to sleep) while a lighter sativa should provide energy.

If you are spending the day at home, try to accomplish something: No slouching on the couch watching TV or playing video games. Instead, work on a long-term project, do some gardening, or clean the house.

self-discovery. ALSO SEE: ANIMATED FLICKS TO WATCH WHILE YOU'RE STONED (P. 160); PINK FLOYD; STONER SYNCHRONICITY (P. 128).

WASTED / *way-sted* / *adj.* The feeling of complete intoxication, whether fueled by marijuana, alcohol, or other drugs. ALSO SEE: BAKED; BLASTED; BLAZED; BURNT; CRISPY; FRIED; HIGH; LIT; LOADED; RIPPED; STONED; TOASTED; ZONKED; ZOOTED.

WATER PIPE / *wah-dur-pipe* / *n.* Technical term for a bong, hookah, bubbler, or any other smoking device that uses a water filtration method. It is the accepted term for any such device in head shops, where paraphernalia must be identified as being for tobacco use only. ALSO SEE: ANATOMY OF A BONG (P. 23); BONG; BUBBLER; GLASS VS. PLASTIC (P. 59); HOOKAH; ROOR.

WEED / *wheed* / *n.* 1. The most popular slang for marijuana, it dates back to the 1930s when prohibitionists referred to cannabis as "the weed with roots in hell," "devil's weed," and "killer weed." Simple usage, minus pejorative adjectives, took hold in the 1990s, as in, "Let's smoke some weed, dude." 2. Name of small Northern California town near Mount Shasta. ALSO SEE: GANJA; GRASS; HEMP; HERB; MARIJUANA; SMOKE; TREES.

WEEDS Critically acclaimed Showtime series starring Mary-Louise Parker, Elizabeth Perkins, and Kevin Nealon about a California suburb that's gone to pot when widowed housewife Nancy Botwin (Parker) becomes the town's main weed dealer. In 2006 Parker won a Golden Globe for the role and the show received a Stony Award for Best TV Series. Conceived by longtime TV writer and producer Jenji Kohan, it is among the network's highest-rated programs. ALSO SEE: MUST-SEE STONER TV (P. 170).

WEED WORLD Marijuana magazine published in Great Britain since 1993.

WHITE WIDOW / *whyte-wi-dough* / *n.* 1. Popular Dutch, mostly indica strain created in 1995 as Peacemaker and renamed by breeder Shantibaba for its famous snowy coat of trichomes. It flowers in nine to eleven weeks and has 18 to 22 percent THC content. 2. Name of a New York–based rock band. 3. Spider (*Latrodectus pallidus*) native to North Africa, southern Russia, the Middle East, Iran, and Cape Verde. Its venom is not toxic. ALSO SEE: ALL-TIME GREATEST STRAINS (P. 124).

> "I'm really in favor of legalizing marijuana. I don't think it's that controversial."
> **—Mary-Louise Parker,** actress

Weed World

WILLIAMS, MONTEL (B. 1956) Daytime TV talk-show host born in Baltimore, Maryland, on July 3, 1956, who has suffered from multiple sclerosis since 1999 and revealed medical-marijuana use for MS in his 2004 memoir, *Climbing Higher.* He has been the featured speaker at numerous MPP benefits and also represents the pharmaceutical industry group Partnership for Prescription Assistance. ALSO SEE: MARIJUANA POLICY PROJECT; MEDICAL MARIJUANA.

WOODSTOCK, NEW YORK Township founded in 1787 that is two hours northwest of New York City in the Catskill Mountains. A counterculture hub for alternative lifestyle seekers, it is home to 6,200 residents and hosts an annual film festival every October. The legendary 1969 rock festival actually took place fifty miles southwest in Bethel, New York. (The festival was originally going to be held in nearby Saugerties, but moved to Bethel instead and retained the Woodstock name.) *Peanuts* cartoonist Charles M. Schulz christened his famous yellow bird after the festival and town. "Woodstock" is also the title of a song written by Joni Mitchell and performed by Crosby, Stills, Nash & Young (1970).

WOOKIE / *wook-ee* / *n.* Derogatory term for a dreadlocked or shaggy-haired hippie. It refers to Chewbacca, *Star Wars's* star and the hairiest of all space creatures.

X

X, XTC / *ex, ex-tee-see* / *n.* SEE ECSTASY.

Y

Yippie cofounder and notorious 1960s provocateur Abbie Hoffman, circa 1968

YERBA / *year-bah* / *n.* 1. Spanish word for herb. 2. Short-lived Spanish edition of *High Times* (1998).

YIN AND YANG / *yin-and-yang* / *n.* In Chinese philosophy, the terms describing the opposite forces contained within all things. The circular symbol for this concept, known in Chinese as the taijitsu, consists of two equal and complementary parts—one black and the other white—the curves of which fit together perfectly. Each part of the circle includes a piece (in the form of a dot) of the other. Many people seeking alternatives to traditional Judeo-Christian philosophies and practices gravitate to this symbol and what it represents, incorporating it into art, fashion, music, and literature.

YIPPIES / *yip-eez* / *pl. n.* Youth International Party founded by Abbie Hoffman, Jerry Rubin, Paul Krassner, Anita Hoffman, Stew Albert, Bob Fass, Phil Ochs, Ed Sanders, Keith Lampe, and Nancy Kurshan in 1967 and noted for pranks such as levitating the Pentagon and running a pig (Pigasus) for president in 1968. *BlackListed News* details the group's history. The current incarnation, based in New York's Lower East Side, runs the annual marijuana rally in May, which has evolved into the Global Marijuana March, coordinated by Cures Not Wars and Dana Beal. ALSO SEE: PAUL KRASSNER; U.S. POT RALLIES (P. 200).

YOUNG, NEIL (B. 1945) Born in Toronto, Canada, on November 12, 1945, the legendary guitarist and singer-songwriter began his career in 1966 with the Mynah Birds, featur-ing future funk star and fellow Canadian Rick James. After moving to Los Angeles, he cofounded Buffalo Springfield with Stephen Stills, Richie Furay, Bruce Palmer, and Dewey Martin. The group had a No. 7 hit with "For What It's Worth" in 1967. He joined Crosby, Stills & Nash in 1969, performing at Woodstock and on *Déjà Vu* (1970) and the live *Four Way Street* (1971). His second and third solo albums, *Heart of Gold* (1970) and *Harvest* (1972), recorded with Crazy Horse, were Top 10 successes. He has since recorded 36 studio albums. Two of his songs—"Roll Another Number (for the Road) (on *Tonight's the Night*, 1973) and "Homegrown" (on *American Stars 'N Bars*, 1977)—are associated with marijuana. Noted for his caustic guitar style, nasal vocals, and socially conscious lyrics, he remains the greatest living singer-songwriter after Bob Dylan. Each year since 1985, he has co-hosted Farm Aid with Willie Nelson. ALSO SEE: RICK JAMES; WILLIE NELSON.

The yin-yang symbol

YOUTUBE / *yoo-toob* / *n.* Heralded by *Time* as the "Invention of the Year" (2006), which quickly prompted Google to purchase it for $1.65 billion, this largely user-fueled Web site allows users to watch and share videos with the rest of the world. ALSO SEE: MYSPACE.

Z

Z / *zee* / *n.* Slang for the abbreviation of one ounce (oz.), which denotes twenty-eight grams. It marks the point of quantity and usually comes with a high-volume discount. ALSO SEE: EIGHTH; GRAM; O.Z., QUARTER; Q.P.

ZIG-ZAG / *zeeg-szahg* / *n.* French rolling paper company founded in 1894 by Maurice and Jacques Braunstein in Paris. Its name stands for the process of interleaving papers in a zig-zag manner. Legend has it that the bearded smoker on all the packaging, Zouave, was a French soldier who rolled a cigarette from gunpowder paper when his clay pipe was smashed by a bullet. Many sizes of paper are available, but the most popular remains French Orange and the 1 ¼ package. ALSO SEE: GUIDE TO ROLLING PAPERS (P. 116).

ZONG BONG / *zahng-bahng* / *n.* Zigzag-shaped glass water pipe famous for the fact that it won't tip over. It was manufactured by seedleSs in the 1990s, a company that was targeted by the DEA's Operation Pipe Dreams in 2003 and now sells clothing only. ALSO SEE: GLASS VS. PLASTIC (P. 59); OPERATION PIPE DREAMS.

ZONKED / *zawn-kd* / *adj.* 1. The sensation of being ultra-stoned. 2. Falling asleep due to physical exhaustion or simply being tired, as in, "I was zonked out, dude." ALSO SEE: BAKED; BLASTED; BLAZED; BLUNTED; BURNT; BUZZED; CRISPY; FRIED; HIGH; LIT; LOADED; RIPPED; STONED; TOASTED; WASTED; ZOOTED.

ZOOTED / *zoo-tid* / *past part. of zoot* Hip-hop slang for being extremely high, as in, "Yo, son, that weed got me zooted." ALSO SEE: BAKED; BLASTED; BLUNTED; BURNT; BUZZED; CRISPY; FRIED; HIGH; LIT; LOADED; RIPPED; STONED; TOASTED; WASTED; ZONKED.

NUMBERS

007 / *dub-bull-oh-se-ven* / *n.* Name of a homemade pipe with a two- to three-foot-long plastic tube—like the one used in a funnel—that is connected to a standard Graffix-like stem and bowl. Marijuana is lit and the smoke is sucked through the tube. Its name has no real significance in the James Bond world. James Bong, maybe.

311 Los Angeles–based alternative rock-rap group with a heavy reggae influence, it consists of Nick Hexum (vocals), Doug "S. A." Martinez (rap vocals), Tim Mahoney (guitar), Aaron "P-Nut" Wills (bass), and Chad Sexton (drums). The group was formed in Omaha, Nebraska, and first came onto the stoner scene in 1993 with the album *Music*, which contains the songs "My Stoney Baby" and "Hydroponic." As their fan base grew , so did their steady string of sold-out live shows, culminating in a yearly event in New Orleans, 311 Day, during which the band has been known to play for more than five hours. Their biggest-selling album, 1995's *311* (known as the blue album), went triple platinum and included the hit single, "Down." The same year they contributed "Who's Got the Herb?" to the NORML benefit CD, *Hempilation: Freedom Is NORML*. It remains a 311 concert staple. ALSO SEE: HEMPILATION; HOW TO MAKE A MUTE (P. 96); STONER BANDS (P. 177).

420 / *fore-twen-tee* / *n.* Code for smoking marijuana and originally believed to be the California police department's code for "marijuana smoking in progress." In actuality, this code doesn't exist. Others think it's connected to the Bob Dylan song "Rainy Day Women #12 & 35" (12 multiplied by 35 equals 420), on which he chants, "Everybody must get stoned." Former San Rafael, California, high school students calling themselves the Waldos claim to have coined the term, which spread through the Deadhead scene and by the late 1980s began circulating at Dead shows. April 20 (4/20) has become the unofficial stoner holiday marked by parties and festivals across the U.S. and Canada. ALSO SEE: WEED SITES ON THE WEB (P. 220).

49:51 / *fore-tee-nyne-fif-tee-won* / *n.* Term describing the pot-to-tobacco ratio in a European or mixed joint (49 percent tobacco to 51 percent marijuana).

5-0 / *five-oh* / *n.* Code for police, as in, "Put the joint down, dude. It's the 5-0!" Popularized through the successful TV cop drama *Hawaii Five-O* (1968–1980) about two Hawaii state police detectives (played by Jack Lord and James MacArthur) who chase down criminals in their home state. The term refers to the fact that Hawaii is the fiftieth state to join the union. Another possible origin could be the 5.0-liter Ford Mustang, which in some jurisdictions is used as a police vehicle.

Above: 49:51 (49 percent tobacco to 51 percent marijuana)
Right: The 4:20 Snack Shop in Negril, Jamaica

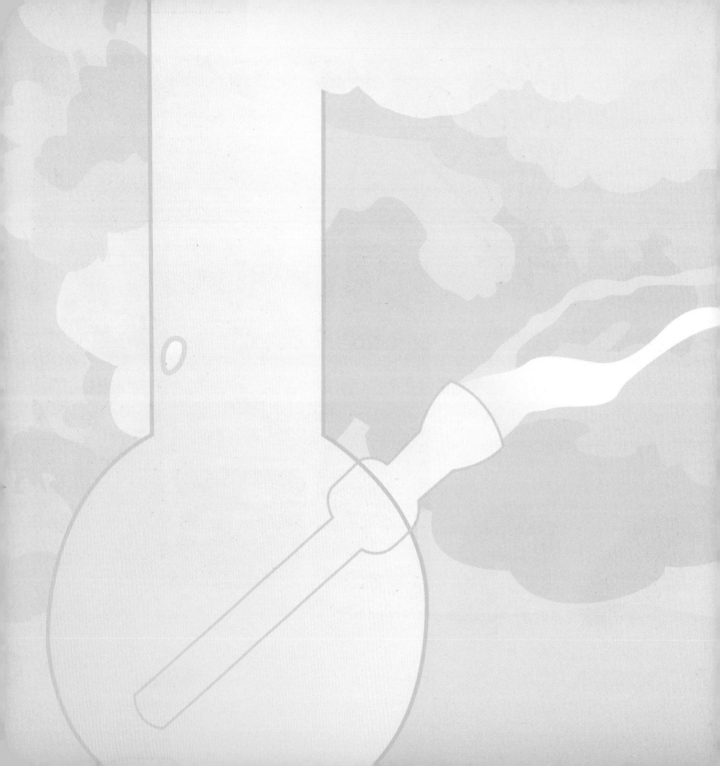

Pot Culture PICKS

Your guide to the best in stoner
movies, TV, music, travel & more

A Brief History of
Stoner Movies

Tommy Chong (left) and Cheech Marin (right) in
Up in Smoke

Up in Smoke (1978)
The one-and-only classic, best-ever, original Cheech
& Chong movie introduced the dopey duo—who had
been a stand-up comedy and album fixture since the
early 1970s—to the silver screen. Huge joints, a van
made out of hemp, and general high jinks and hilarity
abound in this Marx Brothers–style comedy.

Classic Line: "Is that a joint, man? That looks like a
quarter pounder!" —Pedro

Fast Times at Ridgemont High (1982)
Jeff Spicoli (Sean Penn)—the blond-haired surfer who
never wears a shirt, hardly comes to class, and always
uses the word *dude* in conversation—redefined the
stoner character in this coming-of-age flick written
by Cameron Crowe (*Almost Famous*) and directed
by Amy Heckerling (*Clueless*) about a group of L.A.
"Valley" teens. The rebellious Spicoli's interactions
with his anal-retentive history teacher Mr. Hand
(Ray Walston) are highlights, as is the scene when
Spicoli spills out of a smoke-filled VW bus. The cast

also includes Jennifer Jason Leigh, Phoebe Cates, and
Judge Reinhold.

Classic Line: "All I need are some tasty waves, a cool
buzz, and I'm fine." —Spicoli

Dazed and Confused (1993)
Richard Linklater's career-defining indie flick about a
group of high schoolers in Austin, Texas, introduced
the world to the ultimate stoner character, Slater
(played by Rory Cochrane), whose quintessential
scene involves a conversation
about George and Martha

Washington being potheads. The film also features
Ben Affleck, Matthew McConaughey, and Parker
Posey in early roles. Even Renée Zellweger makes an
uncredited first appearance.

Classic Line: "Behind every good man there is a
woman, and that woman was Martha Washington,
man. And every day when George would come home,
she would have a big fat bowl waiting for him, man,
when he comes in the door, man. She was a hip, hip,
hip lady, man." —Slater

Friday (1995)
This first and best in the series of three "Friday"
movies was directed by F. Gary Gray and written by
hip-hop heavyweight Ice Cube (with D. J. Pooh). It
costars Ice Cube as Craig, who's introduced to weed
by his constantly high buddy, Smokey, played by the
hilarious Chris Tucker in a breakout role. The cast
also includes John Witherspoon and Nia Long.

Classic Line: "Puff puff, give. Puff puff, give.
You're fuckin' up the rotation." —Smokey

Half Baked (1998)
The movie that introduced stand-up comedian Dave
Chappelle to stoners was cowritten by Chappelle
(with Neal Brennan). Chappelle costars as Thurgood
and Sir Smoke-a-Lot in a double role. When
Thurgood's friend Kenny (Harland Williams) gets
busted, Thurgood and his other buds (including
Jim Breuer) rip off a hospital's medical-marijuana
stash in order to start a weed delivery service so that

they can spring Kenny from jail where he is being protected by the Squirrel Master (Tommy Chong). Meanwhile, Snoop Dogg, Jon Stewart, and Willie Nelson are among their customers.

Classic Line: "Did you ever see the back of a $20 bill . . . *on weed*?" —Stewart

The Big Lebowski (1998)

This Coen brothers cult comedy (directed by Joel and cowritten with brother Ethan) introduced the ultimate slacker-stoner, a Creedence-loving, unemployed bowling enthusiast known to his friends only as "the Dude," played masterfully by Jeff Bridges. The Dude tokes while crashing his car, being attacked by a marmot (essentially a large squirrel) in the bathtub, and postcoitus. The terrific cast includes bowling buds Walter (John Goodman) and Donny (Steve Buscemi), as well as Julianne Moore, Philip Seymour Hoffman, and John Turturro as rival bowler, Jesus. This film has inspired a cult following of pot-toking, bathrobe-wearing White Russian drinkers and the semiannual Lebowski Fest.

Classic Line: "Well, you know, the Dude abides." —The Dude

Road Trip (2000)

Stoners head out on the highway to retrieve a naughty video accidentally sent to one character's girlfriend. Along the way, they trash their car, smoke out with a grandpa and his dog, and hang with a black fraternity. It features Tom Green, D.J. Qualls, Seann William Scott, Amy Smart, Breckin Meyer, and Paolo Constanzo as smart-stoner Rubin, and is directed by Todd Phillips (*Old School*, *Starsky & Hutch*, and *Bittersweet Motel*).

Classic Line: "Are you gonna pass that doobie, or what?" —Grandpa

Jay and Silent Bob Strike Back (2001)

After supporting roles in *Clerks*, *Mallrats* and *Dogma*, Jay (Jason Mewes) and Silent Bob (Kevin Smith) took center stage in Smith's fifth film. Upset that a comic book about their lives, "Bluntman and Chronic," is being made into a movie, they take off on a cross-country trip that ultimately lands them in Hollywood where the dopey duo end up using bong sabers to win control of the movie within the movie. Heavy on the cameos, George Carlin, Ben Affleck, Jason Lee, Judd Nelson, and Carrie Fisher all make appearances.

Classic Line: "You guys need to turn those frowns upside down. And I got just the thing for that. We call them Doobie Snax." —Jay

How High (2001)

Bob Dylan's son Jesse chose hip-hop legends Method Man (Silas) and Redman (Jamal) to anchor this stoner comedy about two blunt smokers who try to matriculate at Harvard. They believe a certain strain of marijuana makes them smarter and they need to grow another crop fast if they're going to get by in the Ivy League. The cast includes Mike Epps, Fred Willard, and Cypress Hill's B-Real and Sen Dog.

Classic Line: "How did I fail women's studies? I love bitches!" —Jamal

Harold & Kumar Go to White Castle (2004)

The story of two twenty-something stoners (Kal Penn plays Kumar and John Cho plays Harold) who get the munchies and an insatiable craving for White Castle burgers. After accidentally chucking their stash, the guys roll through New Jersey, crashing Princeton University in pursuit of a pot refill. Along the way, they pick up hitchhiker Neal Patrick Harris (playing himself as a coke-snorting, stripper-loving jerk), the guys ride and smoke out a cheetah, and in the movie's stoniest scene, Kumar imagines making love to a quarter-pound bag of weed.

Classic Line: "Did Doogie Houser just steal my fucking car?" —Harold

Kal Penn (left) and John Cho (right) in *Harold & Kumar Go to White Castle*
Opposite: Matthew McConaughey and Joey Lauren Adams in *Dazed and Confused*

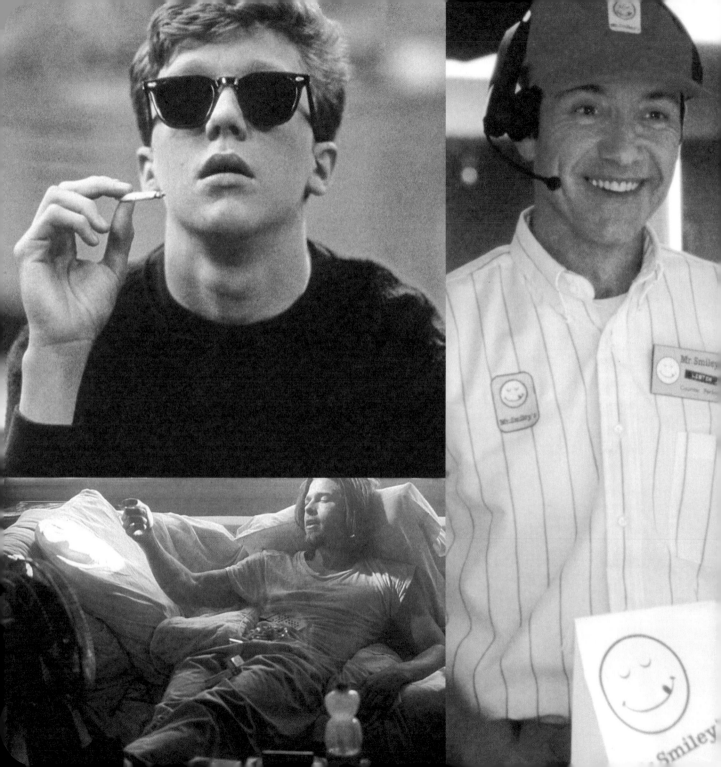

A Brief History of Stoner Scenes in Non-Stoner Movies

Annie Hall (1977)
Annie (Diane Keaton) doesn't like to have sex when she's not high. Annie offers Alvy (Woody Allen) a joint. He refuses, joking, "If I have grass I get too wonderful for words."

Animal House (1978)
Professor Jennings (Donald Sutherland) smokes out his students in his candlelit house. Larry (Tom Hulce) has an epiphany, and then asks, "Could I buy some pot from you?"

Nine to Five (1980)
Secretaries Doralee (Dolly Parton), Violet (Lily Tomlin), and Judy (Jane Fonda) share a joint and vivid dreams of offing their bean-counter boss (Dabney Coleman).

History of the World, Part 1 (1981)
Josephus (Gregory Hines) rolls an enormous bomber of "Roman Red" in this hilarious Mel Brooks spoof, narrated by Orson Welles.

The Breakfast Club (1985)
Bad-boy leader of the detention squad John (Judd Nelson) sparks one up over the objections of goody-goodies Claire (Molly Ringwald), Brian (Anthony Michael Hall), and Andrew (Emilio Estevez). "Chicks cannot hold the smoke," says a stoned Brian.

Platoon (1986)
Sgt. Grodin (Willem Dafoe) initiates Pvt. Taylor (Charlie Sheen) into the stoner platoon with a potent shotgun hit of Vietnamese grass literally from a rifle.

True Romance (1993)
This cocaine caper starring Christian Slater and Patricia Arquette features Brad Pitt as slacker stoner Floyd who offers a honey-bong toke to hit man Virgil (James Gandolfini).

Jackie Brown (1997)
Melanie (Bridget Fonda) offers Louis (Robert De Niro) a bong hit, advising him to inhale deeply. "Coughing's good," she says. "Gets ya higher."

American Beauty (1999)
When Lester (Kevin Spacey) cops pot from his teenage next-door neighbor Ricky (Wes Bentley), he selects the extremely overpriced $2,000 bag.

The Beach (2000)
Richard (Leonardo DiCaprio) stumbles upon a huge pot plantation in Thailand and almost gets killed by armed guards who chase him.

Mr. Smiley's

Stoner Character Actors

Cheech & Chong

Movies: *Up in Smoke* (1978), *Cheech & Chong's Next Movie* (1980), *Cheech & Chong's Nice Dreams* (1981), *Still Smokin'* (1983)

Richard "Cheech" Marin and Tommy Chong embody the 1970s ethos of sex, drugs, and rock and roll. Chong played the zonked-out "straight" man to Cheech's zany, over-the-top Chicano stoner. Since their run of "hit" movies, Marin went mainstream (*Nash Bridges* and *Tin Cup*), while Chong never left his character (*That '70s Show* and *Far Out Man*). In 2003 and 2004 Chong served nine months in jail for selling bongs.

Bridget Fonda

Role/Movie: Melanie, *Jackie Brown* (1997)

Following in the considerable footsteps of her iconic father, Peter Fonda, who starred in *Easy Rider*, Bridget Fonda portrays a pot-smoking nymph in Quentin Tarantino's follow-up to *Pulp Fiction*. After Melanie instructs jailbird Louis (Robert De Niro) to hold in the bong hit because it gets you higher, they have sex. Later in the film, Louis murders her.

Dennis Hopper

Roles/Movies: Max, *The Trip* (1967); Billy, *Easy Rider* (1969); photojournalist, *Apocalypse Now* (1979); Frank Booth, *Blue Velvet*, (1986)

The original movie stoner, Hopper directed and costarred with Peter Fonda and Jack Nicholson in *Easy Rider*. He preceded that role with one in the acid adventure, *The Trip*, with Fonda and Bruce Dern. He's the jittery photographer in *Apocalypse Now* and creeped

Dennis Hopper in *Easy Rider*

out audiences with his gas mask in *Blue Velvet*. Fast-talking and paranoid, Hopper's characters embody the fear and loathing inside every pothead's heart.

Frances McDormand

Role/Movie: Jane, *Laurel Canyon* (2002)

McDormand plays a pot-smoking, record-producing mom opposite her straight son Sam (Christian Bale) and his impressionable fiancée Alex (Kate Beckinsale), who gets caught up in Jane's bohemian lifestyle.

Jason Mewes & Kevin Smith

Role/Movies: Jay and Silent Bob in *Clerks* (1994), *Mallrats* (1995), *Dogma* (1999), *Jay and Silent Bob Strike Back* (2001), and *Clerks II* (2006)

Costarring in no less than five Kevin Smith–directed flicks, the dynamic duo of jive-talking Jay (Mewes) and the seemingly mute Bob (Smith) are two stoners looking for adventure, a good time, and trouble. They sell weed in front of the Quick Stop convenience store in the *Clerks* series, hunt down the Hollywood makers of superheroes Bluntman and Chronic in *Jay and Silent Bob Strike Back*, and help save the world from impending doom in *Dogma*.

Sean Penn

Roles/Movies: Spicoli, *Fast Times at Ridgemont High* (1982); Daulton, *The Falcon and the Snowman* (1985); David, *Carlito's Way* (1993); Eddie, *Hurlyburly* (1998)

Frances McDormand in *Laurel Canyon*

After Dennis Hopper and Cheech & Chong, Penn defined the stoner character with his humorous portrayal of the loopy surfer-dude Spicoli in *Fast Times*. He followed with numerous druggy roles that usually required that he shovel copious amounts of fake coke up his nose. Penn is arguably at his best as the addicted state-secrets dealer in *The Falcon and the Snowman*.

Seth Rogen

Role/Movie: Cal, *The 40-Year-Old Virgin* (2005); Neil, *You, Me and Dupree* (2006); Ben Stone, *Knocked Up* (2007)

Canadian-born Rogen plays a stony store manager who shows fellow employee Andy (Steve Carrell) how to smoke out of an apple in *The 40-Year-Old Virgin*; a whipped husband who has to hide the stench of pot from his overbearing wife in *You, Me and Dupree*; and the pot-smoking lead character in *Knocked Up*, who gets his one-night stand (Katherine Heigl) pregnant and decides to give parenting a try.

Chris Tucker

Role/Movie: Smokey, *Friday* (1995)

It wasn't until the 1990s that black actors began to play potheads, and Tucker was the first. In his one and only stoner role, he urges his homeboy, Craig (Ice Cube), to light up and lighten up. Hard times in South Central Los Angeles become high times with a little of that indo smoke.

Owen Wilson

Role/Movie: Hansel, *Zoolander* (2001)

In the competitive world of male modeling, Wilson portrays the acid-taking, adventure-seeking dimwit Hansel. While you never see him actually toking, a tea he commands be spiked with some sort of hallucinogen gives a sense of his psychedelic tendencies.

Sean Penn in *Fast Times at Ridgemont High*

Classic Stoner Dialogues

Easy Rider (1969)

At a campfire, Wyatt (Peter Fonda), Billy (Dennis Hopper), and George (Jack Nicholson) sit around talking. Wyatt offers a joint.

George: "How do I do it?"
Wyatt [smokes and passes the joint]: "Here."
George: "That's got a real nice taste to it. Though I don't suppose it'll do me much good. I'm so used to the booze."
Wyatt: "You've got to hold it in your lungs longer."

Up in Smoke (1978)

Pedro (Cheech) picks up Anthony (Chong) hitchhiking. Then Anthony lights a fatty.

Anthony: "Hey, you wanna get high? I've got a joint here I've been saving for a special occasion."
Pedro: "Is that a joint, man? That looks like a quarter pounder. Is it heavy stuff? Will it blow me away?"
Anthony: "Toke—toke it up, man. It grabs you by the boo-boo, don't it?"

Animal House (1978)

Professor Jennings (Donald Sutherland) invites students over for some private tutoring that turns into a pot session.

Larry (Tom Hulce) [high]: "OK—that means that our whole solar system could be like one tiny atom in the fingernail of some giant being. That's too much. That means that one tiny atom in my fingernail …"
Jennings: "Could be one tiny little universe."
Larry: "Can I buy some pot from you?"

Caddyshack (1980)

Carl (Bill Murray), the golf course's groundskeeper, gives Ty (Chevy Chase) a lesson about the country club's unique greenery.

Ty: "I've felt grass like this before. I've played on this stuff."
Carl: "This is a hybrid. This is a cross of Bluegrass, Kentucky Bluegrass, Featherbed Bent, and Northern California Sinsemilla. The amazing stuff about this is that you can play holes on it in the afternoon, take it home, and just get stoned to the bejeezus at night on this stuff. I've got pounds of this stuff."

Dazed and Confused (1993)

Wooderson (Matthew McConaughey) and Pink (Jeremy London) pick up Mitch (Wiley Wiggins) and head out for a night on the town and a late-night kegger.

Wooderson: "Say man, you got a joint?"
Mitch: "Ah, no, not on me, man."
Wooderson: "It'd be a lot cooler if you did."

The Big Lebowski (1998)

The Dude (Jeff Bridges) and Maude (Julianne Moore) are in bed. They're talking about the mysterious case that has brought them together. He picks up a White Russian off the bedside table.

Maude: "Jeffrey …"
Dude: "It's a complicated case, Maude. Lotta ins, lotta outs. Fortunately, I've been adhering to a pretty strict, uh, drug regimen to keep my mind, you know, limber."

American Beauty (1999)

Lester (Kevin Spacey) goes to the house next door to buy pot from his teenage neighbor Ricky (Wes Bentley).

Ricky: "This shit is top of the line. It's called G-13. Genetically engineered by the U.S. Government. Extremely potent. But a completely mellow high, no paranoia."
Lester: "Is that what we smoked last night?"
Ricky: "This is all I ever smoke."
Lester: "How much?"
Ricky: "Two grand."
Lester: "Jesus, things have changed since 1973."

Curb Your Enthusiasm (2005)

Larry (Larry David) is trying to buy marijuana from a street dealer (Jorge Garcia) for his father who has glaucoma.

Dealer: "I can get you an ounce of, you know, some real hydroponic, scientific stuff, but that'll run you five hundred bucks."
Larry: "Hydroponic?"
Dealer: "Yeah."
Larry: "I'm not looking for a sound system, my friend."

The 40-Year-Old Virgin (2005)

As Andy (Steve Carrell) helps Cal (Seth Rogen) carry a new TV set to a customer's car, Cal gives him dating tips.

Jeff Bridges in *The Big Lebowski*

Cal: "You're not gonna get with anyone unless you play the odds on this, man. You need to plant a lot of seeds. It's like this: When I was growing pot, I realized that the more seeds I planted, the more pot I could ultimately smoke."
Andy: "I think I have all the advice that I can handle right now."

Reno 911!: Miami (2007)

The crooked deputy mayor of Miami aims to shoot Lieutenant Dangle and officers Garcia, Wiegel, Kimball, Jones, Johnson, and Junior, but first allows them their last words.

Officer Clementine Johnson: "Legalize it?"

Opposite: Tommy Chong (left) and Cheech Marin (right) in *Up in Smoke*; Right: Rory Cochrane in *Dazed and Confused*

A Brief History of Druggy Dramas

Easy Rider (1969)

Dennis Hopper's apocalyptic hippie-biker flick begins with a coke deal (Hopper cops from Phil Spector) before Hopper (Billy) and Peter Fonda (Wyatt) head east looking for America. They meet Jack Nicholson (George), who smokes a joint with them for the first time; stop at a commune; trip out in New Orleans; and ultimately run afoul of rednecks. It remains the quintessential 1960s counterculture movie.

The Harder They Come (1972)

Jimmy Cliff's breakout role as Ivanhoe Martin in Perry Henzell's gripping island drama was instrumental in importing reggae music and Rastafarian culture from Jamaica to the U.S. Ivanhoe just wants to play music, but mercenary record producers and pot dealers stand in his way. When Ivanhoe kills a cop, he becomes an antihero. As the target of a manhunt, he makes a brave stand. The terrific sound track features the brilliant title song by Cliff.

Apocalypse Now (1979)

Francis Ford Coppola's Vietnam epic put a dagger through the dark heart of that unfortunate war. Willard (Martin Sheen) travels upriver in search of Kurtz (Marlon Brando), a deranged colonel who's become the leader of a Cambodian tribe deep in the jungle. Along the way, the boat is attacked several times, they stop for a U.S.O. show featuring *Playboy* Playmates (and a cameo by impresario Bill Graham), encounter a tiger in the woods, and generally experience the tense environment with nervousness and naiveté, smoking joints and tripping on acid along the way. When they meet Dennis Hopper's raving photographer at the end of the river, there's no turning back.

True Believer (1989)

James Woods plays pot-smoking lawyer Eddie Dodd, who makes his living defending drug dealers. A former civil rights attorney, Dodd takes on the case of a Korean man he believes has been wrongly convicted of murder. Challenged by his straight-laced assistant, Roger (Robert Downey Jr.), Dodd rises to the occasion, finding the spirit he lost along the way.

GoodFellas (1990)

With this film based on Nicholas Pileggi's book *Wiseguy*, Martin Scorsese gave the gangster movie a new counterculture coat of paint. Henry Hill admires the group of Italian-American mobsters growing in his neighborhood and, despite being part Irish-American, eventually joins them. He runs with Jimmy (Robert De Niro) and Tommy (Joe Pesci), two hardened criminals who pull off a $5 million Lufthansa robbery in 1978. When Hill goes to jail, he

Johnny Depp (right) and Benicio Del Toro (left) in *Fear and Loathing in Las Vegas*

begins selling drugs to other inmates. The second half of the movie, fired up by a Rolling Stones sound track including "Gimme Shelter" and "Monkey Man," follows Hill's growing cocaine operation before the walls finally cave in on him and his associates.

Pulp Fiction (1994)

In Quentin Tarantino's ultra-violent, multi-layered masterpiece, Vincent (John Travolta) and Jules (Samuel L. Jackson) are hit men who playfully take on their opponents, until the fun runs out. But what fun it is, especially when Vincent takes Mia (Uma Thurman), the girlfriend of his boss, Marsellus (Ving Rhames), to a dinner club, where they famously win the dance contest. Later that night, when Mia ODs, Vincent frantically revives her—with the help of his reluctant dealer, Lance (Eric Stoltz)—with a shot of adrenalin to the heart.

Fear and Loathing in Las Vegas (1998)

Three years before *Blow*, Johnny Deep stretched his druggy wings portraying Raoul Duke, Hunter S. Thompson's alter ego, in Terry Gilliam's adaptation of Thompson's 1971 book by the same name. Duke and his lunatic sidekick/lawyer Dr. Gonzo (Benicio Del Toro) tear through Las Vegas on a doped-up bender, demolishing their hotel suite in between attempts at covering a dirt-car race Duke has come to write about. While it's all pretty outrageous, the film lacks the slapstick humor of the original novel and the earlier take on Thompson's life, *Where the Buffalo Roam* (1980), starring Bill Murray.

American Beauty (1999)

Sam Mendes's Oscar-winning treatise on suburban angst stars Kevin Spacey (Lester) and Annette Bening (Carolyn) as a married couple on the rocks. Lester expresses his rebellion by smoking pot with his teenage neighbor Ricky (Wes Bentley) and fantasizing about one of his daughter's flirtatious friends Angela (Mena Suvari). Lester's pursuit of pot is a highlight, especially when he buys an overpriced bag of kind bud for $2,000 from Ricky.

Traffic (2000)

Steven Soderbergh's sweeping polemic about the drug war is adapted from the British TV miniseries of the same name (spelled *Traffik*). Stephen Gaghan's Oscar-winning screenplay changed the story to focus on Mexico rather than Pakistan, and on cocaine rather than heroin. Three stories converge: one about new drug czar Robert Wakefield (Michael Douglas) and his druggy daughter Carolyn (Erika Christensen); another about corrupt *federales* in Mexico and one cop (Benicio Del Toro) not on the take; and the third about a drug dealer in San Diego (Steven Bauer) and his wife (Catherine Zeta-Jones) sought by the DEA. By the end, Wakefield quits, telling the press: "If there is a war on drugs, then our own families have become the enemy. How can you wage war on your own family?"

Blow (2001)

Johnny Depp stars as George Jung in Ted Demme's adaptation of Bruce Porter's book about a pot and coke smuggler. The first half is upbeat and cheery until Jung's maiden bust. He emerges from jail friends with Colombians who introduce him to Pablo Escobar, thus beginning his descent into the cocaine underworld. The film also stars Penélope Cruz (Mirtha) as his wild wife, Paul Reubens (Derek) as his partner, and Ray Liotta (Fred) as his father. Sadly, and ironically, Demme died of a cocaine overdose in 2002, shortly after the film's release.

A Scanner Darkly (2006)

Richard Linklater assembled a cast of Hollywood stoners for this adaptation of Philip K. Dick's futuristic novel about an addictive drug and the government's complicity in its widespread use. Keanu Reeves is perfectly cast as the dumbfounded cop, Bob Arctor, who's hooked on Substance D, as are his friends Charles (Rory Cochrane of *Dazed and Confused* fame), James (Robert Downey Jr.), and Donna (Winona Ryder). A hilarious Ernie (Woody Harrelson) is content to just smoke pot. As he did in *Waking Life* (2001), Linklater had every image in the film painted over (a technique called rotoscoping), creating a unique psychedelic tableau.

Johnny Depp in *Blow*

Comedies to Watch While You're Stoned

Monty Python and the Holy Grail (1975)

Based on the hit Brit TV series *Monty Python's Flying Circus* (1969–74), Terry Gilliam and Terry Jones directed this film, their first and best movie. Often nonsensical, but nonetheless hysterical, the original ensemble of John Cleese, Eric Idle, Michael Palin, Graham Chapman, Carol Cleveland, Gilliam, and Jones play knights of King Arthur's round table instructed by God to find the Holy Grail. While they're not quite successful, the laughs keep coming as they travel the countryside. The comedy troupe followed with *Life of Brian* (1979) and *The Meaning of Life* (1983). The cast embarked on solo careers, and Gilliam, Python's animation genius, would go on to direct *Brazil* (1985), *Time Bandits* (1981), *The Adventures of Baron Munchausen* (1988), and *Fear and Loathing in Las Vegas* (1998). In 2005 *Monty Python's Spamalot*, a musical, opened on Broadway.

Animal House (1978)

"Toga, toga!" Directed by Jon Landis (*The Blues Brothers* and *Trading Places*), this *National Lampoon*–produced farce features the late John Belushi, Tim Matheson, Karen Allen, Tom Hulce, Peter Riegert, and Donald Sutherland as the stoner professor. A ragtag fraternity shakes the university to its core with sex, drugs, and rock and roll, and suffers the wrath of the constantly perplexed Dean Wormer (John Vernon), who places them on "double-secret probation" and conspires with the ROTC frat to toss Delta House off campus. "Louie Louie" and "Shout" performed by Otis Day & the Nights never sounded better.

Verna Bloom (left) and Tim Matheson (right) in *Animal House*

Caddyshack (1980)

Two years after cowriting the hilarious *Animal House*, director Harold Ramis (*Stripes*, *Ghostbusters*, *Vacation*, and *Club Paradise*) turned his attention to the wacky exploits, eccentric

characters, and one very persistent gopher at the Bushwood Country Club. Chevy Chase (Ty) plays a golf aficionado with a taste for blondes; Rodney Dangerfield (Al) is an obnoxious club member; and Bill Murray (Carl), when he's not smoking some of his Kentucky bluegrass weed, attempts to rid Bushwood of the tunneling rodents wreaking havoc on the golf course.

Outside Providence (1999)
Cowritten by Peter and Bobby Farrelly (*There's Something About Mary*, *Kingpin*, and *Dumb and Dumber*) and directed by Michael Corrente, this high school comedy set in Providence, Rhode Island, follows Timothy (Shawn Hatosy) and his stoner friends, including a character aptly named Drugs Delaney (Jon Abrahams). Timothy rebels against his working-class dad (Alec Baldwin) who ships him off to a boarding school, where he falls for a stoner chick played by Amy Smart (she also appears in *Road Trip*), who gives him dental roach clips for a graduation present.

Owen Wilson (left) and Ben Stiller (right) in *Zoolander*

Shawn Hatosy in *Outside Providence*

Scary Movie & Scary Movie 2 (2000, 2001)
This series started by the Wayans Brothers hit the mark the first two times around, spoofing the horror-movie genre with the broadest comic brush possible. Shorty (Marlon), the movies' stoner, wears a weed-leaf necklace and, in the second installment, gets rolled up into a massive joint. Besides Marlon and Shawn Wayans, Anna Faris and Regina King appear in both flicks directed by big brother Keenan Ivory Wayans (*I'm Gonna Git You Sucker* and TV's *In Living Color*).

Zoolander (2001)
An inside look at the world of male modeling in which no detail is spared, no matter how ludicrous. Sniveling pretty boy Derek Zoolander (Ben Stiller, who also directs) faces off against his archrival, the hippie-dippie Hansel (Owen Wilson). Ultimately, Hansel brings down evil designer Mugatu (Will Ferrell) and saves the prime minister of Malaysia from being assassinated by Derek.

Super Troopers (2001)
This zany send-up of dopey cops, directed by Jay Chandrasekhar (*Club Dread*, *The Dukes of Hazzard*, and *Beerfest*) pits two troupes of troopers against each other. One runs drugs, the other smokes them. The cast consists of members of the Broken Lizard comedy ensemble. The opening faux pot-bust scene is a classic, as is the scene when the governor of Vermont (played by Lynda Carter) makes a pitch for legalization. *Super Troopers 2* is scheduled to be released in 2008.

The 40-Year-Old Virgin (2005)
Andy (Steve Carrell), who works in an electronics store, has never gotten laid. This is a great source of humor for his fellow employees, David (Paul Rudd), Jay (Romany Malco of *Weeds* fame), and Cal (Seth Rogen), who smokes pot whenever possible. Andy receives a crash course in grooming and partying and, ultimately, falls for Trish (Catherine Keener). It's not the act of Andy finally losing his virginity that makes the movie worthwhile, but rather how he gets there.

Borat: Cultural Learnings of America for Make Benefit Glorious Nation of Kazakhstan (2006)
One of British comedian Sacha Baron Cohen's

three outrageous characters on *Da Ali G Show*, Borat had been embarrassing himself and everyone he came into contact with for two seasons. A faux Kazakh, Borat tours America, making a mess everywhere he goes. The beauty of this mockumentary, directed by Larry Charles (TV's *Curb Your Enthusiasm*), is that Cohen truly fooled people into thinking he was actually Borat, which resulted in legal suits upon the film's release.

Grandma's Boy (2006)

An overgrown videogame-tester, Alex (Allen Covert), moves in with his Grandma Lilly (Doris Roberts) and her two spinster friends. Directed by Nicholaus Goossen, the film is full of silly stoner antics, like when Lilly and pals accidentally get high on Alex's stash and turn a bong into a vase, or when Alex's dealer, Dante, smokes

a fatty with a chimp. It culminates in a geeky gamer showdown during which Lilly saves the day.

Tenacious D in The Pick of Destiny (2006)

From the fertile minds of Jack Black (JB) and Kyle Gass (KG) comes this goof of a rock movie in which they declare their band, Tenacious D, the greatest of all time and seek a magic guitar pick that will help them win a band contest. Along the way, they take plenty of bong hits and, in an animated fantasy scene, JB eats mushrooms and goes on a colorful, *Alice in Wonderland*—style trip.

Trailer Park Boys: The Movie (2006)

Americans have been slow to pick

up on the Canadian comedy phenomenon *Trailer Park Boys*, mostly because the TV series, which this movie is based on, doesn't air in the U.S. (The movie was released in Canada a year before its U.S. release.) But it's time to catch up on the stony antics of Ricky (Robb Wells), Julian (John Paul Tremblay), and Bubbles (Mike Smith), who send up life in a trailer park. Ricky, fresh out of jail, discovers his stripper girlfriend Lucy (Lucy Decoutere) has been banging her boss. He wins her back on the strength of a shotgun hit of B.C. bud. They end up having a trailer park wedding, while cops attempt to arrest them for sundry crimes.

Knocked Up (2007)

Judd Apatow's follow-up to *The 40-Year-Old Virgin* is about schlubby pothead Ben (Seth Rogen), who impregnates an extremely attractive TV personality (Katherine Heigl) during a one-night stand. Ben lives with a group of stoners and inhales bong hits, joints, and even puffs out of a gas mask before he moves out and leaves his smoked-out lifestyle behind.

Kyle Gass (left) and Jack Black (right) in *Tenacious D in The Pick of Destiny*

Stoner Movies to Avoid

Midnight Express (1978)

What happens when you get caught with hash in Turkey? You spend an entire movie in jail. This harrowing screenplay by Oliver Stone is a major bummer until Billy (Brad Davis) escapes from prison.

Rude Awakening (1989)

Cheech Marin and Eric Roberts star in this film about two hippies who escape to a jungle in 1969 to evade the FBI only to reemerge twenty years later and find that all their friends have turned into Yuppies.

The Stoned Age (1994)

A ridiculously hokey attempt to cash in on the success of *Dazed and Confused*, this blasé look at a group of 1970s teenage stoners reveals nothing more than an obsession with Blue Öyster Cult.

Homegrown (1998)

Good cast (Billy Bob Thornton, Hank Azaria, and Ryan Phillippe), bad stoner movie about a bumbling gang of pot growers. The booty goes up in smoke at the end, a definite no-no. Directed by Maggie and Jake Gyllenhaal's dad, Stephen.

Brokedown Palace (1999)

Same story as *Midnight Express*, different country (Thailand). Alice (Claire Danes) takes the rap for Darlene (Kate Beckinsale) when they get busted with heroin.

Saving Grace (2000)

Grace (Brenda Blethyn) has a green thumb. When she gets caught growing pot, the crop becomes a bonfire with neighbors dancing around stoned. Written by *The Late Late Show* host Craig Ferguson.

Dude, Where's My Car? (2000)

Disney-style stoner movie starring dumber (Seann William Scott) and dumbest (Ashton Kutcher), who, uh, get stoned and, uh, can't, uh, find their, uh, hmmm, uh—oh yeah—car!

Waiting… (2005)

Dopey restaurant staff, including Andy Milonakis as a stoner, just want to have fun. Even smooth-talking Ryan Reynolds can't save this lame farce.

Strangers with Candy (2006)

A cult cable show becomes a big-screen movie starring Amy Sedaris's overgrown high schooler Jerry Blank, who tokes, loses it, and trashes a room *Reefer Madness*–style. Not funny, even with a script cowritten by Stephen Colbert.

Kate Beckinsale (left) and Claire Danes (right) in *Brokedown Palace*

Animated Flicks to Watch While You're Stoned

Fantasia (1940)

Multiple stories of mysticism, evolution, and the apocalypse set to classical music masterpieces by Bach (*Toccata and Fugue in D Minor*), Stravinsky (*Rite of Spring*), Tchaikovsky (*Nutcracker Suite*), and Beethoven (*Symphony No. 6*), and illustrated by

Disney's finest animators are trippy from beginning to end, thanks to surreal images of brooms marching and animals dancing. To the strains of Paul Dukas's "The Sorcerer's Apprentice," Mickey Mouse is almost overwhelmed by a flood. Who knew Walt Disney's greatest work would be a stoner favorite all these years later?

Yellow Submarine (1968)

The Beatles battle the Blue Meanies in an attempt to bring love and music back to Pepperland, a paradise deep in the sea. Complete with underwater psychedelia and a killer sound track, George Dunning's classic holds up four decades later. No drugs are taken during the voyage, but you have to be high to enjoy sequences backed by stony Beatles' gems "Lucy in the Sky with Diamonds" and "With a Little Help from My Friends."

Pink Floyd The Wall (1982)

Pink Floyd's epic 1978 rock opera was brought to the silver screen by Alan Parker with glorious visuals (only half animated) that tell the fictional tale of Pink (Bob Geldof), a washed-up rock star who's tortured by memories of his dead father, smothered by his mother, wronged at school, addicted to drugs, and on an out-of-control life spiral. He retreats into a fantasy world of fascism, building and later knocking down the wall in his mind. The sound track includes Floyd classics such as "Comfortably Numb" and "Another Brick in the Wall." ALSO SEE: STONER SYNCHRONICITY (P. 128).

Heavy Metal (1982)

Loosely based on popular storylines from the sci-fi/fantasy magazine of the same name, *Heavy Metal* chronicles the travel and influence of an evil force that is glowing green through multiple dimensions. In a universe populated by interstellar hippie trash-men, warrior women on dragons, zombie WWII air force

fighters, noir hover-taxi drivers, and buxom babes, the emphasis is on sex and violence. This Canadian film, with a sound track by Blue Öyster Cult and Devo, was super trippy for the time, the first hint of the larger world of anime to come.

Beavis and Butt-Head Do America (1996)

The brilliant mind of Mike Judge hatched the animated series about America's favorite couch potatoes, *Beavis and Butt-Head*, an MTV staple from 1993 to 1997. In the movie spin-off, Beavis and Butt-Head road trip around the U.S. Classic drug scenes feature Beavis on peyote and pills, completely losing it, but managing to stay out of protective custody. Judge followed with TV's *King of the Hill* (1997 through the present), *Office Space* (1999), and *Idiocracy* (2006).

Scenes from *Yellow Submarine* (left) and *Heavy Metal* (above)

Sci-Fi Flicks to Watch While You're Stoned

Plan 9 From Outer Space (1959)

Ed Wood's mishmash of an outer space horror flick is complete with cheap effects, utterly baffling editing, and an almost Dadaist script full of zombified performances by a cast full of Z-list stars at the end of their rope. It's so bad it's good.

2001: A Space Odyssey (1968)

Glacially slow and visually stunning, this Stanley Kubrick (A Clockwork Orange and The Shining) classic is the gold standard for depicting the surrealism of space flight. Through the main character's de-evolution from grown man to E.T. space baby, and the all-knowing, all-seeing HAL 9000 computer's schizoid breakdown, your head will spin like the space station headed to Jupiter.

THX 1138 (1971)

George Lucas's dystopian future is an exercise in minimalism, where most sets are vast expanses of white, all characters are either bald in white smocks or faceless head-busting cops, sex is forbidden, and everyone is just a number on mood-altering pills, except for the title character played by Robert Duvall, who stops taking the pills and breaks free. Six years later, Lucas launched his Star Wars franchise.

Star Wars (1977)

Wise-cracking robots, glorious space battles, the ominous Death Star, hyperspace travel, and light sabers (with trails!), plus heroes you can really root for—all intertwined with an epic story of good versus evil. The cast includes Harrison Ford (Han Solo), Mark Hamill (Luke Skywalker), Carrie Fisher (Princess Leia), Alec Guinness (Ben Obi-Wan Kenobi) and, of course, those lovable robots, 3-CPO and R2-D2. Five sequels later, Star Wars remains the benchmark for all American sci-fi.

Close Encounters of the Third Kind (1977)

Steven Spielberg (E.T. the Extra-Terrestrial) keeps his tongue planted firmly in his cheek for most of this movie, until the aliens are unveiled, and then wonderment takes over. Inexplicably drawn to Devil's Tower in Wyoming, where it turns out the government is preparing for a spaceship landing, a manic Richard Dreyfuss (Roy) drives his wife, Ronnie (Teri Garr), and family crazy (he forms the Devil's Tower out of a mound of mashed potatoes) before hitting the road in search of the lost chord (deh dih duh doh deh).

Blade Runner (1982)

Han Solo turns private eye in Ridley Scott's sci-fi noir thriller starring Harrison Ford as replicant hunter Rick and Rutger Hauer as replicant leader Roy in a rainy, futuristic Los Angeles. With its slow pace and dreamy sound track by Vangelis, it's easy to lose yourself in the dense and complicated imagery. The cast also includes Daryl Hannah, Sean Young, and Edward James Olmos.

Keanu Reeves in *The Matrix*
Opposite right: Sigourney Weaver
in *Galaxy Quest*

Dune (1984)

Epic in scope and vision, but hard to follow, the characters on the sandy planet known as Dune spend half the time hallucinating on "spice" (a drug called *mélange*, which is needed for interstellar travel) or manifesting psychic powers. Directed by David Lynch (*Blue Velvet* and TV's *Twin Peaks*) and starring Kyle MacLachlan and Sting, it's creepy, weird, and haunting.

Starship Troopers (1997)

Insectoid aliens! Heavy weaponry! Square-jawed youngsters on a mission to defend humanity! Directed by Paul Verhoeven (*Total Recall* and *Basic Instinct*), this not-so-faithful adaptation of Robert A. Heinlein's novel by the same name mashes up ultraviolent and fascist overtones into a cartoony satire of military and propaganda films.

Galaxy Quest (1999)

The washed-up cast of *Galaxy Quest*, a fictional *Star Trek* knockoff TV show, finds out that aliens really do exist when a band of Thermians, after seeing "historical documents" (or "episodes" as we call them on Earth), recruit the actors to help save their planet. Goofball special effects along with Tim Allen, Sigourney Weaver, and a spaced-out Tony Shalhoub in campy costumes, make this a sleeper worth seeking out.

The Matrix (1999)

Take the red pill and find out that reality is just a sham and all of humanity is being farmed for power to keep intelligent machines alive. Directed by Andy and Larry Wachowski, the film stars Keanu Reeves as Neo, the constantly harassed protagonist; Carrie-Anne Moss as Trinity, his running mate; Laurence Fishburne as fearless leader Morpheus; and Hugo Weaving as Neo's rival, Agent Smith, who has the flexibility of an East German gymnast. Innovative special effects and manic action sequences make the sequels (*The Matrix Reloaded* and *The Matrix Revolutions*) pale by comparison.

Fantasy Flicks to Watch While You're Stoned

The Wizard of Oz (1939)

Iconic in every way and revolutionary for the time, *The Wizard of Oz* remains a classic of psychedelic proportions. From happy-go-lucky munchkins to flying monkeys, the Tin Man, Scarecrow, Cowardly Lion, Wicked Witch of the West, to, of course, the impressionable Dorothy and her little dog, Toto, too, it's a cast of characters as colorful as the land of Oz itself. A spell of poppies puts the gang to sleep as they make their way to the Emerald City. Play the movie simultaneously with Pink Floyd's *Dark Side of the Moon* and get ready for some surreal synergy.

Jason and the Argonauts (1963)

Widely regarded as stop-motion animator Ray Harryhausen's masterpiece, this live-action telling of the Greek myth of Jason and the Golden Fleece features epic battles with clay monsters and a sequence with seven animated skeletons that took four months to shoot. Bernard Hermann's score is an added bonus.

Watership Down (1978)

Who would have thought that an animated film about rabbits in the English countryside could be so dark and violent? But this bloody epic directed by Martin Rosen, about militaristic rabbit warfare and psychic rabbit seers, freaked out countless parents everywhere. Full of muted tones and dense English fog, danger is everywhere and beauty fleeting.

Clash of the Titans (1981)

Loosely based on the Greek myth of Perseus, who must perform a number of near-impossible deeds to please Zeus and the Gods on Mount Olympus, Perseus (Harry Hamlin) tries to save Princess Andromeda (Judi Bowker), while encountering metallic mechanical owls, sea monsters, giant scorpions, and Medusa. The campy cast, directed by Desmond Davis, also includes Laurence Olivier, Claire Bloom, Maggie Smith, Ursula Andress, and Burgess Meredith.

Conan the Barbarian (1982)

Set in a shifting unnamed desert, this swords-and-sorcery classic directed and written by John Milius (he wrote *Apocalypse Now*) stars Arnold Schwarzenegger as Conan and James Earl Jones as the villainous cult leader Thulsa Doom, who commands the army that killed Conan's parents. Equipped with a massive sword, Conan fights off giant snakes, hordes of bad guys, and anything that gets between him and a cup of mead.

The Dark Crystal (1982)

Directed by Jim Henson (*The Muppets*) and Frank Oz (*Little Shop of Horrors*), this involved story is about the redemption of a planet populated by puppets plunged into darkness. Jen, the last of the gentle Gelflings, makes the creepy journey to heal the broken crystal at the precise moment the three suns align, dodging lizardlike Skekses along the way.

Krull (1983)

The Beast and his army of invading Slayers kidnap Princess Lyssa (Lysette Anthony), and Prince Colwyn (Ken Marshall) comes to her rescue. The Beast's Black Fortress, which appears magically in a different place on planet Krull every day, is destroyed in an orgy of explosions and deadpan heroics. Surreal sets designed under the direction of Peter Yates (*Breaking Away*) include visual effects like a spinning five-sided blade and a giant glass spider in a chaotic web.

Legend (1985)

The screen is awash with fairies, elves, and goblins moving through slow-motion snow, endless dark forests, and clouds of flower petals. Shot on blurry

Ian McKellan in *The Lord of the Rings*
Opposite: (left to right) Ray Bolger, Jack Haley, Judy
Garland, and Bert Lahr in *The Wizard of Oz*

film stock, a simple tale of defending a unicorn and rescuing a princess becomes a heady psychedelic experience in the hands of Ridley Scott (*Blade Runner* and *Gladiator*). Tim Curry plays the evil Lord of Darkness with elegant abandon.

Labyrinth (1986)

David Bowie, in full-on 1980s hair-metal mode, plays Jareth the Goblin King who steals the baby brother of Sarah (a fifteen-year-old Jennifer Connelly). Jim Henson provides a tableau of riddles, puzzles, and psychosexual Freudian analogies, centering on Sarah's tortured romance with the king. In one sequence, drugged by a poisoned peach, Sarah is romanced at a masked ball full of romping monsters. Spurning Jareth's advances, she throws a chair through a spherical mirror, undoing the entire reality.

The Lord of the Rings (2001, 2002, 2003)

Peter Jackson's adaptation of J. R. R. Tolkien's epic makes you feel like you're in Middle Earth, riding across the sweeping plains of Rohan or lost in the treacherous mountains of Mordor. The films star Elijah Wood as Frodo, the keeper of the ring; his fellow hobbits, Sam (Sean Astin), Merry (Dominic Monaghan), and Pippin (Billy Boyd); Ian McKellen as the great and powerful Gandolf the Grey; Viggo Mortensen (Aragorn); Orlando Bloom (Legolas Greenleaf); Cate Blanchett (Galadriel); Liv Tyler (Arwen); Ian Holm (Bilbo); and Andy Serkis as the sniveling Gollum. Filmed all at once, this series was conceived as a trilogy, as opposed to one film followed by cash-it-in sequels. A couple of stony scenes occur in the first film, *The Fellowship of the Ring*: Gandolf smokes pipe-weed and the hobbits gobble magic mushrooms as they leave their beloved Shire with the goal of returning the ring to Mordor, and hopefully ending the war that plagues them.

Documentaries

Don't Look Back (1967)

D. A. Pennebaker (*Monterey Pop*) had an all-access pass to Bob Dylan's 1965 British tour and shot the experience guerrilla-style, capturing a sometimes-detached Dylan holding court like a true royal. Wildly influential, like its subject, the black-and-white film is credited with virtually inventing the modern rock documentary.

Heavy Metal Parking Lot (1986)

More of a short than a full-length documentary (the original clocked in at sixteen minutes), the premise is simple: Jeff Krulik and John Heyn took their cameras into the parking lot of a Judas Priest concert in Maryland to ask fans about their love of heavy metal. The result is one of the most important anthropological documents of "wasted youth" ever filmed. Classic line: "My name is Gram, like a gram of dope."

Grass (1999)

Ron Mann's overview of antimarijuana hysteria, narrated by Woody Harrelson, was culled from hours upon hours of amazing antidrug footage and classic newsreels. Featuring hilarious graphics and an excellent sound track, it follows the history of government enforcement from the beginning of the twentieth century to the Clinton era, spending considerable time rhapsodizing about the decriminalization movement of the 1970s.

a/k/a Tommy Chong (2006)

The pot comic spent nine months in jail in 2003 and 2004 for selling bongs. Josh Gilbert documents the government's campaign against Tommy Chong and other paraphernalia companies and also traces the comedian's career back to his days in Vancouver in the late 1960s when he met "Cheech" Marin and the duo took their Cheech & Chong act on the road, ultimately making many albums and movies together. After they split up, Chong found work in television (*That 70s Show*) and started his own company, Chong Glass.

An Inconvenient Truth (2006)

What self-respecting stoner isn't an environmentalist, too? Former vice president and presidential candidate Al Gore has always had a passion for ecology, and this doc by Davis Guggenheim brings Gore's opinions expressed in his 1993 book, *Earth in the Balance*, to the screen. It is primarily a lecture about global warming, but also goes after tobacco for causing the lung-cancer death of his sister.

Above: Grass
Opposite: Bob Dylan (left) and D. A. Pennebaker (right) in *Don't Look Back*

Bob Dylan (left) and D. A.
Pennebaker (right) in
Don't Look Back

Music Movies

Monterey Pop (1968)

The first rock festival movie, directed by D. A. Pennebaker (*Don't Look Back*), shows John and Michelle Phillips of the Mamas and the Papas running the event that would kick off the Summer of Love in 1967. Incendiary performances by Jimi Hendrix and the Who—Hendrix literally lights his Strat on fire and Pete Townsend breaks his in half—top off a stellar lineup that includes Janis Joplin, Jefferson Airplane, Simon & Garfunkel, and the Mamas and the Papas.

Woodstock (1970)

Not the first but still the best festival movie ever made, featuring a who's who of 1960s rock bands and performers including Jimi Hendrix; Sly & the Family Stone; and Crosby, Stills, Nash & Young. Michael Wadleigh captures the counterculture in full flower, with split-screen images and shaky camera interviews. Santana's version of "Soul Sacrifice" in the rain remains a major highlight.

The Last Waltz (1978)

Martin Scorsese (*GoodFellas*) documented the Band's final concert in 1976 featuring Bob Dylan, Neil Young (he's high—just look real close), Eric Clapton, Emmylou Harris, Van Morrison, Neil Diamond, Joni Mitchell, Ringo Starr, and Dr. John. Live performances and fascinating backstage footage tell the melancholy story of the end of one of the era's most revered bands.

This Is Spinal Tap (1984)

Pioneering the mockumentary format, director Rob Reiner takes the laughable behind-the-scenes antics of your average washed-up 1980s hair-metal band to eleven. Starring Michael McKean, Christopher Guest, Harry Shearer, and Reiner himself, with cameos by Paul Simon, Fran Drescher, and Billy Crystal, it's a backstage pass to rock and roll at its funniest.

Dave Chappelle's Block Party (2005)

For several years Dave Chappelle ever so quietly produced a hip-hop concert in Brooklyn. After he left *Chappelle's Show*, he decided to film the concert, with Michel Gondry (*Eternal Sunshine of the Spotless Mind*) directing. Chappelle's taste for conscious hip-hop and R&B—Kanye West, Common, Erykah Badu, Mos Def, the Fugees, and the Roots—takes center stage. But the comedian's narrative and antics, such as importing a high school marching band and random white people from the Midwest, provide laughs to go along with the positive music.

Left: Woodstock event poster
Opposite: (left to right) Michael McKean, Harry Shearer and Christopher Guest in *This Is Spinal Tap*

Must-See Stoner TV

Chappelle's Show, Seasons 1 and 2

For two incredible seasons (2003–2004), Dave Chappelle's skit comedy show was the talk of television. But when it came time to produce the third, Chappelle bolted, shutting down one of the greatest TV comedy series of all time. An unrepentant pot smoker, Chappelle's characters flaunt laws and question authority. His coked-up impersonation of Rick James ("I'm Rick James, bitch!") is particularly memorable. And his musical guests include some of the most conscious hip-hop performers.

Da Ali G Show

Before *Borat*, there was *Da Ali G Show* (2003–2004) featuring Kazakhstani doofus Borat, rabidly gay Austrian reporter Bruno, and the titular faux hip-hop wigger host Ali G—all the brilliant creations of British bad-boy comic Sacha Baron Cohen. Fake news was never more hysterical than in the hands of Ali G, who regularly pranks congressmen, journalists, and astronauts with his dumb-and-dumber questions. Plus, he loves to skin up a spliff, yo. Booyakasha!

Entourage

Living in Hollywood as an A-list actor with boundless cash, starlet girlfriends, and weed at your disposal is the way to be, and Doug Ellin has captured every sight, smell, and sound of this fairy-tale world since the series began in 2004. Loosely based on the real-life experiences of Mark Wahlberg and his cronies back in Boston, Adrien Grenier's posse includes Kevin Connolly, Kevin Dillon, and Jerry Ferrara, who plays Turtle, the crew's hip-hop–digging pothead.

Family Guy

Created by Seth MacFarlane in 1999, this oft-canceled show (in 2000 and again in 2002) focuses on the Griffin family—Peter, Lois, Meg, Chris, and Stewie, plus Brian their talking dog. Like *The Simpsons* before it, *Family Guy* has become a stoner favorite due to its tangential humor and odd characters.

Real Time with Bill Maher

No one on television is more open about marijuana use than Bill Maher. His standard joke is, "The worst thing about pot is it makes you eat cookie dough." During an interview with Jane Fonda on his HBO talk show, he asked, "Ted Turner—pothead?" Fonda responded, "Are you?" Maher paused for a second before declaring, "Well, yeah!" Since 2003 Maher has regularly addressed the issue of marijuana prohibition on this very left-of-center show.

South Park

TV's most irreverent show—animated or otherwise—comes from the creative and

Sacha Baron Cohen of *Da Ali G Show* in 2002

Left: The cast of *Family Guy*
Right: The cast of *Weeds*

controversial minds of Trey Parker and Matt Stone. Since 1997 no issue of the moment has escaped their weekly episodes. Four tykes with dirty mouths—Stan, Kyle, Kenny, and Cartman—get into all kinds of trouble. Only these kids are *really* troublemakers.

The Daily Show with Jon Stewart

The king of "fake news," Jon Stewart has been spinning current events out of control since 1999. Popular correspondents doubling as droll stand-up comics have branched out to movies and sit-coms (Steve Carell, who stars in *The Office*) and their own talk shows (Stephen Colbert's *The Colbert Report*). Like Maher, Stewart tackles thorny drug issues—he just does it with more humor and less anger. Plus, Stewart loves to remind viewers about his cameo in *Half Baked*.

The Sarah Silverman Program

Raunchy, racy, and laugh-out-loud funny, comedian Sarah Silverman not only pushes the envelope, but also every one of your buttons as she navigates the challenges of everyday life. The characters in Silverman's deranged world include her actual sister Laura, gay neighbors played by Brian Posehn and Steve Agee, and a host of random innocents who are regularly confronted by Silverman's crass take on everything and anything that crosses her path. In the pilot episode (2007), Silverman has a minor obsession with cookies, and a major addiction to cough syrup, which causes her to hallucinate in bright, vivid cartoons.

The Simpsons

Stoners love to kick back with a bong and watch cartoons. The most popular animated prime-time TV series ever, *The Simpsons*, springs from the imagination of Matt Groening and the show's clever writing staff. Homer, Marge, Bart, and Lisa are the all-American nuclear family with a twist. Since 1989 the show has skewered popular culture, occasionally sharpening its pencils to comment on controversial subjects such as drugs, usually pot.

Weeds

This critically acclaimed Showtime series, created by Jenji Kohan in 2005, features a main character who deals pot, a first for television, cable, or otherwise. Mary-Louise Parker won Golden Globe and Stony awards for her role as suburban housewife Nancy Botwin, chief supplier of fictional Agrestic, California, with local councilman Kevin Nealon (Doug) playing one of her regular customers. Pot, the PTA, and politics? Perfect.

A Brief History of Classic Stoner TV

(Left to right) Leonard Nimoy, William Shatner, and James Doohan in *Star Trek*

Get Smart (1965–70)

James Bond meets the Pink Panther in this satire created by comic geniuses Mel Brooks and Buck Henry about a bumbling undercover agent Maxwell Smart (Don Adams) and his understanding and understated female partner, Agent 99 (Barbara Feldon). Physical comedy and absurd plots keep Smart (Agent 86) and 99 busy foiling the evildoings of their nemesis organization, KAOS, which is led by Siegfried (Bernie Koppell). Outfitted with futuristic Bond-like gadgetry

(the shoe phone, for instance) that never work as planned, the dimwitted 86 is usually saved by the superior intelligence and cunning of 99. Look for reruns of the 138 half-hour episodes on TV Land and other cable channels, and a feature-length movie adaptation starring Steve Carell and Anne Hathaway in 2008.

The Monkees (1966–68)

For three years, the Monkees were America's answer to the Fab Four. Their half-hour NBC sitcom, partly based on the Beatles' hit movies *A Hard Day's Night* and *Help*, features mop-tops Davy Jones, Micky Dolenz, Michael Nesmith, and Peter Tork, and was the first exposure for many Americans to psychedelic sounds and fashions. Endlessly silly and perhaps a little repetitive (how many times can you watch these guys get chased by screaming girls), the show may look dated, but the music ("Daydream Believer" and "Last Train to Clarksville") still rocks.

Star Trek (1966–69)

Gene Roddenberry's novel series about space exploration earned its own cult of Trekkies, and was followed by ten big-screen movie adaptations and other variations, such as *Star Trek: The Next Generation* (1987–94). But *Star Trek* was never better than during its four-year, eighty-episode run on NBC. Captain Kirk (William Shatner) and the pointy-eared logician Mr. Spock (Leonard Nimoy) hold together the starship *Enterprise* crew that also includes Scottie (James Doohan), Dr. McCoy (DeForest Kelley), Uhuru (Nichelle Nichols), and Sulu (George Takei). Classic Kirk line: "Beam me up, Scottie!"

The Smothers Brothers Comedy Hour (1967–70)

Before *Laugh-In* and Dick Cavett, Smothers Brothers Tom and Dick turned TV on its ear with on-air Vietnam protests and other controversies over censorship that would eventually lead to the variety show's cancellation by CBS. The folk duo/comedians played

(Left to right) Micky Dolenz, Davy Jones, Peter Tork, and Michael Nesmith in *The Monkees*

to the burgeoning youth culture with hip guests like Steve Martin, Rob Reiner, and Pat Paulsen, and even hipper bands like the Who, Jefferson Airplane, and Cream. One recurring performer, Leah French, was the show's resident hippie best known for the skit, "Share a Little Tea with Goldie."

The Dick Cavett Show (1968–72)

Dick Cavett was the Charlie Rose of his day, but way hipper and wittier. He liked to wear turtlenecks and keep the set informal which helped when he had notoriously media-shy guests like John Lennon and Yoko Ono, who were repeat visitors, and Salvador Dalí, who made his entrance holding an anteater on a leash. Where most talk shows book musical acts solely for the purpose of closing out the program, Cavett was famous for putting his rock-and-roll guests on the couch and chatting with them. Just hours after the Woodstock festival, he had Jefferson Airplane, David Crosby, and Steve Stills on the show. An outlet for many voices in the American counterculture of the 1960s and 1970s, this ninety-minute show is as fascinating to watch today (on DVD) as it was the first time.

Rowan & Martin's Laugh-In (1968–73)

No TV show reflected the counterculture outbreak of the late 1960s better than *Laugh-In*, courtesy of the stand-up comedy team of Dan Rowan and Dick Martin. Totally slapstick and full of colorful Pop Art and flower-power imagery, the show introduced Goldie Hawn and featured a wacky cast that included Judy Carne, Arte Johnson, Ruth Buzzi, Jo Anne Worley, and Alan Sues. They routinely roasted Nixon, and when the doors swung open to the weekly party scene, it turned positively groovy, baby.

M*A*S*H (1972–83)

Set in a Mobile Field Hospital during the Korean War, this much-loved and long-running half-hour show (249 episodes) flips from serious to funny in a heartbeat. Though based in comedy, M*A*S*H tackles the futility and human cost of war. Most of the story lines are actually taken from interviews with real medics, who attest to the shenanigans that went on and the amount of partying people did to let off steam. Based on Robert Altman's 1970 movie, the TV version stars Alan Alda as Hawkeye Pierce, Loretta Swit as Hot Lips Houlihan, and Harry Morgan as Colonel Potter. The final episode is still the most viewed show in American TV history with 77 percent of the population tuning in.

Saturday Night Live (1975–present)

Saturday Night Live had its heyday on NBC in the 1970s and 1980s, faltered in the 1990s, and came back in a big way in the twenty-first century with a stellar ensemble that has included Will Ferrell, Amy Poehler, Jimmy Fallon, and Tina Fey. This cast gave birth to

George Harrison (left) and Dick Cavett (right) on *The Dick Cavett Show* in 1971

recurring skits like "Jared's Room," featuring Horatio Sanz as the bong-ripping Gobi. And whenever there's a marijuana-related story on "Weekend Update," Poehler delivers the stony punch line. "Lazy Sunday," a faux hip-hop video that features Andy Samberg and Chris Parnell rapping about cupcakes and "the Chronic-what-cles of Narnia," became one of the most viewed clips on YouTube. Fans of *Saturday Night Live*'s early years with Chevy Chase, John Belushi, Billy Murray, and Gilda Radner can always find classic shows on cable networks like E!

SCTV (1976–82)

Before Canada had the *Trailer Park Boys*, there was *Second City TV*, or simply *SCTV*, the funniest sketch-comedy TV show of all time. Not to knock *Saturday Night Live*, but for thirty-five episodes over seven years, the Canadians had the edge over the Americans on Saturday nights, when the two shows ran back-to-back (*SCTV* followed SNL). Consider the cast: John Candy, Eugene Levy, Martin Short, Catherine O'Hara, Andrea Martin, Joe Flaherty, and Dave Thomas. *SCTV* is about a fictional TV station in Western Canada that's, let's say, less than professionally operated. But it's the dead-on impersonations and unique characters (Short's Ed Grimley or O'Hara's Lola Heatherton) that set the show apart. All the episodes, available on DVD, are highly recommended.

Twin Peaks (1990–91)

Freaky, surreal, and dense, *Twin Peaks* brought out the inner geek in countless stoners of the early 1990s when the David Lynch–created "dramedy" became a national phenomenon. But somewhere along the plot line, this murder mystery set in a small border town in northwest Washington state turned into a tale of intense psychodrama and unexplainable paranormal subtexts that even the most passionate of followers could not decipher, perhaps leading to its cancellation after just two seasons.

Stoner-Friendly Cartoons

Aqua Teen Hunger Force

The hottest show on Comedy Central's late-night "Adult Swim" lineup, Matt Maiellaro and Dave Willis's *Aqua Teen Hunger Force* has hit a chord with munched-out stoners (since 2000) caught up in the zany adventures of three fast-food–themed characters: Frylock, Meatwad, and Master Shake. After six seasons, the show hit the big screen in 2007 with the aptly named *Aqua Teen Hunger Force Colon Movie Film for Theaters.*

Beavis and Butt-Head

The brainchild of Dallas-based animator and director Mike Judge (*Office Space*) was a sensation for MTV from 1993 to 1997, comprising 199 ingenious half-hour episodes following the dopey exploits of two metalhead/couch potatoes who have way too much spare time on their hands. The TV show was spun off into the movie, *Beavis and Butt-Head Do America*, in 1996.

Scooby-Doo

This classic from the Hanna-Barbara animation studio has united generations since first appearing on CBS in 1969. Featuring a dog (Scooby-Doo) and his loyal friends who travel around the country in their van known as the "mystery machine," the show has gone through changes over the years, but one thing that's remained constant is Scooby's beatnik best bud Shaggy (considered to be one of the first TV stoners), who always wears a green T-shirt and bell-bottoms and has an insatiable appetite for "scooby snacks." In the 2002 movie, Shaggy (played by Matthew Lillard) meets his dream girl, Mary Jane.

SpongeBob SquarePants

He's a talking sponge that wears pants and lives in a pineapple deep in the Pacific Ocean "town" of Bikini Bottom. Thanks to *SpongeBob's* trippy deep-sea characters and scenery, the cartoon created by marine biologist and animator Stephen Hillenburg and intended for an audience of seven-year-old kids has become a stoner staple since it premiered on Nickelodeon in 1999.

The Ren & Stimpy Show

A 1990s Nickelodeon success story, Canadian animator John Kricfalusi brought the dog and cat team of Ren Hoek (a chihuahua) and Stimpson J. Cat (a, um, cat) to television. Brilliantly drawn and colored, these two rascals captured the imagination of children and adults alike from 1991 to 1996, paving the way for adult-themed cartoon series to follow.

Scenes from *The Ren & Stimpy Show* (above) and *SpongeBob SquarePants* (right)

Stoniest Simpsons Episodes

"Homer's Barbershop Quartet"
Date Aired: September 30, 1993
Written By: Jeff Martin

Homer to Bart: "What'd you kids get?"
Bart: "I bought this cool pencil holder."
Homer: "Heh-heh, far out, man. I haven't seen a bong in years."

"Lemon of Troy"
Date Aired: May 14, 1995
Written By: Brent Forrester

Abe: "It all began when Jebediah Springfield first came to these lands with his partner, Shelbyville Manhattan . . ."
[Flash to pilgrims approaching a hilltop]
Jebediah: "People, our search is over! On this site we shall build a new town where we can worship freely, govern justly, and grow vast fields of hemp for making rope and blankets."

Pop culture icon
Homer Simpson

"Thirty Minutes Over Tokyo"
Date Aired: May 16, 1999
Written By: Donick Cary and Dan Greaney

[In the airport, each of the Simpsons is dressed in the clothes of the place they hope to be going]
Marge: "Hawaii, here we come!"
Lisa: "No, no! We're going to Paris, I can feel it!"
Bart: "Come on, Transylvania."
Homer: "No, mon, let's go home to Jamaica. I been in Babylon too long. I want to pass the dutchie on the left-hand side!"

"Bart to the Future"
Date Aired: March 19, 2000
Written By: Dan Greaney

Lisa [as president] to Bart: "What can I do to thank you?"
Bart: "Legalize it."
Lisa: "Legalize what?"
Bart: [smiles]
Lisa: "Ohhh, oh. Consider it done."

"Weekend at Burnsie's"
Date Aired: April 7, 2002
Written By: Jon Vitti

Entire episode is about Homer's use of medical marijuana.

Stoner Bands

Black Crowes: Like Cypress Hill, they spearheaded the bands-for-weed movement of the 1990s. Lead singer Chris Robinson wore pot-leaf pants, a huge leaf was unfurled during shows, and they cleverly marketed Black Crowes custom rolling papers for each tour.

Cypress Hill: They were named NORML's spokesband in 1992 and have always flown the pot leaf high. In concert, a large smoking plastic Buddha sits onstage and during their lengthy weed-song segment, they break out bongs and joints.

Kottonmouth Kings: Following Cypress Hill's lead, this hip-hop/punk-rock ensemble probably push the weed envelope more than any band with their string of pot-themed albums, and stony stage antics including fake pot plants, a huge smoking joint, and the vaporizing "Visual Assassin" Pakelika.

Sublime: Though lead singer Brad Nowell died of a drug overdose in 1996, this So-Cal ska-punk trio are revered by potheads many years after the group broke up. Their versions of "Smoke Two Joints" and "Legalize It" are cannabis classics.

311: These longtime pot advocates form a trifecta with Cypress Hill and the Black Crowes, who all came up in the early 1990s. They often encore with "Who's Got the Herb?" and use pot-leaf lighting effects to highlight their support.

Sublime—(left to right) Eric Wilson, Brad Nowell, and Bud Gaugh—in 1995

A Brief History
of the Greatest Marijuana Songs

"I Like Marijuana," *Have a Marijuana* (1968)
David Peel & the Lower East Side
Based on the singsong "Peanut Butter" (by the Marathons, 1961), Peel was the first musician to openly extol marijuana in song on his pot-obsessed debut album.

Ozzy Osbourne in 1998

Pot Lyric: "I like marijuana / You like marijuana / We like marijuana too."

"Don't Bogart Me," *Fraternity of Man* (1968)
Fraternity of Man
Generally known as "Don't Bogart That Joint" because of the lyric, "Don't bogart that joint, my friend / Pass it over to me," written by the band that included former and future members of Frank Zappa & the Mothers of Invention and Little Feat. Inclusion on the *Easy Rider* sound track (1969) catapulted the song to infamy.

Pot Lyric: "Rooooooooooll another one / Just like the other one."

"One Toke Over the Line," *Tarkio Road* (1970)
Brewer & Shipley
Folksy duo hit the Top 10 (No. 10) with this catchy tune that popularized the word "toke," for a drag of pot on a joint or pipe. The title presumably means that the song's protagonist had one puff too many.

Pot Lyric: "Awaitin' for the train that goes home, sweet Mary / Hopin' that the train is on time / Sittin' downtown in a railway station / One toke over the line."

"Sweet Leaf," *Master of Reality* (1971)
Black Sabbath
The classic heavy metal ode to marijuana is the first

track on this album, written by the band with lyrics by Ozzy Osbourne.

Pot Lyric: "Straight people don't know what you're about / Soon the world will love you, sweet leaf."

"Panama Red," *The Adventures of Panama Red* (1973)
New Riders of the Purple Sage
This Grateful Dead side project became its own band and devoted an entire album to the exploits of a smuggler named Panama Red. The lead track, written by Peter Rowan, tells about a red-haired rogue who will, "steal your woman, then rob your head." Also recorded by Old and In the Way, featuring Jerry Garcia, in 1975.

Pot Lyric: "Nobody feels like workin' / Panama Red is back in town."

"Legalize It," *Legalize It* (1976)
Peter Tosh
The lead track on this album says it all: "Legalize it, don't criticize it." Tosh was a former member of Bob Marley and the Wailers and also cowrote "Get Up, Stand Up" (1973) with Marley.

Pot lyric: "Doctors smoke it / Nurses smoke it / Judges smoke it / Even the lawyers too."

Peter Tosh blazes on stage in 1978

"Mary Jane," *Come Get It!* (1978)
Rick James
Love ballad to James's favorite lady, the smokeable variety, plays with double entendres. It's been sampled and covered by numerous hip-hop artists.

Pot Lyric: "I'm in love with Mary Jane / She's my main thing / She makes me feel all right / She makes my heart sing."

"Pass the Dutchie," *The Youth of Today* (1982)
Musical Youth
Cover version of "Pass the Kutchie" changed the song title to the less offensive "dutchie." It was a Top 10 (No. 10) hit for the British teens.

Pot Lyric: "Pass the dutchie on the left-hand side."

"Smoke Two Joints," *The Toyes* (1983)
The Toyes
Reggae-tinged song written and originally performed by the Portland, Oregon–based Kay Brothers (Mawg and Sky) humorously describes smoking not one, but two joints on virtually every occasion. It was covered by Sublime on their debut album, *40 Oz. to Freedom* (1992).

Pot lyric: "I smoke two joints in the morning / I smoke two joints at night / I smoke two joints in the afternoon / It makes me feel all right."

"Hash Pipe," *Weezer* (2001)
Weezer
Rivers Cuomo took Weezer fans by surprise when he devoted a song to a piece of paraphernalia. The lyrics are obtuse at best, rhyming "ass wipe" with hash pipe. The song dented the Top 40 (No. 31) and is played at the end of *The Marijuana-Logues* show.

Pot lyric: "I've got my hash pipe."

179

Favorite Stony Lyrics

"La Cucaracha" (early 20th century):
This traditional Mexican song was popularized by Pancho Villa's army during his country's revolution.

Stony Lyric: "La cucaracha ya no puede caminar, porque no tiene porque lefalta marihuana por fumar" [The cockroach can't walk anymore, because he doesn't have any marijuana to smoke].

"Rainy Day Women #12 & 35,"
Blonde on Blonde (1966)
Bob Dylan
Dylan brazenly sang about getting stoned on this hit that rose to No. 2 on the charts.

Stony Lyric: "But I would not feel so all alone / Everybody must get stoned."

"Light My Fire," *The Doors* (1967)
The Doors
The Doors' first and biggest hit broke all kinds of barriers with its nearly seven-minute length and suggestive subject matter.

Stony Lyric: "Girl, we couldn't get much higher."

"The Pusher," *Steppenwolf* (1968)
Steppenwolf
This grungy track first appeared on Steppenwolf's self-titled debut album and on the *Easy Rider* sound track in 1969.

Stony Lyric: "You know I've smoked a lot of grass / Oh Lord, I've popped a lot of pills."

"Coming into Los Angeles,"
Running Down the Road (1969)
Arlo Guthrie
Woody Guthrie's son made a name for himself with songs like this one as well as his more famous "Alice's Restaurant Massacree" (1967).

Stony Lyric: "Bringing in a couple of keys / Don't touch my bags if you please / Mr. Customs Man."

"Illegal Smile," John Prine (1971)
John Prine
The lead track of his debut album remains one of the folk singer's most beloved songs.

Stony Lyric: "And you may see me tonight with an illegal smile / It don't cost very much, but it lasts a long while."

"Taxi," *Heads & Tales* (1972)
Harry Chapin
The emotional centerpiece of Chapin's second album imagined what it was like to drive a big yellow taxi . . . on weed.

Stony Lyric: "Taking tips, and getting stoned / I go flying so high, when I'm stoned."

"Late in the Evening," *One Trick Pony* (1980)
Paul Simon
Simon-sans-Garfunkel's nod to pot.

Stony Lyric: "And I stepped outside and smoked myself a jay."

"Champagne & Reefer," *King Bee* (1981)
Muddy Waters
The blues singer's ode to his two favorite intoxicants was covered by Ian Moore on *Hempilation 2: Free the Weed* (1995).

Stony Lyric: "Bring me champagne when I'm thirsty / Bring me reefer when I want to get high."

"I Wanna Get High," *Black Sunday* (1993)
Cypress Hill
Using a sample from "One Draw" (written by Bob Marley and performed by his wife Rita in 1981), Cypress Hill added their own lyrics to go along with the Marley chorus.

Stony Lyric: "I want to get high, so high."

"Gin and Juice," *Doggystyle* (1993)
Snoop Dogg
When he was still known as Snoop Doggy Dogg, this was the L.A. rapper's breakout hit (No. 8).
    Stony Lyric: "Rollin' down the street, smokin' indo / Sippin' on gin and juice."

"Low," *Kerosene Hat* (1993)
Cracker
David Lowery left Camper Van Beethoven to form the band Cracker. Their only hit topped off at No. 64.
    Stony Lyric: "Hey hey hey, like being stoned."

"You Don't Know How It Feels,"
Wildflowers (1994)
Tom Petty
Petty's last Top 20 single (No. 13) clearly demonstrates the singer's stance on weed.
    Stony Lyric: "Let's get to the point / Let's roll another joint."

"Champagne Supernova,"
(What's the Story) Morning Glory? (1995)
Oasis

The final epic track on Oasis's sophomore album is more than seven minutes long.
    Stony Lyric: "Where were you while we were getting high?"

"Killer Weed,"
The Sauce (2004)
Eddie Spaghetti
The Super-suckers's lead singer/guitarist has a knack for writing great pot songs.
    Stony Lyric: "I got some killer weed / It's exactly what you need."

Snoop Dogg, with blunt, in 2002

The Greatest Pot-Themed Album Covers

Have a Marijuana

David Peel & the Lower East Side (1968):
First photo of a pot plant on the cover of an album.

Catch a Fire

Bob Marley and the Wailers (1973):
Tuff Gong smokes a humongous spliff on
this classic album cover.

Toledo Window Box

George Carlin (1974):
Counterculture comic shows his true colors,
pointing to a T-shirt with pot planted in the so-
called "Toledo Window Box." On the back cover,
a stoned-looking Carlin wears a shirt with all
the leaves trimmed off the plant.

Big Bambu

Cheech & Chong (1972):
Famous takeoff on the Bambu rolling paper pack, it
includes a 10 × 18" faux rolling paper tucked inside.

Good High

Brick (1976):
Lead singer Jimmy "Lord" Brown poses with
a kilo package of weed featuring the band's
logo and a pot-leaf pattern.

Fire It Up

Rick James (1979):
The funky maestro smokes a joint on his second album while wearing thigh-high white boots and a cowboy hat. The inner sleeve glossary of terms defines "Mary Jane" as "Cannabis delectus, 'ummmmmmmmmm good.'"

Road Island

Ambrosia (1982):
The Los Angeles–based pop-rock band known for hits like "Biggest Part of Me" (1980) hired Ralph Steadman to illustrate its fifth album. Hunter S. Thompson's favorite artist included a large sativa leaf, snapped off from its tree-length stem.

Skull & Bones

Cypress Hill (2000):
Hip-hop's stoniest band's fifth album features its trademark upside-down pot leaf painted on a skull.

Legalize It

Peter Tosh (1976):
Reggae star smokes his pipe in a Jamaican pot field.

The Chronic

Dr. Dre (1992):
The 1990s version of *Big Bambu* is a takeoff on the Zig-Zag rolling paper image of the French smoker set inside a mirror frame. Inside, the CD is adorned with a pot leaf.

Countryman

Willie Nelson (2005):
The stony star of country music waited until he was seventy-two to plaster a pot leaf on one of his albums, which happens to be devoted to reggae.

Blunted Hip-Hop Classics

"Cheeba Cheeba," *Loc-ed After Dark* (1989) by **Tone Loc**: On his No. 1 debut album *Loc-ed After Dark* featuring "Wild Thing" and "Funky Cold Medina," the gruff-voiced L.A. rapper was among the first to praise the herb in song.

Weed Lyric: "When it comes to smokin' cheeba / You know my shit is legit."

"How to Roll a Blunt," *Whut? Thee Album* (1992) by **Redman**: New Jersey's "Funk Doc" jumped on the blunt bandwagon with this instructional song on his CD debut.

Weed Lyric: "Seal it, dry it wit ya lighter if ya gotta / The results, mmmmmmmm . . . proper."

"Take Two and Pass," *Daily Operation* (1992) by **Gang Starr**: The Brooklyn duo—Guru and DJ Premier—were quick to recognize the weed explosion in hip-hop, including this song on their third joint.

Weed Lyric: "Take two and pass / So the blunt will last."

"Pack the Pipe," *Bizarre Ride II the Pharcyde* (1992), **The Pharcyde**: Alternative L.A. rappers took a distinctly humorous approach on their debut CD when it came to documenting their favorite way to smoke.

Weed Lyric: "The bud is just the tasty tantalizer / The bud not the beer 'cause the bud makes me wiser."

"Hits from the Bong," *Black Sunday* (1993) by **Cypress Hill**: On their second album, Los Angeles' hip-hop hempsters declared their love for all things marijuana, while steering away from blunts with a more enlightened outlook. It follows the "Legalize It" spoken-word interlude.

Weed Lyric: "Goes down smooth when I get a clean hit / Of the skunky, phunky, smelly green shit."

"Many Clouds of Smoke," *Total Devastation* (1993) by **Total Devastation**: San Francisco rap group followed Cypress Hill's activist lead with a debut album full of pot songs, the best of which is this single that hit the R&B charts.

Weed Lyric: "I want to get blunted my brother / Roll up a fat one pass it around."

"Indo Smoke," *Poetic Justice* sound track (1993) by **Mista Grimm**: One of three singles released from the movie that stars Tupac and Janet Jackson, this joint was recorded by a protégé of Warren G, who wrote, produced, and rapped on the track, which hit No. 56 on the pop charts.

Weed Lyric: "And that's no joke / Because Mista Grimm takes flight from the indo smoke."

"I Got 5 on It," *Operation Stackola* (1995) by **The Luniz**: Oakland-based rappers Yukmouth and Knumskull had a No. 8 hit with this ode to a dime bag of weed on their debut CD.

Weed Lyric: "I got five on it / Potna, let's go half on a sack."

"Mad Izm," *Station Identification* (1995) by **Channel Live**: Brooklyn duo—Hakim and Tuffy— were joined by KRS-One for this moderate pot hit (No. 54) off their debut CD.

Weed Lyric: "Wake up in the morning got the yearning for herb / Which loosens up the nouns, metaphors, and verbs."

"Hay," *The Final Tic* (1996) by **Crucial Conflict**: Chicago hip-hoppers had a one-hit wonder (No. 18) with this rollicking rural rap track.

Weed Lyric: "Smokin' on / Haaayy in the middle of the barn."

"Blueberry Yum Yum," *The Red Light District* (2004) by **Ludacris**: This Atlanta-based rapper spent significant time in Amsterdam, hence the album title and his tribute to sweet-smelling Blueberry buds.

Weed Lyric: "Get ya lighters, roll the sticky, let's get high."

Cypress Hill—(left to right) B-Real, Sen Dog and DJ Muggs—circa 1991

Ganja Reggae Classics

"Legalize It," *Legalize It* (1976) by **Peter Tosh**: The No. 1 marijuana song of all time is a reggae classic by virtue of the power of its enduring and hopefully attainable message.

Ganja Lyric: "Doctors smoke it / Nurses smoke it / Judges smoke it / Even the lawyers too."

"Kaya," *Kaya* (1977) by **Bob Marley**: The reggae legend named an album and song after marijuana, which he called "kaya."

Ganja Lyric: "Got to have kaya now / Kaya, kaya."

"Macka Splaff," *Handsworth Revolution* (1978) by **Steel Pulse**: British group headed by David Hinds misspelled spliff on this track from their debut CD.

Ganja Lyric: "Mister collie, collie collie man / Me want some herbs to smoke tonight."

"The International Herb," *International Herb* (1979) by **Culture**: Song written and sung by the late Joseph Hill, it is similar in spirit and style to "Legalize It."

Ganja Lyric: "I took a spliff this morning of the international herb / It make I feel so groovy, man / It gives me explanation in music, man / So dats why I can't refuse it, man."

"Sinsemilla," *Sinsemilla* (1980) by **Black Uhuru**: Penned by Michael Rose, this was the first song to acknowledge the evolution of marijuana from seeded to seedless.

Ganja Lyric: "I've got a stalk of sinsemilla growing in my backyard."

"One Draw," *Who Feels It Knows It* (1981) by **Rita Marley**: Written by Bob Marley for his wife the year he died, the opening line was later sampled by Cypress Hill on "I Wanna Get High."

Ganja Lyric: "Hey Rastaman, hey whatcha say / Give mi some of your sensi."

"Pass the Kutchie," *Changes* (1982) by the **Mighty Diamonds**: Originally recorded by this Jamaican group the same year the U.K.–based Musical Youth had an international hit with it.

Ganja Lyric: "Pass da kutchie pon da left hand side."

"Under Mi Sensi," *Here I Come* (1985) by **Barrington Levy**: Early dancehall DJ followed Black Uhuru's lead on this catchy track. The song was covered by the Long Beach Dub Allstars on *Hempilation 2: Free the Weed*.

Ganja Lyric: "Hey, Babylon, you no like ganja man / But we bring da foreign currency pon di island."

"We Be Burnin'," *The Trinity* (2005) by **Sean Paul**: Sequel to the dancehall star's "Gimme the Light" (2002), it was censored because of its pro-marijuana lyrics and hit No. 7 on the charts.

Ganja Lyric: "Legalize it, time to recognize it."

"Iron Bars," *Mind Control* (2007) by **Stephen Marley**: Bob Marley's second son sings about being busted and jailed for marijuana possession with his younger brother Julian in 2002.

Ganja Lyric: "Let me out, let me out / I'm an angry lion."

Bob Marley relaxes with a
spliff in Kingston
Opposite: Peter Tosh (left)
and Bunny Wailer (right)
in Jamaica in 1978

Willie Nelson takes a hit

Cannabis Country Classics

"Shanty," *Jonathan Edwards* (1971) by **Jonathan Edwards**: Minnesota folkie went country for this song about hanging around the cabin getting stoned.

Herbal Lyric: "Well, pass it to me baby / Pass it to me slow / Cuz we gonna lay around the shanty, mama / And put a good buzz on."

"Wildwood Weed," *Jim Stafford* (1974) by **Jim Stafford**: Performed as "Wildwood Flowers" by the Carter Family, Stafford changed the title of the tune written by Don Bowman and popularized it as a pot song.

Herbal Lyric: "Smokin' them wildwood flowers got to be a habit / We didn't see no harm / We thought it was kind of handy / Take a trip and never leave the farm."

"Me and Paul," *Me and Paul* (1985) by **Willie Nelson**: Though he's known for his marijuana advocacy, Nelson rarely sings about it. But on this song, which also appeared on *Hempilation 2: Free the Weed* (1998) as a live version, he refers to a run-in with the police.

Herbal Lyric: "Almost busted in Laredo / But for reasons that I'd rather not disclose."

"The Dope Smokin' Song" (1998) by **Hank Flamingo**: This offbeat track by the Nashville singer was recorded live especially for *Hempilation 2: Free the Weed*.

Herbal Lyric: "Let's all get stoned and listen to George Jones."

"Weed with Willie," *Shock'n Y'all* (2003) by **Toby Keith**: Famous for his personal marijuana stash, Willie Nelson invited Keith to give it a try. Keith barely survived and wrote this humorous song about the experience.

Herbal Lyric: "I always heard that his herb was top shelf / And Lord I just could not wait to find out for myself / Don't knock it till you tried it / Well, I tried it, my friend / I'll never smoke weed with Willie again."

"Grandma," *A Lil Sump'm Sump'm* (2005) by **Jon Nicholson**: Nashville-style singer's poignant song about getting his grandmother high at a ripe old age.

Herbal Lyric: "Sittin' here old as I am / And never been stoned / I waited too damn long / So bring it on / Grandma's gonna fly."

Cab Calloway leads his big band

Reefer Jazz Classics

"Muggles" (1928) by **Louis Armstrong**: A jazz-era euphemism for weed, this smokin' instrumental was recorded in 1928 by trumpeter Armstrong with Earl "Fatha" Hines on piano. It was named after Armstrong's favorite substance, which he claimed was a medicine and generated warm feelings between him and other vipers.

"Reefer Man" (1932) by **Cab Calloway and his Orchestra**: The "Hi-De-Ho Man" himself was probably high when he recorded this weed anthem back in 1932. A year later, the flamboyant singer/bandleader performed the song in the movie *International House*. It's the first tribute to a pot dealer, a theme Calloway returned to in "The Man from Harlem." Another early jazz big-band leader, Don Redman, covered "Reefer Man," as did the long-forgotten group Baron Lee & the Blue Rhythm Band.

Reefer Lyric: "Have you ever met that funny reefer man?"

"Sweet Marijuana" (1934) by **Gertrude Michael**: Michael debuted this enchanting Latin tune in the film *Murder at the Vanities* (1934) in a risqué dance number featuring topless chorus girls. Julia Lee not only updated the song, but renamed it "Lotus Blossom." Years later, Bette Midler camped it up under the title "Marahuana" on *Songs for a New Depression* (1976).

Reefer Lyric: "Soothe me with your caress / Sweet marijuana, oh marijuana / Help me in my distress."

"If You're A Viper" (1938) by **Stuff Smith & his Onyx Club Boys**: Originally recorded in 1938 by violinist Smith, this delightful ode to potheads, then called vipers by jazz cats, was written by Rosetta Howard, Horace Malcolm, and Herbert Moren, and also recorded by Rosetta Howard and Bob Howard (separately) and then renamed "The Reefer Song" by pianist Fats Waller for his 1943 version. The original is alternately called "You're a Viper" and "If You'se a Viper," and namechecks Mezz Mezzrow, the notorious pot dealer to the jazz stars. It was revived by Manhattan Transfer ("You're a Viper," 1969) and by former MC5 guitarist Wayne Kramer ("If You're a Viper" on *Hempilation 2: Free the Weed*, 1998).

Reefer Lyric: "I dreamed about a reefer five foot long / The mighty mezz but not too strong / I'll be high but not for long / If you're a viper."

"Viper Mad" (1938) by **Sidney Bechet & Noble Sissle's Swingsters**: The first jazz musician to popularize the soprano saxophone, by 1938, Bechet was just another self-confessed viper praising the almighty herb in song. He blew hot on this tune and was accompanied by Noble Sissle's Swingsters.

Reefer Lyric: "Wrap your chops 'round this stick of tea / Blow this gage and get high with me."

Famous Pot Busts

Actor Robert Mitchum at his sentencing for marijuana-possession charge in 1948

Louis Armstrong

When: 1931
Where: Los Angeles
Amount: An unknown number of marijuana joints
Verdict: Guilty
Sentence: Nine days in jail
FYI: Arrest outside jazz club was the first-known celebrity pot bust.

Robert Mitchum

When: 1948
Where: Los Angeles
Amount: Marijuana joints
Verdict: Guilty, but conviction overturned in 1951
Sentence: Sixty days in jail
FYI: The sting that reeled in Mitchum also got actress Lila Leeds.

Grateful Dead

When: 1967
Where: San Francisco
Amount: One pound of marijuana
Arrested: Bob Weir, Ron "Pigpen" McKernan, and nine others
Verdict: Charges dismissed
FYI: The raid was a setup. It took place at the Grateful Dead house at 710 Ashbury Street with reporters and TV crews in tow.

John Sinclair

When: 1969
Where: Ann Arbor, Michigan
Amount: Two joints
Verdict: Guilty
Sentence: Ten years, but commuted after two years
FYI: Three days after the Ten for Two

concert featuring John Lennon and Yoko Ono, Sinclair was freed.

Paul McCartney

When: 1980
Where: Tokyo Airport
Amount: Almost one-half pound of marijuana
Verdict: Guilty
Sentence: Ten days in jail, deportation
FYI: Eleven Wings shows scheduled for Japan had to be canceled.

Carlos Santana

When: 1991
Where: Houston Airport
Amount: Five grams
Verdict: Guilty
Sentence: Six months deferred, $100 fine, community service
FYI: Santana was returning from Mexico.

David Lee Roth

When: 1993
Where: New York City
Amount: $10 worth of marijuana
Verdict: Charge dismissed
FYI: Roth was arrested in Washington Square Park trying to cop an old-fashioned dime bag.

Whitney Houston

When: 2000
Where: Kona Airport, Hawaii
Amount: Fifteen grams of marijuana
Verdict: Charge dismissed
FYI: Houston was traveling with then-husband, R&B star Bobby Brown. Airport security found marijuana

Paul McCartney handcuffed and flanked by Japanese police officers after his 1980 arrest

in their luggage, but only she was charged.

Willie Nelson

When: 2006
Where: Breaux Bridge, Louisiana
Amount: One-and-a-half pounds of marijuana and three ounces of magic mushrooms
Verdict: Guilty
Sentence: Suspended. He and road manager David Anderson were each fined $1,024 and placed on six months' probation.
FYI: Nelson's bus was boarded and he and four others were arrested for the amount confiscated.

Snoop Dogg

When: 2006
Where: Bob Hope Airport, Burbank, California
Amount: Unknown quantity of marijuana
Verdict: No contest
Sentence: Three years suspended sentence, five years probation, and eight hundred hours of community service
FYI: In 2007 Snoop Dogg was detained for possessing marijuana in Stockholm, Sweden.

George Michael

When: 2006
Where: London
Amount: Two small bags containing marijuana and GHB
Verdict: One hundred hours community service, loss of driver's license for two years
FYI: Michael was found slumped over the wheel of a car three times in 2006.

Stoner Legends

Tommy Chong: One half of the famous comedy duo Cheech & Chong, he costarred in *Up in Smoke* (1978) and spent nine months in jail for bong sales (2003–2004).

Jerry Garcia: Grateful Dead guitarist who was a key figure in the Summer of Love and San Francisco's psychedelic music revolution. He died in 1995.

Jack Herer: Known as "The Hemperor," due to his influential book, *The Emperor Wears No Clothes*

(1985), which inspired a new generation of stoners to learn why marijuana is really prohibited. (Hint: It's a conspiracy.)

Ken Kesey: Merry Prankster and psychedelic improviser who wrote *One Flew Over the Cuckoo's Nest* (1962) and organized bus tours and Trips Festivals. He died in 2001.

Timothy Leary: He advised the 1960s generation to "Turn on, tune in and drop out" and cowrote *The Psychedelic Experience* (1964), recommending LSD and mushroom use as a way to reach higher consciousness. He died in 1996.

Bob Marley: Jamaican musician and ganja smoker who introduced reggae culture and Rastafarian beliefs to the world in the 1970s. He died of cancer in 1981.

Willie Nelson: Always on the road, he tours from city to city performing for adoring fans, many of whom share his fundamental belief that marijuana should be legal for recreational and medical use, and that farmers should be allowed to grow hemp.

Dennis Peron: Gay activist who led the campaign to legalize medical marijuana in California. He cowrote Proposition 215 and opened the first pot dispensary, the Cannabis Buyers' Club, in 1993.

Keith Stroup: The founder of NORML opened the discussion to decriminalizing marijuana and "responsible" marijuana use by adults.

Left: Dennis Peron; Above: Ken Kesey; Right: Hunter S. Thompson

Hunter S. Thompson: Counterculture writer who penned *Fear and Loathing in Las Vegas* (1972) and influenced many generations of would-be "gonzo" journalists. He committed suicide in 2005.

Stoner Festivals

Bonnaroo Music & Arts Festival

Duration/Date: Four days, starting on Thursday night and ending on Sunday. Typically held on the third weekend of June.

Location: Manchester, Tennessee (sixty miles southeast of Nashville)

Price: $185–$215, depending on when you purchase your ticket, plus a $22 service charge per ticket; VIP tickets sold in pairs for $1,122.

Capacity: 80,000

Camping: Yes

Vibe: Music goes on for sixteen hours a day, from noon to the wee early-morning hours, on thirteen different stages. Started as a jam-band fest in 2003, it has evolved to include a wider range of alt-rock. The festival site is a farm, but it is not picturesque. Campgrounds sprawl for miles. The festival is well run with a relatively friendly staff. Bring food, unless you want to eat unhealthy vender chow for four days. Good microbrew draft beer selection. Tends to rain, so take appropriate gear.

Historic Past Performances: Bob Dylan, Radiohead, the Police, the White Stripes, Tom Petty (with Stevie Nicks), Dave Matthews Band, the Black Crowes, Wilco, Neil Young, James Brown, and Steve Winwood

Weed-friendly Level: High. Psychedelics like magic mushrooms are plentiful.

Burning Man

Duration/Date: Eight days, leading up to Labor Day

Location: Black Rock City, Nevada (ninety miles northeast of Reno)

Price: Free

Capacity: 35,000

Camping: Yes

Vibe: The more outrageous the better is the credo of Burning Man, where art installations have lit up the night and personal expression has been at its most extreme since 1986. Bring food and cook it up with your camp. Be prepared for desert conditions: hot days, cold nights, and possible sandstorms. Psychedelics go really well with the neon configurations and, of course, the burning of the man.

Weed-friendly Level: Extremely high

Coachella Music and Arts Festival

Duration/Date: Recently expanded from two to three days. Typically held on the last weekend in April.

Location: Indio, California (twenty miles east of Palm Springs)

Price: $85 per day; VIP, $125 per day

Capacity: 55,000

Camping: Yes

Vibe: Founded in 1999 and set against a picturesque desert backdrop, nonaggressive alternative and indie bands (both classic and up-and-comers) rock on two stages, with more dance-oriented acts taking over in three tents. Also on the grounds: a sculpture garden, small film festival, and dozens of vendors.

Historic Past Performances: Iggy Pop, Radiohead, Beastie Boys, Madonna, Queens of the Stone Age, Flaming Lips, Kraftwerk, and the Pixies' first reunion show

Weed-friendly Level: Low. Andy Dick was arrested in 2005 and many concertgoers have complained of aggressive searches at the entry gates. Be careful.

Gathering of the Vibes

Duration/Date: Four days. Typically held during the first weekend of August.

Location: Bridgeport, Connecticut

Price: $125; VIP, $385

Capacity: 8,000

Camping: Yes

Vibe: Founded by Terrapin Presents in 1996 after the death of Jerry Garcia, GOTV has moved a lot, from rural locations in New York State to an urban venue in Bridgeport, Connecticut (Seaside Park), where it currently resides. A full slate of jam bands play on four stages, starting Thursday night. Usually there's an emphasis on the Dead.

Historic Past Performances: Phil Lesh and Friends, the Allman Brothers, Bob Weir & Ratdog, James Brown, and George Clinton.

Weed-friendly Level: High.

Glastonbury Festival of Contemporary Performing Arts

Duration/Date: Three days. Typically held on the last weekend in June.

Location: Pilton, England (125 miles west of London)

Price: 150 pounds ($298)

Capacity: 175,000

Camping: Yes

Vibe: Set on a site steeped in history (King Arthur may be buried on the former farm), lush green hills and flowing streams accent one of the world's oldest and most revered musical events (founded in 1970). Featuring more than 300 performers on thirty themed stages throughout the eight-mile perimeter, every form of performance and visual art is represented as well as dozens of charities looking

Festival-goers at the Bonnaroo
Music & Arts Festival in 2006

to raise awareness and money for their causes. The festival's mission—to bring together, stimulate, and entertain a diverse international crowd for one blow-out weekend—as well as its massive physical space encourages attendees to let loose. However, beware of rain and muddy conditions.

Historic Past Performances: The Who, Paul McCartney, Oasis, Radiohead, the Smiths, the Cure, Coldplay, and David Bowie

Weed-friendly Level: High

High Sierra Music Festival

Duration/Date: Four days. Typically held during the first weekend of July.

Location: Quincy, California (eighty miles northwest of Reno)

Price: Four days, $156; weekend, $131; VIP, $650

Capacity: 8,000

Camping: Yes

Vibe: Tucked away in the Sierra Mountains, this is one of the most beautiful and pristine locations for any music festival in America. Ten stages alternate between day and night, with an emphasis on jam bands, acoustic music, and bluegrass. In addition to music, there's plenty of hiking, biking, rock climbing, and swimming to enjoy in the area. Being this is Northern California, you can imagine a surplus of kind buds keeping the festival, (founded in 1991), extremely high.

Historic Past Performances: String Cheese Incident, Medeski Martin & Wood, Gov't Mule, and Widespread Panic

Weed-friendly Level: High, but in 2005 police arrested numerous festivalgoers for possession while driving in and out of the site.

New Orleans Jazz & Heritage Festival

Duration/Date: Six days total. Typically held during the last weekend of April and the first weekend of May.

Location: New Orleans, Louisiana

Price: $35–45 per day; VIP, $600 per weekend

Capacity: 100,000 per day

Camping: No

Vibe: Founded in 1970, the best music festival in America is not a campout and you won't hear many jam bands. Instead, feast on the glorious regional music and food of Louisiana. Eleven stages are uniquely positioned at the Racetrack Fairgrounds (just minutes from the French Quarter) so that you seamlessly fade out of one and fade into another, with styles ranging from jazz to blues to gospel to Cajun and zydeco and to marching bands and Mardi Gras Indians sporting amazing feathered outfits and drumming up a storm. It's a heady brew, washed down with an Abita draft beer or sweetened ice tea. Bring your dancing shoes and an umbrella.

Historic Past Performances: Bruce Springsteen's Seeger Sessions Band, the Neville Brothers, Dr. John, Santana, Bonnie Raitt, Lenny Kravitz, the Meters, and B. B. King

Weed-friendly Level: Moderate. Since Katrina there's been a shortage of kind bud, plus New Orleans has always had an overload of Mexi-schwag.

Rainbow Gathering

Duration/Date: One week, leading up to July 4.
Location: National Forests in the lower forty-eight states
Price: Free

Capacity: 10,000
Camping: Yes
Vibe: Since 1972 the Rainbow Family of Living Light—a loosely organized confederation of local "families"—meets in a carefully selected section of prime U.S. National Forest. You must park and pack everything in to the main site. Many camps are set up with kitchens and a central Main Circle is where people are fed en masse. The "magic hat" is passed, paying for the next meal. You're also expected to help with food preparation and other

Naked attendees at Burning Man in 1997

tasks. But mostly this is a paradise for people who want to strip away their clothes and belongings, commune with nature, smoke some good bud, trip out on mushrooms, and think about ways of saving the world.

Weed-friendly Level: Extremely high

Reggae on the River

Duration/Date: Three days. Typically held during the first weekend of August.

Location: Piercy, California (seventy-five miles south of Eureka)

Price: $165; VIP, $225

Capacity: 14,000

Camping: Yes

Vibe: America's premier reggae festival, founded in 1984, takes place in the heart of marijuana country, at French's Camp in Humboldt Country. The river it's named after, the Eel, is narrow and shallow but is still nice to take a dip in on hot days. It does get cool at night. Music on multiple stages by the best reggae performers in the world keep the festival irie, and Ital food and locally grown ganja are plentiful for seasoned taste buds.

Historic Past Performances: Jimmy Cliff, Toots & the Maytals, Third World, Israel Vibration, Burning Spear, Steel Pulse, the Marley Brothers, Bunny Wailer, Femi Kuti, and Common

Weed-friendly Level: The highest of the high

South By Southwest Music Conference and Film Festival

Duration/Date: Typically held during the second two weeks of March. The film festival runs for nine days and overlaps with the music conference, which is held from Wednesday through Saturday.

Location: Austin, Texas

Price: $425 to $550 for the music festival badge, $225 to $350 for the film festival badge, up to $850 for the platinum package, which includes the interactive

A colorful "wizard" at the Rainbow Gathering in 2001

conference as well. Wristbands offering limited access to the music festival cost $150.

Capacity: 21,000

Camping: No

Vibe: Known as Spring Break for the music industry since 1987, the four-day music festival features more than 1,500 bands performing in seventy different local venues and stages nightly. During the day, badge holders can attend music business panels at the Convention Center, check out the Flatstock rock poster trade show, catch an indie flick, or simply be entertained by countless parties offering free booze, barbeque, and great tunes.

Historic Past Performances: Keynote addresses by Johnny Cash, Neil Young, Robbie Robertson, Chrissie Hynde, Pete Townsend, and Robert Plant; club sets by Beck, Elliott Smith, Spoon, Los Lonely Boys, the Flaming Lips, Polyphonic Spree, Fastball, and the Stooges.

Weed-friendly Level: Moderate. Austin tolerates thousands of intoxicated out-of-towners taking over their streets, but bike patrols (especially in the downtown area) are on the lookout for people puffing outdoors. And with a new city smoking ordinance in place, partying inside the clubs and bars isn't much better.

U.S. Pot Rallies

Boston Freedom Rally

Founded: 1992 by MASS CANN NORML
Date: Third Saturday of September
Location: Boston
Crowd: 15,000–20,000
Vibe: One stage centrally located in Boston Common features bands and speakers for six hours, starting at high noon. Unfortunately, police routinely arrest fifty to seventy-five revelers. The night before, MASS CANN gives out awards to local and national activists.
Noteworthy Bands and Speakers: Letters to Cleo, Herbal Nation, the 360s, John Sinclair, Wayne Kramer, and Robby Roadsteamer

Fourth of July Smoke-In

Founded: 1970 by the Yippies
Date: July 4
Location: Washington, D.C.
Crowd: 5,000
Vibe: The oldest U.S. marijuana rally takes place in the festive nation's capital on the country's birthday, which makes for a combustible environment. Speakers from 12 noon until 3 p.m. at Lafayette Park followed by a march and concert at 23rd Street and Constitution Avenue. Due to the large police presence, it's easier to light up fireworks than joints.
Noteworthy Speakers: Chris Conrad, Mikki Norris, Ed Rosenthal, Dana Beal, and John Pylka

Hash Bash

Founded: 1971
Date: First Saturday of April
Location: Ann Arbor, Michigan
Crowd: 5,000
Vibe: Intimate college rally on the University of Michigan's Diag runs from high noon until 1 p.m. No bands, just speakers, lots of signs, and ganja smoke. There's a $25 fine if you're caught smoking pot in Ann Arbor, but getting busted on campus carries a harsher penalty, so be careful if you're going to light up in public.
Noteworthy Speakers: Gatewood Galbraith, Chef RA, and Adam Brook

Angel Raich (center) leads marijuana protest in Missoula, Montana, on April 20, 2007

A view from the stage of the crowd and the Puget Sound at the Seattle Hempfest

Marijuana March

Founded: 1971 by the Yippies
Date: First Saturday of May
Location: New York City
Crowd: 1,000
Vibe: What began as the New York Smoke-In has evolved into a worldwide phenomenon including more than two hundred cities, known as the Global Marijuana March. In New York, the rally begins in Washington Square Park at 11 a.m., marches east, and continues in Tompkins Square Park. When Rudolph Giuliani was mayor, his strong-arm tactics led to as many as three hundred arrests and scared people away from the event.
Noteworthy Bands: Richie Havens, the Chambers Brothers, the Cannabis Cup Band, and David Peel & the Lower East Side

Seattle Hempfest

Founded: 1991 by Peace Heathens
Date: Third weekend of August
Location: Seattle
Crowd: 50,000 per day
Vibe: Four stages feature music and speeches for two days in narrow Myrtle Edwards Park on Puget Sound. Arrests are rare and weed is plentiful.
Noteworthy Bands and Speakers: Woody Harrelson, Fishbone, Kottonmouth Kings, Jack Herer, Elvy Musikka, and Vivian McPeak

Stoner Beaches

Dahab, Egypt: Long considered a bohemian hot spot for neighboring Israeli backpackers, this tiny former fishing village in the south of Egypt's Sinai peninsula features a two-mile stretch of oceanside Bedouin-style tents that cater to your every need. There's not much to do here but sit back, relax, read a book, puff hash from a hookah, and enjoy the hot, dry air. Nearby attractions include the Blue Hole, a mind-blowing and highly dangerous deep-sea reef-diving center; Sinai's biggest city, Sharm El-Sheik; and Terabin, a smaller, less-populated version of Dahab.

How to Get There: Fly to Cairo and take an eight- to ten-hour bus ride from there to Dahab; or fly to Tel Aviv, and either drive or take a shared taxi seven hours south to Dahab. It takes two hours from the Eilat/Taba border to Dahab, and you'll pass Terabin on the way.

Goa, India (Anjuna Beach): Almost seventy-five miles of beaches line the Indian province of Goa in southwestern India, but Anjuna, which lies thirty miles north of Goa's capital Panaji, is the most popular among the hippie crowd. First popularized by bohemian tourists in the 1950s and 1960s (who also started the tradition of full-moon parties that rage late into the night), Anjuna continues to host all-night raves and beach parties. Prime weather starts in November and runs through New Year's, which typically sees a massive influx of partyers. During the day, visitors sip from exotic fruit drinks, dine at one of the many thatched open-air tents, visit the nearby flea market and, of course, sample the local charas.

How to Get There: Fly to New Delhi or Chennai and then take a domestic flight to Goa. The nearest airport is Dabolim, which is about forty-five miles from Panaji and seventy-five miles from Anjuna. You can also get to Anjuna by rail (the closest train station is in Karmali) or bus, which goes directly to Anjuna from Mapusa. Once in Goa, travel is easy and affordable, with taxis and bikes for hire at every corner.

Maui, Hawaii, U.S. (Red Sand Beach): This super-isolated beach (also known as Kaihalulu, meaning roaring sea) near Hana is one of Maui's treasured secrets. Notoriously hard to find on the far side of Ka'uiki Hill south of Hana Bay, you have to hike a quarter mile down a short, steep, and muddy slope to get to the bottom. There, sun worshippers (some in the nude), snorklers, and nature-loving stoners sit in awe of the trippy red sand, which is the result of the crumbling cinder that accents the hill above the bay. Visitors describe the overlooking cliff, nearby cave, and surf-breaking boulders as a "trip to the moon." Take a couple hits of some local Maui Wowie and you'll see what they mean.

How to Get There: Fly into Maui's Kahului Airport, then drive fifty-two miles east on Maui's north coast along the famous (and sometimes treacherous) Hana Road.

Negril, Jamaica: On the western tip of the island—where white-sand beaches shimmer in the blistering sun, reggae sounds abound, and wafts of ganja smoke float through the air—Negril is Jamaica's stoner paradise. Heads will prefer the smaller cliffside hotels to the touristy all-inclusive resorts on Seven Mile Beach, though herb is easily found just about anywhere, anytime. Still, keep it on the d.l.

How to Get There: Fly to Montego Bay, rent a car, and drive southwest on fifty miles of winding roads, accented by gorgeous sugar plantations, to Negril.

Venice Beach, California, U.S.: One of California's most recognized tourist spots has been a counterculture nexus since the *Beach Blanket Bingo* days of the early 1960s. But even today, you'll see more than your share of surfers, bikini babes, sidewalk musicians, rollerbladers, and body builders along the wide So-Cal shoreline. Plenty of head shops cater to stoners' needs (no trouble finding paraphernalia) and a puff or two makes the sunny day so much more enjoyable.

How to Get There: Fly into LAX, then take a bus or drive to the heart of Venice, a mere seven miles from the airport.

Above: Anjuna Beach in Goa, India
Right: Paradise Beach in Dahab

Stoner Colleges

Humboldt State University, Arcata, California: Nestled among northern California's redwood forest and overlooking the Pacific Ocean nearly three hundred miles north of San Francisco, the natural beauty of this Humboldt County campus, located in the heart of California growing country and founded in 1913, is among the stoniest spots in the state. And as one of only two California colleges to offer a botany major, it's no wonder. HSU's 6,400 students can also take pride in a long history of activism, most notably a 1970 student protest against the United States advance into Cambodia that shut the campus down, and an emphasis on the arts, thanks to Arcata's and nearby Eureka's many galleries and museums as well as monthly art festivals.
Famous Alumni: Raymond Carver, Mike Patton, and *SpongeBob SquarePants*'s creator Stephen Hillenburg.

New York University, New York, New York: A private university founded in 1831, NYU is located in Manhattan's Greenwich Village and is home to 20,000 undergraduates. Known for its performing arts programs, from which a number of successful actors and musicians have graduated, it is also among the nation's top business and law schools. Academics aside, the city that never sleeps promises an uncompromising party scene.
Famous Alumni: Woody Allen, Philip Seymour Hoffman, Angelina Jolie, Burt Lancaster, Billy Crystal, Whoopi Goldberg, Billy Crudup, Gina Gershon, Ethan Hawke, Felicity Huffman, Neil Diamond, Melissa Manchester, Martin Scorcese, Ang Lee, Tom Ford, and Saul Williams.

Oberlin College, Oberlin, Ohio: A private liberal arts school founded in 1833, it has a student body of 2,800 and houses the world-renowned Oberlin Conservatory of Music. With a reputation for being the hipster's Ivy League school, as a result of the many indie-rock bands who have come out of its halls (Yeah Yeah Yeahs, Trans Am, and the Sea and Cake), it was one of the first U.S. colleges to admit African-American students (1835) and today enjoys a thriving gay and lesbian community.
Famous Alumni: Eric Bogosian, William Goldman, Julie Taymor, Thornton Wilder, and Ben & Jerry's cofounder Jerry Greenfield.

Reed College, Portland, Oregon: A small school of 1,400 undergraduates outside of Portland, it was founded in 1908 and offers a liberal arts curriculum on a picturesque one-hundred-acre campus that's been traditionally left-leaning.
Famous Alumni: Steve Jobs, Ry Cooder, Barbara Ehrenreich, and Dr. Tod Mikuriya.

University of California, Santa Cruz: Founded in 1965 and located seventy-five miles south of San Francisco among rolling hills and redwood groves overlooking the Pacific Ocean and Monterey Bay, this public college with 13,600 undergraduates reaches an elevation of almost 2,000 feet at its northernmost point. Among the nation's top schools for space studies, UCSC has a history of political activism. Interesting boarding bonus: There's an area on the grounds where students can live out of RVs.
Famous Alumni: Maya Rudolph, and musicians Gillian Welch and Wayne Horvitz.

University of Colorado, Boulder: The flagship of Colorado's state school system with a student population numbering almost 30,000, this top-ranked institution founded in 1876 sits in the foothills of the Rocky Mountains mere miles from some of America's best ski slopes and hiking trails. Offering courses in 150 different disciplines, the school is known for its physics and chemistry programs, which, aside from real-life experiments at campus parties, have yielded a number of Nobel laureates and astronauts. Boulder is known as the second pot-smokingest city in 2005 (Boston is No. 1).
Famous Alumni: Robert Redford, Judy Collins, and *South Park*'s Trey Parker and Matt Stone.

University of Michigan, Ann Arbor: The oldest university in Michigan, it was founded in 1817 and is now home to some 25,000 undergraduates. Known for political activism, this is where John F. Kennedy first proposed the formation of the Peace Corps while campaigning for the presidency in 1960. A more doobie-ous honor: The annual Hash Bash (first Saturday of April on the Diag), a full-blown smoke-fest started in 1971 as a way to celebrate Michigan's reclassification of pot infractions from a felony to a misdemeanor, is still going strong.
Famous Alumni: Madonna, Iggy Pop, Gerald Ford, James Earl Jones, Mike Wallace, Arthur Miller, Lucy Liu, Selma Blair, Tom Brady, Ann Coulter, and Tom Hayden.

University of Vermont, Burlington: A public university of 8,800 undergraduates, it is set in the Green Mountains and located in the town where Phish first formed in the early 1980s. The school was founded in 1791 and merged with the Vermont Agricultural College in 1865, making it a pretty good place to study botany. It lures countless hippies and ski bums looking for a little crunch to go with their academics.

Famous Alumni: Mike Gordon, Ben Affleck, Howard Dean, and Gail Sheehy.

University of Wisconsin, Madison:

This Big Ten college founded in 1848 has long been considered one of the top party schools in the country. Home to some 29,000 undergrads, beer reigns at UW, especially at the school's two annual events, the Mifflin Street Block Party, which was started in 1969 as a protest to the Vietnam War and now serves as a way for students to blow off steam before finals, and the State Street Halloween party, which is held on the Saturday before Halloween and, at last count, drew almost 100,000 people. The school is also the birthplace of *The Onion*, the satirical newspaper started by two UW juniors in 1988 and now based in New York. In addition, the Great Midwest Harvest Festival pot protest has been taking place in Madison since 1970.

Famous Alumni: Frank Lloyd Wright, Boz Scaggs, Steve Miller, Joan Cusack, Jane Kaczmarek, Joyce Carol Oates, and Ben Sidran.

HONORABLE MENTION: Evergreen State College (Olympia, Washington), Lewis & Clark College (Portland, Oregon), New College of Florida (Sarasota), Massachusetts Institute of Technology (Cambridge), SUNY New Paltz (New York), University of California (Berkeley), University of Florida (Gainesville), University of Massachusetts (Amherst), University of Missouri (Columbia), University of Oregon (Eugene), University of Texas (Austin), Warren Wilson College (Asheville, North Carolina), and Wesleyan University (Middletown, Connecticut).

The first-ever "Hash Bash" at University of Michigan, April 1, 1971

Pot Books Through the Ages

The Hasheesh Eater (1857) by Fitz Hugh Ludlow

Really the Blues (1946) by Mezz Mezzrow and Bernard Wolfe

Red-Dirt Marijuana and Other Tastes (1967) by Terry Southern

A Child's Garden of Grass (1969) by Jack S. Margolis and Richard Clorfene

Marihuana Reconsidered (1971) by Lester Grinspoon

Grass: The Official Guide for Assessing the Quality of Marijuana on the 1 to 10 Scale (1973) by Jack Herer and Al Emmanuel

Weed (1974) by Jerry Kamstra

Marijuana Grower's Guide (1978) by Mel Frank and Ed Rosenthal

Reefer Madness: A History of Marijuana (1979) by Larry "Ratso" Sloman

High Culture: Marijuana in the Lives of Americans (1980) by William Novak

High in America (1981) by Patrick Anderson

Budding Prospects (1984) by T. Corraghessen Boyle

The Emperor Wears No Clothes: The Authoritative Historical Record of Cannabis and the Conspiracy Against Marijuana (1985) by Jack Herer

Marijuana Botany: Propagation and Breeding of Distinctive Cannabis (1993) by Robert Connell Clarke

Hemp: Lifeline to the Future (1994) by Chris Conrad

The Great Book of Hemp: The Complete Guide to the Environmental, Commercial and Medicinal Uses of the World's Most Extraordinary Plant (1995) by Rowan Robinson

Brownie Mary's Medical Marijuana Cookbook, Dennis Peron's Recipe for Social Change (1996) by Mary Rathburn and Dennis Peron

Indoor Marijuana Horticulture: The Indoor Bible (1996) by Jorge Cervantes

Smoke and Mirrors: The War on Drugs and the Politics of Failure (1996) by Dan Baum

Hemp for Health: The Medicinal and Nutritional Uses of Cannabis Sativa (1997) by Chris Conrad

The Hemp Manifesto: 101 Ways That Hemp Can Save Our World (1997) by Rowan Robinson

Marihuana: The Forbidden Medicine (1997) by Lester Grinspoon and James B. Bakalar

Marijuana Myths, Marijuana Facts: A Review of the Scientific Evidence (1997) by Lynn Zimmer and Dr. John Morgan

Mr Nice: An Autobiography (1997) by Howard Marks

Cannabis Spirituality: Including 13 Guidelines for Sanity and Safety (1998) by Stephen Gaskin

Drug Crazy: How We Got Into This Mess and How We Can Get Out (1998) by Michael Gray

Hashish! (1998) by Robert Connell Clarke

The Healing Magic of Cannabis (1998) by Beverly Potter and Dan Joy

Paradise Burning: Adventures of a High Times Journalist (1998) by Chris Simunek

Shattered Lives: Portraits from America's Drug War (1998) by Mikki Norris, Chris Conrad, Virginia Resner, and R. U. Sirius

Amazing Dope Tales (1999) by Stephen Gaskin

The Hemp Cookbook (1999) by Ralf Hiener, Bettina Mack, Matthias Schillo, and Stefan Wirner

The Hemp Cookbook: From Seed to Shining Seed (1999) by Todd Dalotto

Get Stoned and Read This Book (1999) by Gordon G. Gourd

Offbeat Marijuana: The Life and Times of the World's Grooviest Plant (1999) by Saul Rubin

Pot Stories for the Soul (1999) edited by Paul Krassner

The Benefits of Marijuana: Physical, Psychological & Spiritual (2000) by Joan Bello

The Botany of Desire: A Plant's-Eye View of the World (2001) by Michael Pollan

The Cannabible (2001) by Jason King

Marijuana Medicine: A World Tour of the Healing and Visionary Powers of Cannabis (2001) by Christian Ratsch

Smokescreen: A True Adventure (2001) by Robert Sabbag

Waiting to Inhale: The Politics of Medical Marijuana (2001) by Alan Bock

Adventures in the Counterculture: From Hip Hop to High Times (2002) by Steven Hager

The Galaxy Global Eatery Hemp Cookbook (2002) by Denis Cicero

Loaded: A Misadventure on the Marijuana Trail (2002) by Robert Sabbag

Pot Planet: Adventures in Global Marijuana Culture (2002) by Brian Preston

The Cannabible 2 (2003) by Jason King

The Cannabis Companion: The Ultimate Guide to Connoisseurship (2003) by Steven Wishnia

Reefer Madness: Sex, Drugs, and Cheap Labor in the American Black Market (2003) by Eric Schlosser

Romancing Mary Jane: A Year in the Life of a Failed Marijuana Grower (2003) by Michael Poole

Saying Yes: In Defense of Drug Use (2003) by Jacob Sullum

Why Marijuana Should Be Legal (2003) by Ed Rosenthal

Can't Find My Way Home: America in the Great Stoned Age, 1945–2000 (2004) by Martin Torgoff

Cannabis: A History (2004) by Martin Booth

Counterculture Through the Ages (2004) by Ken Goffman

The Last Free Man in America Meets the Synthetic Subversion (2004) by Gatewood Galbraith

Spliffs: A Celebration of Cannabis Culture (2004) by Nick Jones

Busted! Drug War Survival Skills from the Buy to the Bust to Begging for Mercy (2005) by M. Chris Fabricant

Cannabis Yields and Dosage (2005) by Chris Conrad

The Hemp Nut Cookbook: Ancient Food for the New Millennium (2005) by Richard Rose

It's Just a Plant: A Children's Story of Marijuana (2005) by Ricardo Cortes

The Marijuana-logues: Everything About Pot That We Could Remember (2005) by Doug Benson, Arj Barker, and Tony Camin

Spliffs 2: Further Adventures in Cannabis Culture (2005) by Tim Pilcher

Understanding Marijuana: A New Look at the Scientific Evidence (2005) by Mitch Earleywine

9021GROW (2005) by Craig X. Rubin

The Cannabible 3 (2006) by Jason King

How to Roll a Blunt for Dummies! (2006) by R. Prince

The I Chong: Meditations from the Joint (2006) by Tommy Chong

Pot Culture: The A-Z Guide to Stoner Language & Life (2007) by Shirley Halperin and Steve Bloom

Stony Recipes

IF YOU CAN'T TOKE, EAT!
Pot-infused food is a great
alternative to smoking, and it can
take as little as a cookie to achieve
the same effect. In recent years,
the variety of weed snacks has
exploded to include everything
from lollipops to pasta. Still,
desserts remain the stoner
delicacy of choice. So, if you are
lucky enough to receive some pot
from your local compassion club,
read on for a few easy recipes and
step-by-step directions for how
to make the essential ingredient
in all of them, cannabutter.
But be forewarned: When
THC is absorbed through the
stomach, the high can be much
more intense. Bong appétit!

🌿 Guide to Measurements 🌿

LIQUID	Teaspoon	Tablespoon	Fluid Ounce	Gill	Cup	Pint	Quart	Gallon
1 Teaspoon =	1	⅓	⅙	1/24	-	-	-	-
1 Tablespoon =	3	1	½	⅛	1/16	-	-	-
1 Fluid Ounce =	6	2	1	¼	⅛	1/16	-	-
1 Gill =	24	8	4	1	½	¼	⅛	-
1 Cup =	48	16	8	2	1	½	¼	1/16
1 Pint =	96	32	16	4	2	1	½	⅛
1 Quart =	192	64	32	8	4	2	1	¼
1 Gallon =	768	256	128	32	16	8	4	1

DRY	1 Gram	⅛ Ounce	¼ Ounce	½ Ounce	1 Ounce	1 Pound	½ Kilogram	1 Kilogram
Grams =	1	3.5	7	14	28	453.6	500	1,000
Ounces =	0.035	⅛	¼	½	1	16	17.5	35
Pounds =	0.002	1/128	1/64	1/32	1/16	1	1.1	2.2
Kilograms =	0.001	0.0035	0.007	0.014	0.028	0.453	½	1

Cannabutter

The key ingredient in all weed-infused foods, cannabutter can be incorporated into any dish that calls for regular margarine or butter. Or just spread it on some toast for a potent morning eye-opener. The process of making it requires patience as it is long and somewhat tedious, but done right (and with quality shake), you can bake to your heart's delight.

INGREDIENTS

⅛ to ¼ ounce ground marijuana *(depending on the quality of the bud)*

½ pound butter

Bring a large pot of water, filled ⅓ full, to boil. Add the marijuana and the butter, and cook at a low boil for 6 hours, stirring every half hour. Pour the liquid through a strainer lined with cheesecloth into a bowl. Dispose of the cheesecloth contents. Cover the bowl well, and refrigerate overnight. The next day, scoop off the top layer of butter and pour out the liquid. Scrape away any sediment left at the bottom of the bowl, and melt the top layer and sediment together in a saucepan. Re-strain, pour into a glass jar, and refrigerate.

Lavender Lemon Bars

This California specialty combines two of the state's finest assets: citrus and weed, plus a little lavender flavor for a from-the-garden twist on this old-time favorite.

INGREDIENTS

Crust

1 cup flour

½ cup confectioners' sugar

⅛ teaspoon salt

4 ounces cold cannabutter, cut into small pieces

Filling

2 large eggs

1 cup powdered sugar

2 tablespoons flour

⅛ teaspoon salt

2 teaspoons grated lemon zest

¼ cup freshly squeezed lemon juice

a pinch of lavender leaves

Preheat the oven to 350 degrees. Line an 8-inch square baking pan with well-greased parchment paper.

Prepare the crust. Mix the flour, confectioners' sugar, and salt. Cut in the cannabutter with a pastry blender or two knives. Combine lightly until the mixture resembles small pebbles. Press evenly into the bottom of baking pan. Bake 18–20 minutes, or until slightly golden. Set aside.

Prepare the filling. In a medium bowl, whisk together eggs, powdered sugar, flour, and salt. Stir in lemon juice and lemon zest until well combined. Pour over crust and sprinkle with lavender leaves. Bake 15–18 minutes, until filling sets. Cool and dust with confectioners' sugar before serving.

Double Chocolate Chip Cookies

No matter what flavor or variety, cookies have been a staple stoner snack for decades. Try these chocolate chip confections that are not only tasty, but also toasty.

INGREDIENTS

8 ounces cannabutter
½ cup brown sugar
1 cup sugar
1 teaspoon vanilla
3 large eggs
2 ⅔ cups flour
1 teaspoon baking soda
1 teaspoon salt
½ teaspoon honey
1 cup white chocolate morsels
1 cup dark chocolate morsels

Preheat the oven to 375 degrees. In a large mixing bowl, cream the cannabutter, brown sugar, sugar, and vanilla. Beat in the eggs, one at a time. In a medium bowl, combine the flour, baking soda, and salt, and add it to the first mixture. Pour a touch of honey into the batter, and stir in the morsels. Drop the batter by rounded teaspoonful onto an ungreased cookie sheet, about 1 inch apart. Bake for 8–9 minutes, or until cookies are puffed up. Cool on baking sheet for 2 minutes, then remove to cool completely.

Banana Bread

Looking to make use of some overripe bananas? Try this easy-to-bake take on a centuries-old recipe.

INGREDIENTS

2 *cups flour*
1 ½ *teaspoon baking soda*
½ *teaspoon salt*
4 *overripe bananas*
1 *cup sugar*
6 *ounces cannabutter, melted*
2 *large eggs*
1 *teaspoon vanilla*
½ *cup pecans and walnuts, finely chopped*
4 *to 8 ounces cognac*
confectioners' sugar

Preheat the oven to 350 degrees and lightly grease a 9 × 5-inch loaf pan. In a large bowl, combine flour, baking soda, and salt. Set aside. In a small bowl, mash two of the bananas with a fork. Set aside. With an electric mixer, whip together the remaining bananas and the sugar, for three minutes. Add the melted cannabutter, eggs, cognac, and vanilla. Beat well. Add the dry ingredients and mix. Fold in the nuts and mashed bananas with a rubber spatula. Pour the batter into the loaf pan. Bake for 75 minutes, or until golden brown and a toothpick comes out clean. Rotate the pan periodically to ensure even browning. Don't worry if the bread cracks down the middle. Cool in the pan for about 10 minutes, then remove to cool completely. Dust with confectioners' sugar, slice, and serve.

Weed Sites on the Web

For more information, visit some of our favorite Web sites about stoner life.

ASA: www.safeaccessnow.org
Cannabis Culture: www.cannabisculture.com
Cannabis News: www.cannabisnews.com
CelebStoner: www.celebstoner.com
Dose Nation: www.dosenation.com
DRCNet: www.drcnet.org
Drug Policy Alliance: www.drugpolicy.org
Famous Friends of Cannabis:
    www.friendsofcannabis.com
Heads: www.headsmagazine .com
IDiggWeed: www.idiggweed.com
Marijuana Madness: www.marijuanamadness.com
Marijuana News: www.marijuananews.com
Marijuana Policy Project: www.mpp.org
NORML: www.norml.org
NORML Audio Stash: www.normlaudiostash.com
Pot or Not: www.potornot.com
Skunk: www.skunkmagazine.com
Treating Yourself: www.treatingyourself.com
Yahooka: www.yahooka.com
Very Important Potheads:
    www.veryimportantpotheads.com
420 Dictionary: www.420dictionary.com
420 Girls: www.420girls.com
420 Magazine: www.420magazine.com

Photography Credits

Unless otherwise noted, images are credited clockwise from bottom left.

Page 6: Brian Jahn (marijuana leaves); **page 7:** Kevin Winter/ Getty Images (Tommy Chong); **page 9:** Gabe Kirchheimer (Steve Bloom and Shirley Halperin); **page 11:** Brian Jahn (Durban Poison); WireImage/Getty Images (Afroman and Jonathan Mewes); Universal Records, 2001 (Afroman single); **page 12:** Bob Berg (Jonah Hill); **page 13:** Gabe Kirchheimer (houseboat); Brian Jahn (bicyclists); Bob Berg (aquapipe); **page 14:** Express/Getty Images (Louis Armstrong); **page 15:** Gabe Kirchheimer (Derry); Jeff Haynes/ AFP/Getty Images (beer bong); Mountain High Map® © 1993 Digital Wisdom®, Inc.; **page 16:** Neal Peters Collection (*Yellow Submarine*); *Revolver* cover designed by Klaus Voorman; *Magical Mystery Tour* cover ©1967, NEMS ENTERPRISES LTD.; **page 17:** BIPs/Getty Images (Beatles); **page 18:** Steve Eichner (Chris Robinson); **page 19:** Billy Tompkins/Retna Ltd. (Jack Black); Mitchell/Getty Images (Humphrey Bogart); Bob Berg (bong); **pages 20–21:** Brian Jahn (Redman); **page 22:** Robb D. Cohen/Retna Ltd. (Bonnaroo); **page 24:** Bob Berg (bubbler); Bob Berg (Sour Diesel); **page 25:** Bruno Press/Getty Images (The Bulldog); Bob Berg (nug jugs); **page 26:** Mike Nelson/AFP/Getty Images (Burning Man); **page 27:** Evening Standard/Getty Images (William S. Burroughs); **page 28:** G.Hanekroot/ Sunshine/Retna Ltd. (Byrds); **page 29:** Bob Berg (Steve-O); **page 30:** Cover courtesy of *Cañamo*; Cover courtesy of *Cannabis Culture*; **page 31:** Brian Jahn (Skunk #1); **page 32:** Brian Jahn (Rob Thomas); **page 33:** Bob Berg (cannabutter); **page 34:** Allen Ginsberg/CORBIS (Timothy Leary and Neal Cassady); Brian Jahn (Dave Chappelle); **page 35:** WireImage/ Getty Images (George Carlin); **pages 36–37:** Paramount Pictures, 1995 (*Up in Smoke* video); Neal Peters Collection (Cheech & Chong); **page 38:** Janez Skok/CORBIS (chillum); **page 40:** Gabe Kirchheimer (Paradise); **page 41:** Gabe Kirchheimer (Rocker T and coffeeshop menu); **page 42:** Splash News (Cameron Diaz and Drew Barrymore with Cameron Diaz); Flynet (Mischa Barton); Splash News (Ryan Phillippe); Fame Pictures (Charlize Theron); Flynet (Paris Hilton taking a hit); Peter Kramer/Getty Images (Paris Hilton posing); **page 43:** Bob Berg (crystals); Courtesy of Columbia Records (Cypress Hill); **page 44:** Mountain High Map® copyright © 1993 Digital Wisdom®, Inc.; **page 45:** Philip Gould/Corbis (Deadheads); **page 46:** Neal Peters Collection (Rory Cochrane, Jason London, and Sasha Jensen); MCA Home Video, Inc., 1994 (*Dazed and Confused* video); Neal Peters Collection (Wiley Wiggins and Christin Hinojosa); **page 47:** Neal Peters Collection (Matthew McConaughey); **page 48:** *Houses of the Holy* cover design by Hipgnosis (Storm Thorgenson, Aubrey Powell) (P) 1973 Atlantic Record Corporation for the U.S. and WEA Int'l Inc., for the world outside the U.S.; **pages 50–51:** Henry Diltz/Corbis (Doors); WireImage/Getty Images (Ray Manzarek); **page 52:** King Collection/Retna Ltd. (Bob Dylan); **page 53:** Bob Berg (dugout); John Springer Collection/Corbis (Dennis Hopper, Peter Fonda, Jack Nicholson); **page 54:** Allen Ginsberg/ CORBIS (William S. Burroughs and Jack Kerouac); **page 55:** Map © Map Resources; Neal Peters Collection (*Fast Times at Ridgemont High*); *Fabulous Furry Freak Brothers* cover courtesy of Rip Off Press; **page 56:** Jeffrey L. Rotman/CORBIS (fatty); Bob Berg (filters); **page 57:** Bob Berg (medical edibles); **page 58:** © Ben Fernandez (Allen Ginsberg); Roger Ressmeyer/ CORBIS (Jerry Garcia); Bob Berg (pipe); **page 59:** Bob Berg (bongs); **page 60:** Map © Map Resources; **page 61:** Gabe Kirchheimer (Arjan Roskam); Michael Ochs Archives/Corbis (Grateful Dead); **page 62:** Bob Berg (Cisco Adler); **page 63:** Bob Berg (grinders); **pages 64–65:** Jan Sturmann/Polaris (outdoor plants and harvested buds); **page 67:** Brian Jahn (seedling); **page 68:** Ted Streshinsky/CORBIS; (Tom Wolfe, Jerry Garcia, and Rock Skully); Brian Jahn (hairs); **page 69:** Gabe Kirchheimer (Woody Harrelson); Brian Jahn (hash); **page 70:** Cover courtesy of *Heads*; **page 71:** Bob Berg (Dementia); Gabe Kirchheimer (hemp products); Allan Tannenbaum/Polaris (Jimi Hendrix); **page 72:** Bob Berg (grinder, scissors, and fingers); Gabe Kirchheimer (Jack Herer); **page 73:** Cover courtesy of *Highlife*; Keystone/Getty Images (Albert Hofmann); **page 74:** Dennis Kleiman (hookah); Bob Berg (honey bottle); Neal Peters Collection (Dennis Hopper); **page 75:** Wendy Sue Lamm (Adam Levine); **page 76:** Angelo Cavalli/Zefa/Corbis (Jamaica); **page 77:** Brian Jahn (Amsterdam); Bob Berg (Venice Beach); Atlantide Phototravel/Corbis (Morocco); **page 78:** Map © Map Resources; **page 79:** Bob Berg (Rainbow); **page 80:** Mountain High Map® copyright © 1993 Digital Wisdom®, Inc.; Freek Arriens/Retna Ltd. (Rick James); **page 81:** Michael Ochs Archives/Getty Images (Jefferson Airplane); **page 82:** Bob Berg (kif); **page 83:** Bob Berg (Sugar Kush); **page 84:** Santi Visalli Inc./Getty Images (Timothy Leary); Michael Putland/Retna Ltd. (Led Zeppelin); **page 85:** Brian Jahn (Arj Barker, Doug Benson, and Tom Camin); **page 86:** Bob Berg (lighters); **page 87:** Filmmagic/Getty Images (Bill Maher); **page 88:** Peter Simon/Retna Ltd. (Bob Marley); **page 90:** Brian Jahn (Stephen and Ziggy Marley); **page 91:** Bob Berg (Pacific Sour Diesel); Map © Map Resources; **page 92:** David Atlas/Retna Ltd. (Melissa Etheridge); **page 93:** Paul Smith/ Featureflash/Retna Ltd. (Melissa Etheridge); **page 94:** Neal Peters Collection (*Midnight Express* and Robert Mitchum); **page 95:** Bob Berg (munchies); **page 96:** Bob Berg (P-Nut); **page 98:** Brian Jahn (Willie Nelson); Map © Map Resources; **page 99:** Columbia Records (Bob Dylan single); **page 100:** Mountain High Map® copyright © 1993 Digital Wisdom®, Inc.; **page 101:** Neal Peters Collection (Jack Nicholson and Dean Stockwell); **page 102:** Bob Berg (one-hitters); **page 105:** Courtesy of Steve Bloom (David Peel); Bob Berg (blunt and dime bag); **page 106:** C. Taylor Crothers (Phish); **page 107:** Courtesy of Sarah Saiger (Disco Biscuits); **page 108:** Gabe Kirchheimer (marijuana leaf); Bob Berg (pope); **page 109:** Bob Berg (proto pipe and pokers); **page 110:** Bob Berg (pipes); **page 111:** Ted Streshinsky/Corbis (Further bus); **page 112:** *Vincebus Eruptum*, photography by John Van Hamersveld, art direction by Gut © 1968 PolyGram Records, Inc.; *Pretties for You* © 1969 Bizarre Records; Lex Van Rossen/Redferns/ Retna Ltd (Bob Pollard); *The Gordons*, a Gordons Project— Copyright all rights reserved to the Artists; *In Search of Space* © 1972 and manufactured by United Artists Records, Inc., Los Angeles, California 90028. Printed in USA; **page 113:** Brian Jahn (Rasta); **page 114:** Neal Peters Collection (*Reefer Madness*); **page 115:** Bob Berg (roach, roach clip, and rolling machine); **pages 116–117:** Bob Berg (rolling papers); **page 118:** JBA/Camera Press/Retna Ltd. (Rolling Stones); **page 121:** Bob Berg (screens); **page 122:** Robb D. Cohen/Retna Ltd. (Joe Trohman); **page 123:** Cover courtesy of *Sinsemilla Tips*; **page 124:** Steve Eichner (Blueberry); **page 125:** Kevin Winter/ Getty Images (Bo Bice); **page 126:** Getty Images (Seth Rogen); **page 127:** Bob Berg (space cake); **page 128:** *Dark Side of the Moon* sleeve design by Hipgnosis and sleeve art by George Hardie N.T.A. (P) 1973 The Gramophone Company, Limited; Neal Peters Collection (Judy Garland); **page 129:** Brian Jahn (Strawberry Cough); **page 132:** Map © Map Resources; Peter Simon/Retna Ltd. (Peter Tosh); **page 133:** Jim McCrary (Gram Parsons); Splash News (Helen Hunt); Daniel Berehulak/Getty Images for MTV (Snoop Dogg); Splash News (Britney Spears); **page 134:** Bob Berg (vaporizer); Mountain High Map® (British Columbia) copyright © 1993 Digital Wisdom®, Inc.; Map (California) © Map Resources; **page 135:** Bob Berg (vaporizer); Barry Underhill (Pakelika and the Kottonmouth Kings); **page 136:** Steve Eichner (orange VW bus); Peter Finger/Corbis (psychedelic VW bus); **page 137:** Bob Berg (innovations); **page 138:** Jennifer Maler/Retna Ltd.(Doug Benson and Adrianne Curry); Christopher Knight (Adrianne Curry); **page 139:** Neal Peters Collection (*The Wall*); **page 140:** Cover courtesy of *Weed World*; Mountain High Map® copyright © 1993 Digital Wisdom®, Inc.; **page 141:** Bettmann/Corbis (Abbie Hoffman); Bob Berg (49:51); **page 143:** Brian Jahn (4:20 Snack Shop); **page 146:** Paramount Pictures (Cheech & Chong); Neal Peters Collection (Matthew McConaughey and Joey Lauren Adams); **page 147:** Neal Peters Collection (Kal Penn and John Cho); **page 148–149:** Neal Peters Collection (Brad Pitt); Neal Peters Collection (Anthony Michael Hall); Movie Star News (Kevin Spacey); **page 150:** Neal Peters Collection (Dennis Hopper and Frances McDormand); **page 151:** Neal Peters Collection (Sean Penn); **page 152:** Paramount Pictures (Cheech & Chong); **page 153:** Neal Peters Collection (Jeff Bridges and Rory Cochrane); **page 155:** USA Films (*Traffic*); Movie Star News (Johnny Depp); **page 156:** Movie

Star News (Verna Bloom and Tim Matheson; Orion Pictures Corporation (*Caddyshack* video); **page 157:** Neal Peters Collection (Shawn Hatosi, and Owen Wilson and Ben Stiller); **page 158:** Michael Caufield/WireImage/Getty Images (Tenacious D); **page 159:** Neal Peters Collection (Kate Beckinsale and Claire Danes); **pages 160–161:** Neal Peters Collection (*Yellow Submarine* and *Heavy Metal*); **page 162:** Neal Peters Collection (*2001: A Space Odyssey*); Movie Star News (Sigourney Weaver); **page 163:** Neal Peters Collection (Keanu Reeves); **page 164:** Neal Peters Collection (*The Wizard of Oz*); **page 165:** Neal Peters Collection (Ian McKellan); **page 166:** HVE/Home Vision Entertainment, package design by Public Media Inc. (*Grass DVD*); **page 167:** Neal Peters Collection (Bob Dylan and D. A. Pennebaker); **page 168:** Getty Images (Woodstock); **page 169:** Neal Peters Collection (*This Is Spinal Tap*); **page 170:** Michel Utrecht/WireImage/Getty Images (Sacha Baron Cohen); **page 171:** Neal Peters Collection (*Family Guy*); Courtesy Showtime (*Weeds*); **page 172:** Neal Peters Collection (*Star Trek*); **page 173:** Henry Diltz/Corbis (The Monkees); Neal Peters Collection (George Harrison and Dick Cavett); **page 174:** Neal Peters Collection (*The Ren & Stimpy Show*); **page 175:** Neal Peters Collection (*SpongeBob SquarePants*); **page 176:** Neal Peters Collection (Homer Simpson); **page 177:** Steve Eichner (Sublime); **page 178:** Dennis Kleiman (Ozzy Osbourne); *Panama Red* © 1973 CBS, Inc./ (P) 1973 CBS, Inc., cover design by Toots and Toots, cover art by Lore and Chris; **page 179:** Andy Freeberg/Retna Ltd. (Peter Tosh); **page 180:** *The Doors*, Elektra Records, front cover photo by Guy Webster; *Running Down the Road*, Reprise Records, a Division of Warner Bros. Inc., photography by Henry Diltz and reissue design by Thomas Molesky; *Black Sunday* © 1993 Sony Music Entertainment, Inc., photography by Anthony Artiaga, and concept and design by Dante Ariola and Jay Pupke; **page 181:** Brian Jahn (Snoop Dogg); **page 182:** *Big Bambu* (P) 1972 Ode Records. The album jacket was created and designed by Wilkes & Braun for Sound Packaging Corp. (permission granted by Gracias, Papeleros Reunidas, S.D.); *Have a Marijuana*, © 1968 Elektra Records, Cannabis sativa courtesy of The American Museum of Natural History; *Catch a Fire* © 1973 Island Records Ltd., photography by Esther Anderson; *Toledo Window Box* © 1974 Little David Records Co., Inc., album design by Pacific Eye & Ear, T-shirt illustration by Drew Struzan, and photography by Gary Sloan; *Good High* (P) 1976 Bang Records, photography by Richard Hoflich; **page 183:** *Fire It Up* (P) 1979 & Trademark Motown Records Corporation, photography by Ron Slenzak; *Legalize It* © 1976 CBS, Inc./P 1976 CBS, Inc., photography by Lee Jaffe; *Road Island* (P) 1982 Warner Bros. Records Inc., cover illustration by Ralph Steadman; *Skull & Bones* © 2000 Sony Music Entertainment Inc., cover illustration by Mr. Cartoon; *Countryman* (P) and © 2005 UMG Recordings, Inc., art direction and design by Craig Allen and photography

by Jim Harrington; *The Chronic* (P) 1992 Death Row Records, art direction and design by Kimberly Holt-Unleasjed, photography by Daniel Jordan; **page 185:** Sony Music Entertainment Inc. (Cypress Hill); **page 186:** Adrian Boot/Retna UK (Peter Tosh and Bunny Wailer); **page 187:** Patrick Chauvel/Sygma/Corbis (Bob Marley); **pages 188–189:** Liason/Getty Images (Willie Nelson); **page 190:** Movie Star News (Cab Calloway); **page 192:** Neal Peters Collection (Robert Mitchum); **page 193:** Bettmann/Corbis (Paul McCartney); **page 194:** Gabe Kirchheimer (Dennis Peron); Ted Streshinsky/Corbis (Ken Kesey); **page 195:** Paul Harris/Liaison/Getty Images (Hunter S. Thompson); **page 197:** Robb D. Cohen/Retna Ltd. (Bonnaroo); **page 198:** Stephen Ferry/Liaison/Getty Images (Burning Man); **page 199:** Bill Schaefer/Getty Images (Rainbow Gathering); **page 200:** Justin Sullivan/Getty Images (Montana Protest); **page 201:** Gabe Kirchheimer (Seattle Hempfest); **page 203:** Jon Hicks/Corbis (Goa); David Silverman/Getty Images (Dahab); **page 205:** David Knapp/Courtesy of the John & Leni Sinclair Collection, Bentley Historical Library, University of Michigan; **page 206:** (left to right) *A Child's Garden of Grass: The Official Handbook for Marijuana Use* by Jack S. Margolis and Richard Clorfene, illustrated by Jack S. Margolis, published in 1970 by Pocket Books, copyright © 1969 Jack S. Margolis and Richard Clorfene; *Weed* (*Adventures of a Dope Smuggler*) by Jerry Kamstra, published in 1975 by Bantam Books, copyright © 1974 Bantam Books, Inc., photographs copyright © 1974 Eugene Anthony; *Really the Blues* by Milton "Mezz" Mezzrow and Bernard Wolfe, published in 1964 by Signet books, copyright © 1964 Henry Miller; *Budding Prospects: A Pastoral* by T. Coraghessan Boyle, published in 1984 by Penguin Books, copyright © 1984 T. Coraghessan Boyle, cover design by Melissa Jacoby based on a detail of *Le Lion Ayant Faim* by Henri Rousseau; **page 207:** (left to right) *Marijuana Myths, Marijuana Facts: A Review of the Scientific Evidence* by Lynn Zimmer and John P. Morgan, published by the Lindesmith Center in 1997, copyright © 1997 Lynn Zimmer and John P. Morgan, cover design and graphics by Mark E. Phillips; *Mr Nice: An Autobiography* by Howard Marks, published in 1997 by Mandarin, copyright © 1996, 1997 Newtext Limited, jacket photograph by Steve Pyke; *Reefer Madness: Sex, Drugs, and Cheap Labor in the American Black Market* by Eric Schlosser, published by First Mariner Books in 2004, copyright © 2004 Eric Schlosser, book design by Robert Overholtzer; *Saying Yes* by Jacob Sullum, published in 2004 by Jeremy P. Tarcher/Penguin Books, copyright © 2004 Jacob Sullum, book design by Michelle McMillian; **pages 210–214:** Bob Berg (recipes); **page 215:** Brian Jahn (marijuana leaves).

Quotation Sources

Page 14: Louis Armstrong (Max Jones and John Chilton, *Louis: The Louis Armstrong Story, 1900–1971*, Da Capo Press, 1988); **page 15:** Jennifer Aniston (Mark Binelli, "How a Class Clown Became Hollywood's Hottest Chick," *Rolling Stone*, September 27, 2001); **page 30:** Josh Groban (Michael Joseph Gross, "Who Does Josh Groban Think He Is?" *Blender*, January/February 2007); **page 34:** Rodney Dangerfield (Jeffrey Ressner, "10 Questions for Rodney Dangerfield," *Time Magazine*, May 17, 2004); **page 39:** Kirsten Dunst ("Kirsten Dunst: I do like weed," *The Sun*, April 9, 2007); **page 40:** Robert Altman (Bernard Weinraub, "When Hollywood Is a Killer," *The New York Times*, April 5, 1992); **page 43:** Ryan Phillippe ("The Hot List: Ryan Phillippe," *Rolling Stone*, October 19, 2006); **page 51:** Ray Manzarek (as told to *Pot Culture*); **page 60:** Arnold Schwarzenegger (Lynn Elber, The Associated Press, November 14, 2002); **page 69:** Woody Harrelson (at the San Francisco premier of *Grass* as quoted in an article in the *Atlanta Journal-Constitution*, June 3, 2000); **page 74:** Bill Hicks (in a stand-up comedy routine); **page 78:** Norman Mailer (Interview with Steven Marcus, July 6, 1963, "The Art of Fiction No. 32: Norman Mailer," *The Paris Review*, © 2004 The Paris Review Foundation, Inc.); **page 81:** Kevin Smith (Rebecca Weiss, "Comedy Connection: Kevin Smith," *The Cornell Daily Sun*, September 18, 2007); **page 87:** Bill Maher (Interview on *Tavis Smiley*, PBS, February 12, 2007); **page 88:** Bob Marley; **page 90:** David Crosby (*Relix*, February/March 2007); **page 91:** Paul McCartney ("Paul McCartney Advocates Marijuana Decriminalization," NORML, September 25, 1997, www.norml.org); **page 94:** Robert Mitchum (in his plea for probation stemming from marijuana possession charges); **page 97:** Willie Nelson; **page 103:** Isaac Brock (Austin Scaggs, "Q&A: Isaac Brock," *Rolling Stone*, March 7, 2007); **page 104:** Barack Obama (in a speech made on January 21, 2004, to students at Northwestern University); **page 120:** Montel Williams ("Taking Action: Montel Williams on Medical Marijuana," The Montel Williams MS Foundation, www.montelms.org); **page 121:** George Michael (Nicola Methven, "Exclusive: George Michael on Drugs," www.mirror.co.uk); **page 129:** Tim Delaughter (as told to *Pot Culture*); **page 136:** Norah Jones (Josh Eels, "Norah Jones: The Devil in Miss Jones," *Blender*, March 2007); **page 140:** Mary Louise Parker ("Parker: 'Legalise Cannabis,'" www.contactmusic.com, January 17, 2006).

Our deepest gratitude . . .

To the many writer friends who helped compile lists and terms: Michael Aldrich, Charlie Amter, Paul Bonanos, Zach Cowie, Jessica Hundley, Mitch Myers, and Ryan Pienciak. To the photographers who so generously let us pillage their archives: C. Taylor Crothers, Steve Eichner, Gabe Kirchheimer, Dennis Kleiman, Brian Jahn, Jeff Kravitz, Kevin Mazur, Scott Cosman, and Bob Berg (who took all of our how-to and still-life shots). To our brilliant illustrator, Steve Marcus (see all of his work at www.smarcus.com). To the celebrities who have unapologetically stood up for pot, many of whom contributed to portions of this book: Tommy Chong, Willie Nelson, Rob Thomas, Melissa Etheridge, Adam Levine and Maroon 5, Matthew McConaughey, Chris Robinson, Woody Harrelson, Snoop Dogg, Adrianne Curry, Bo Bice, P-Nut and 311, Steve-O, Tim Delaughter, Redman, Pakelika and the Kottonmouth Kings, Shooter Jennings, Cisco Adler and Whitestarr, Joe Trohman and Fall Out Boy, Bob Pollard, Jonah Hill, Seth Rogen, and *The Marijuana-Logues'* Doug Benson, Arj Barker, and Tony Camin. To our agent, Sarah Lazin, and the good folks at Harry N. Abrams (Leslie Stoker, Eric Himmel, Susan Homer, Neil Egan, Eva Prinz, Scott Auerbach, Francis Coy, E.Y. Lee) for seeing this book through, and also to Robbie Hamilton for additional help. To Sarah Saiger and Bambu for the generous use of their trademark image on this book's cover. And finally to Meg Handler, our ever-so-patient photo editor, without whom we couldn't have done this book.

Shirley Halperin would like to thank:

Thom Monahan, the greatest husband in the world; transcriber extraordinaire Michelle Lanz; friends and colleagues who helped and provided endless support: Ron Feiner, Michael Lippman, Jordan Feldstein, Fred Kharrazi, Shawn Tellez, Phil Viardo, Adam and Peter Raspler, Bill Leopold, Steven Girmant, Matt Labov, Daniel Weiner, Dvora Vener and the BWR music department, Kevin Beggs, Jenji Kohan, Jay Faires, Stu Zakim, Liz Rosenberg, Gina Orr, David Newgarden, Gayle Boulware, Ian Drew, Amy Sultan, Jason Roth, Heidi Wahl, Carleen Donovan, Joe D'Angelo, Matthew Mills, Polly Parsons, Brian Sarkin, Guy Blakeslee, Otto Hauser, Adam Shore, Simon Cardwell, Mike and the staff at Dementia, the *Rolling Stone* crew (Joe Levy, Jason Fine, Jenny Eliscu, and Austin Scaggs); all of my bosses throughout this project who've each taken "being cool" to an entirely new level: Lori Majewski, Rick Tetzeli, Mike Steele, and Janice Min; my EBHS buds (Merg, Pablo, Whitty) and teachers (Janet Koenig, John Calimano, and Steve Michaud); the lovable, huggable Super Dave; Anne Toder, Michael Greenberg, Mary Monahan, my brother Shai and the Capitol Years, and my parents for letting me run amuck for most of my life.

Steve Bloom would like to thank:

All the stoners I've ever known, but especially: Ed Bender, Ian Lago, Tom Martin, Adam Orenstein, and David Smith. All of the Blooms and my greater family, but especially: Lenny, Gloria, Barry, Alicia, Joanna, and Rafael. The *Clinton News* and my De Witt Clinton High School journalism teacher, Ada Chirles. The Lehman College newspaper, *The Meridian*. All those who helped out with this project, but especially: James Ellis, Debby Goldsberry, John Maybee, Felicia Nalivansky, and Kevin Zinger. All my favorite activist groups, but especially: NORML, CAN, DPA, SSDP, and MASSCANN. All the great marijuana-reform heroes, but especially: Jack Herer, Dr. Tod Mikuriya, Elvy Musikka, Ethan Nadelmann, Angel Raich, Irvin Rosenfeld, Allen St. Pierre, and Keith Stroup.